150 YEARS
OF PHOTOGRAPHY
IN SPAIN

The translation of this book was made possible by the assistance of the General Director of Books, Archives & Libraries of the Spanish Ministry of Education and Culture.

ISBN: 84-7782-678-1
Registration number: B-27937-2000

LUNWERG EDITORES
Beethoven, 12 - 08021 BARCELONA - Tel. (93) 201 59 33 - Fax (93) 201 15 87
Sagasta, 27 - 28004 MADRID - Tel. (91) 593 00 58 - Fax (91) 593 00 70

Printed in Spain

Available throught D.A.P./Distributed Art Publishers
155 Sixth Avenue, 2nd Floor, New York, N.Y. 10013
Tel. (212) 627 19 99 - Fax (212) 627 94 84

150 YEARS
OF PHOTOGRAPHY
IN SPAIN

Publio López Mondéjar

LUNWERG
EDITORES

J. LAURENT. The Alms Collector. *Córdoba, ca. 1870. (Private Collection.)*

FOREWORD TO THIS EDITION

This is the third edition of the book now in your hands, following on the excellent reception accorded the first two editions by the public and the media. When we first contacted Publio López Mondéjar in 1985 to propose the compilation of this first comprehensive history of photography in Spain, we were well aware of the difficulties that such an all-encompassing project would present, at a time when the study of Spain's photohistory was still in its infancy. From that now distant meeting was born the idea of the initial publication of the monumental tetralogy *Las Fuentes de la Memoria (The Wellsprings of Memory)*, of which the first three volumes have now been published: *Photography and Society in 19th Century Spain* (1989), *Photography and Society in Spain from 1900 to 1939* (1992), and *Photography and Society in Spain under Franco* (1996). In view of the great success of these books and their editions in other languages, we decided at the end of 1997 to publish this *History of Photography in Spain*, which sold out in just a few months. This new edition coincides with an exhibition of the photographs reproduced in the book, with the title *150 Years of Photography in Spain*, which opened at the Círculo de Bellas Artes in Madrid in December 1999. Three months later, we find it necessary to publish yet another edition, along with the first edition in English and another edition with a similar content entitled *150 Years of Photography in Spain*, to serve as the catalogue for the exhibition, which is scheduled to visit Spain, Europe and America over the next three years.

For this edition, the author has carefully revised the texts published in the previous two editions, adding new photographs, updating information and qualifying quite a few of his opinions and observations in the light of recent discoveries. It is an honour for Lunwerg Editores to continue offering the public this ambitious, meticulous and analytical work, one that was first conceived ten years ago in conjunction with Spain's most highly respected and widely known photographic historian. Our sincerest thanks both to him and to all of the many individuals and institutions who have generously provided their invaluable assistance. And we must not forget our particular indebtedness to the photographers themselves; they are the true authors of this work

LUNWERG EDITORES

For Consuelo and Lucía

TABLE OF CONTENTS

PART THREE

PART ONE

"The Peepshow", *engraving by Ortego, ca. 1860.*

In 1839, after a half-century of ascendancy by the bourgeoisie had paved the way for economic liberalism and the industrial revolution, the time was ripe for the arrival of photography. Photography had not appeared earlier simply because the economic and financial structure of society was not propitious to its integration and development. Since the 15th century, there had been repeated attempts to capture the image of nature with the greatest possible fidelity, attempts that had led to the invention of dozens of methods that were the precursors of photography, such as the camera lucida, the graphic telescope, the diagraph, the physiognomograph, the graphic mirror, the periscopic camera and the dozens of pantographic instruments produced by the fertile imagination of the protagonists of 19th century industrial development. The long-standing obsession of artists and scientists with the camera obscura smoothed the way for the acceptance of photographic images at a time when the incessant and vertig-

ANONYMOUS. Portrait of Nicéphore Niepce, ca. 1875.

JEAN-BAPTISTE SABATIER BLOT. Portrait of Daguerre. Daguerreotype, 1884.

inous progress of science and technology was demanding a new means of representing reality.

This technological progress and the growing political influence of the middle class contributed decisively to the success of the experiments carried out by people such as Hyppolyte Bayard, Louis-Jacques-Mandé Daguerre, Nicéphore Niepce, William Henry Fox Talbot and John F. William Herschel. Niepce first obtained images on paper in the spring of 1816 using a camera obscura, although the only example of his work that has survived dates from 1826, the famous *View from the window*, which required an eight-hour exposure. At the beginning of the 1820s, Talbot began producing his celebrated "photogenic drawings", and in 1823, the same year that he invented the diorama, Daguerre made his first attempts at capturing images on polished copper plates. When Daguerre heard of Niepce's heliographic works, he approached him with the proposal of working together, after acknowledging him as the inventor of "a new means of capturing the vistas offered by nature without the aid of a draftsman". Niepce died in 1833 and

*Camera used by Alabern to take
the first Spanish daguerreotype.
(Observatorio Fabra, Barcelona.)*

Daguerre was left to work at perfecting the new invention on his own. In 1837, he obtained an almost perfect image of a still life composition that can still be seen in the collection of the Société Française de Photographie in Paris. It is the oldest example of what its creator was then beginning to call the daguerreotype, consigning to oblivion Niepce's decisive contribution to the birth of this revolutionary method of depiction.

The artistic advantages offered by the daguerreotype and its industrial utility as the basis for a new and lucrative business were decisive when it came to obtaining the official backing that was needed in order to turn this invention into a reality, an invention that, in the words of Paul Delaroche, "was to be of immeasurable service to the arts". On 7 January 1839, François Arago, astronomer, republican member of parliament and outstanding member of the democratic opposition to the monarchy under Louis-Philippe, informed the Académie des Sciences in Paris of Niepce and Daguerre's invention. Five months later, on 15 June, he presented it to the National Assembly itself and proposed that the State acquire the rights to the invention in return for a lifetime annuity for Daguerre and for Niepce's son. This event was to have widespread repercussions, since it led to State involvement in the promotion and development of the daguerreotype. Daguerre also proved himself very adept at promoting his own invention, through public demonstrations and an extensive network of followers and agents, such as Louis Sachse in Berlin, Antoine Claudet in London, and François Gouroud and Samuel Morse in the United States. News of the invention of the daguerreotype made an immediate and profound impression around the world. It was received with such great enthusiasm in the larger cities of Europe and America that within one and a half years Daguerre's original technical manual had been published in 39 editions and 8 translations. Samuel Morse wrote in the 7 March 1839 edition of the New York newspaper *The Observer*: "The daguerreotype bears a certain resemblance to aquatint etchings, but the exquisite detail of its lines is admirable and defies the imagination. No painter or etcher has ever achieved such detail. It is truly prodigious."

While Arago was busy describing the daguerreotype process to the French National Assembly, Spain was witnessing a fierce struggle between the supporters of the pretender to the throne, Don Carlos, and the defenders of the dynastic rights of Queen Maria Cristina of Naples. In spite of the ravages of war, Spain's population had reached 14,600,000. Although it had as yet made only minor inroads, progress was beginning to empty the countryside and concentrate the population within the constricting boundaries of the cities. In the space of just a few years, Madrid and Barcelona – the symbols *par excellence* of the century's sweeping demographic revolution – had doubled their populations, at the expense of the villages and towns of Aragon, Valencia, Murcia and Andalusia. This exodus from the countryside, made easier by the considerable improvement of transportation facilities during the reign of Isabella II, would eventually break down the stubborn regional barriers that had been so effectively impermeable up until that time. Under the regency of Maria Cristina, a new historical era began that was to revolutionise the country's social structure. The overbearing influence of the nobility was to be replaced by the belated ascendancy of the middle class, who promoted the industrial transformation that so drastically altered the country's immutable landscape. Bankers, businessmen and scholars took the place of the hoary nobility that the legions of that century's Romantic travellers had so disliked. For lack of the talent-based aristocracy advocated by Larra, a new financial aristocracy was to lay the foundations for the country's incipient industrialisation. Steam mills began replacing Don Quixote's legendary windmills. But this process of industrial development, begun cautiously around the turn of the century, was set in motion by foreign capital, as the Spanish were at the time still caught up in the endless struggle between old and new, between Carlism and liberalism, between oppression and freedom. "Let us weep, then, and translate," wrote Larra in 1836; thus, the Spain that moved *Figaro* to tears

of despair and lamentation and provoked Espronceda's furious *tears of fire*, busied itself with translating and copying, in an attitude that prefigured Unamuno and characterised the national spirit of the century. It is not surprising, then, that the very first attempts at photography in Spain were made by foreigners, with the exception of a small number of liberal scientists and literary figures closely linked to Parisian intellectual circles.

The Daguerreotype in Spain

The news of the invention of the daguerreotype caused such profound and immediate repercussions that just nineteen days after Arago had presented it to the Académie des Sciences in Paris, the newspaper *El Diario de Barcelona* published a short article on the subject. An anonymous journalist wrote: "We cannot give a more accurate description except to say that this invention has fixed on paper an image of natural and artistic objects that is absolutely faithful, reproducing all of the original shading and delicacy of lines with total accuracy of shapes, perspective and varying tones of light." The following day, *El Semanario Pintoresco Español* gave a more detailed description of a daguerreotype: "Daguerre does not work with paper, but rather with burnished copper plates; after three minutes in summer and somewhat longer in autumn or winter, he removes the piece and shows it now bearing a beautiful depiction of the object that the apparatus was trained on. With a brief and superficial washing, the view taken so quickly is fixed permanently, proof against even the strongest sunlight."[1]

Pedro Monláu Roca, a prestigious doctor, Professor of Literature and Hygiene and the Paris correspondent for the Barcelona Academy of Arts and Sciences, informed the Academy of the discovery on 24 February. In his report, Monláu gave an exhaustive description, along with a series of interesting comments on possible future uses for the new technique. He considered the daguerreotype without a doubt to be the greatest invention of the century, while lamenting: "It is a shame that in this grand drama of life and industrial progress the Spanish should be relegated, for reasons that have nothing to do with their ability, to the obscure role of spectators."[2] The Academy organised the first public demonstration of the daguerreotype in Barcelona, given by Ramón Alabern, who had learned the technique in Paris at one of the demonstrations given by Daguerre himself. *El Diario de Barcelona* announced the event the same day in its entertainment section. The newspaper advised: "In order to ensure the success of the event, spectators watching from the windows and balconies of the Lonja and the Casa de Xifré [the buildings that were being photographed] should withdraw for the few minutes that the plate is being exposed in the camera obscura. The process is so exact that if any spectator fails to heed this recommendation, their recalcitrance will be indelibly preserved for posterity on the resulting plate."[3] The daguerreotype was raffled among the fortunate witnesses of this historic occasion who had bought tickets for the considerable sum of 6 silver reales. There has been no further trace of this first photograph taken in Spain, which required an exposure lasting 22 minutes.

Six days later the newspaper *El Corresponsal* published a detailed account of the first attempt at taking a daguerreotype in Madrid, by Professors Mariano de la Paz Graells, José Camps and Juan María Pou y Camps.[4] This is the first documented photographic image of Madrid. On 16 December of the same year, Mariano de la Paz Graells and Joaquín Hysern y Molleras took what is assumed to be the second daguerreotype of Madrid. The exposure took 95 minutes and the results, according to Hysern, were perfect.[5] During the first months of the following year, members of the Liceo de Madrid took several more daguerreotypes of such emblematic sites as the Puerta de Alcalá, the Prado Museum and the Fuente de Nep-

ANONYMOUS. View of the Casa Xifré, next to the sea wall. Daguerreotype, Barcelona, September 1848.
(Courtesy of the Museu d'Art Modern de Tarragona.)

tuno. According to their authors, these experiments were rather less than successful and the results have unfortunately not survived.

The rapid spread of the daguerreotype in Spain is evident in the various translations of Daguerre's manual published in 1839. Outstanding among these is the translation by Hysern y Molleras, who produced an excellent version of the *Historical and Descriptive Account of the Various Processes of the Daguerreotype and the Diorama*, in which he included a series of very interesting notes on his own experiments, providing crucial information for reconstructing the daguerreotype's beginnings in Spain. Two other versions of the manual were published the same year, translated by Eugenio de Ochoa and Pere Mata, both of them leading scientists and liberal activists as well as major proponents of Spanish progressive Romanticism.[6]

In March 1839, the Valencia newspaper *El Diario Mercantil* announced the publication of Hysern's book – a paperback edition sold at a price of 12 silver reales – and on 7 September, the same newspaper published an unsigned article on Daguerre's invention "for fixing the image captured by a camera obscura". This article must have piqued the curiosity of certain Valencians, such as Juan José Vilar, who travelled to Paris to learn the secrets of the new technique. He returned to Valencia several months later, bringing with him a camera, copper plates and chemicals, to begin carrying out his own experiments. On 26 February 1840, Vilar sent his first efforts to the Sociedad Económica de Amigos del País, and one month later the press published news of his work.[7] José Montserrat and José Gil carried out similar experiments using cameras that they had built themselves, following instructions contained in a manual "printed in Paris". Later in life, Montserrat was elected as a senator and used photography for scientific ends. The Sociedad itself showed a great deal of interest in these early experiments with daguerreotypes and went so far as to offer two thousand silver reales to anyone who could invent "a method of capturing natural colour in the images obtained using M. Daguerre's device or any other more advanced one".[8] The first daguerreotype taken in Seville was made by Vicente Mamerto Casajús in June 1842. One year earlier, Granada's Sociedad Económica de Amigos del País had offered honorary membership to "anyone who could successfully take two daguerreotypes in the presence of a committee assembled by the Sociedad".[9]

The First Professionals

The daguerreotype was quick to make a profound impression on the scientific, artistic and cultural life of the time. None of our Spanish pioneers in the field of the daguerreotype, however, practised photography professionally. Most of them were liberal and progressive scientists whose interest in the new technique was based on purely cultural motives. It was left to foreign daguerrotypists to photograph our great-great-grandparents during that era of the beginnings of photography as a business in Spain. With very few exceptions, these professionals were photographers who had been unable to establish prestigious studios in their own countries – France, Switzerland, Germany or England – and who had moved to Spain in search of an unexploited market where they could work without competition. Most of them were highly mobile and combined their work as photographers with other activities, from selling all sorts of products to giving classes in the new art and selling cameras, copper plates and all of the material required for taking daguerreotypes. In support of their professional prestige, they stressed their supposed academic and artistic qualifications, even going so far as to use spurious titles. They were, in reality, the driving force behind the photographic revolution in a country with no enthusiasm for scientific experimentation and suffering from a severe and long-standing technological backwardness.

Among the more interesting members of that numerous and stirring legion of itinerant daguerreotypists were M. Gairoard – self-proclaimed "member of the Paris Athenaeum" – who arrived in Malaga in 1837 and later worked in such distant cities as Valencia, Santander and Zaragoza; Mr. Constant – "Parisian portraitist" – who worked in Pamplona, San Sebastian, Zaragoza and Vitoria between 1843 and 1845; Etienne Martín – "photographer of the Royal Theatre in Paris" and Woelker, from Switzerland, both of them arriving in Valencia at the beginning of the 1840s; the German Joseph Widen, who worked in several cities in Andalusia, Valencia and Tenerife, "on his way to Havana"; Taylor and Lowe – "Bavarian opticians" – established in Zaragoza (1849), Cádiz and Barcelona, where they were still selling cameras and phantasmagorias in 1850; Mr. Anatole – "Parisian artist" – who offered his services in cities such as Murcia, Valencia and Zaragoza; Schmidt, from Switzerland – "daguerreotypist offering portraits in colour" – who travelled the towns of Navarre in 1848, claiming to have taken over two thousand three hundred portraits "to the entire satisfaction of his customers"; Madame Fritz, who arrived in Valencia from Lisbon in 1845 and who was working two years later in Barcelona. Worthy of special mention here are the Briton Charles Clifford – "English daguerreotypist" – who worked in Madrid and other cities in Spain, beginning in 1851; the Pole Louis Lippa Fardzenyiski – the self-styled Count Lippa; and Eugenio and Enrique Lorichon, French miniaturists who worked in such distant cities as Barcelona, Seville and Santander between 1848 and 1859.[10]

Aside from these itinerant artists, the list of foreign daguerreotypists working in Spain during the 1840s and 50s is interminable. As mentioned earlier, most of them also sold cameras and gave improvised classes to our grandparents, who saw in photography a way of "broadening their education" or were interested in joining the rapidly growing number of those who were converting the new technique into a profession. The instructive efforts of these disciples of Daguerre were truly vast and, moved by the prosaic need to earn a living, they were, in the end, the ones who established photography in Spain.[11]

Madame Fritz, Clifford, Leygonier, Gairoard, Schmidt, Le Masson, Grozat, Taylor, Lowe, Bonneville, Galtier, Sardin and particularly Count Lippa were among those pioneers of instruction in the art of photography who, in the course of their itinerant professional lives, offered their potential customers "brief lessons". Most of them offered this instruction without charge and it was precisely this fact that was the principal draw of these impromptu teachers in their efforts to sell cameras, tripods, plates and other equipment for taking portraits. The exception proves the rule, and thus we see how the Swiss Schmidt, in 1848, was charging 320 silver reales for lessons in the secrets of the new technique. Judging by Woelker's advertisements in 1844, it was an exceedingly simple technique: "Daguerreotypes. This art has been simplified to such an extent that [Woelker] offers a complete course in photography lasting two weeks, after which the student will have learned everything that they need to know to take photographs and views and make all other uses of this unusual and useful science."[12]

These lessons, the inevitable spread of knowledge on the street and a few initial brief courses given by Alabern at Barcelona's Academy of Sciences provided the technical background for the Spanish daguerreotypists who followed – albeit with very different motives – in the footsteps of the liberal scientists who, flying in the

ANONYMOUS. *Jabel Hogg taking a portrait with a daguerreotype camera. Daguerreotype, 1843.*
(*Bokelberg Collection. Hamburg.*)

face of official indifference, had brought the good news of the daguerreotype to Spain. Arandes, Antonio Gálvez, José Beltrán, Manuel Herrero, Rafael Escriche, José and Salvador Albiñana, in Madrid; Mauricio Sagristá, Juan Parés, Severo Bruguera, Fernando and Anaïs *Napoleon*, Eusebio Planas, Rafael Alvareda, Parcerissas, Ignacio Mariezcurrena and E. Martí in Barcelona; González Ragel in Jerez; Casimiro de Ibarra in Cantabria; García Peribáñez and Fernández de Neira in Valladolid; Perote in Extremadura; Pedro Alliet and Miguel Sanz y Benito in Pamplona; J. Rom in Cádiz; Genaro Ximénez in Jaén; Díaz and Sabaté in Zaragoza; and Juan J. Barrera in Valencia were among the first Spaniards to enter the photography business and compete with the multitude of foreign daguerreotypists. Some of them were already working by the beginning of the 1840s, among them Mauricio Sagristá (1842), José Beltrán (1843) and Severo Bruguera (1844), although most of them set up shop after 1845.

CH. CLIFFORD ("English daguerreotypist").
Unknown subject. Madrid, 1851.
(Alberto Shommer Collection.)

The fierce competition was reflected in prices, which dropped steadily as the number of active portraitists grew. In any case, the price of a daguerreotype was determined by the photographer's prestige, the city that they worked in, the number of subjects, colouring and format, which could be a full plate (21.5 × 16.5 cm), half plate (16 × 14 cm), quarter plate (10.8 × 6.3 cm), a sixth of plate (8 × 7 cm) or even a ninth of a plate (6 × 5 cm). Most prices were in the neighbourhood of the 60 silver reales charged by Mr. Constant in 1842, the 50 charged by Bruguera in 1846 or the 30 charged by Clifford in 1852. We can reasonably suppose that these prices corresponded to quarter or sixth plate portraits, the commonest formats used in Spain. In 1844, the Frenchman Rousson charged 60 reales for quarter plate portraits, 48 for sixth plate portraits and 80 for two subjects on one quarter plate, while the price for portraits of larger groups was "negotiable". These prices represented rather substantial sums, in view of the normal purchasing power of Spaniards at the time and in comparison with the prices of other products. At the middle of the 19th century, daily wages were around 6 reales for city employees, 8 reales for construction foremen and 10 reales for a foreman in a tobacco factory. Labourers in Catalan industries at the time earned between 4 and 7 reales for working days of up to 11 hours, while agricultural workers in Andalusia earned no more than 2 reales daily, not to mention the thousands who were paid in kind or simply worked for their keep. It is therefore easy to understand why the customers of those early photographic studios were exclusively from the more affluent classes: landowners, senior civil servants, or members of the aristocracy or the burgeoning bourgeoisie. These are the people immortalised in the metallic reflections of the daguerreotypes. Photography, which always outlives its own times, bears witness to their likenesses, facing their own immortalisation in all seriousness, dignified, surprised, immobile in their interminable poses.

Photography was becoming a serious rival to painted portraits. Aside from the novelty and the clarity offered by daguerreotypes, they were rather less expensive than painted miniatures, which cost between 80 and 175 silver reales at mid-century. As a result, many painters began turning their hands to photography, a situation that clearly influenced the quality of these early daguerreotypes, taken as they were by professionals versed in the fundamentals of portraiture. Nevertheless, the spread of the daguerreotype was not as effortless as might be supposed. The original process was costly and complicated, requiring bulky equipment and exposures lasting up to thirty minutes. Newhall cites the example of one of the earliest victims of the incipient art, during a session that took place on 2 February 1840, in S. Wolcott's studio: "He sat for a full eight minutes with the sun on his face and tears rolling down his cheeks, while the photographer paced about the studio, counting off the time aloud at five-second intervals."[13] Several years would pass before the process was perfected, thanks to innovations by Baron de Séguier and Louis Fizeau, who built much lighter cameras using gold chloride to produce clearer images. At the same time Wolcott, Fritz, Petval and Voigtländer were producing finer lenses that corrected for the reversal of the image. By 1843, exposures had been reduced to between one second and two minutes, depending on the lighting and the type of copper plate. Only then could the daguerreotype portrait become firmly established as the professional occupation of the hundreds of photographers who followed in the footsteps of Robert Cornelius and Richard Bearn, who opened the first studios in Philadelphia and London in 1840 and 1841, respectively.[14]

By the middle of the century dozens of daguerreotypists were working as portraitists in almost all Spanish cities, although it was in Madrid, Barcelona, Seville, Valencia, Zaragoza, Málaga, Pamplona and Santander that the taking of portraits was most commonly found as a livelihood. Among these cities, the largest number of daguerreotypists, and the best among them, set up shop in Barcelona. At least, it is this city that has best preserved its heritage of daguerreotypes and the memory of its first photographers. Outstanding among them were Lorichon, *Franck*, the members of the Fernández family – known as the *Napoleóns* – and Rafael Alvareda. Eugenio Lorichon began working in Barcelona around 1848 and produced some of the most beautiful daguerreotype portraits that have survived in Spain. From 1853 to 1860 he worked assiduously in Málaga with his son Enrique and made a continuous round of visits to other Spanish cities, in association with Mattey (1866) and Marqueti (1857). François Alexandre de Villecholes (better known under his pseudonym *Franck*) arrived in Spain around 1848, fleeing the revolutionary upheavals that ushered in the Second French Republic. Unlike his contemporaries, he did not emigrate strictly for financial reasons, but instead had clearly political motives. He worked for years in partnership with Wigle in their luxurious portrait studio in the Paris of the Second Empire. Fernando and Anaïs *Napoleón* established themselves in Barcelona in 1853. The *Napoleóns* were excellent portraitists and were succeeded by several generations of their descendants, who maintained the family firm's prestige until the turn of the century, when Emilio *Napoleón* opened another portrait studio in Madrid.

The daguerreotypists of Madrid never rivalled the importance of Barcelona's. This appears to be borne out by the surviving work of Arandes, Rafael Escriche, Juan Martí, Manuel Herrero and the brothers Salvador and José Albiñana, although the latter achieved a certain degree of prestige in his lifetime and received extensive praise for the pieces that he showed at the 1855 Universal Exposition in Paris. Francisco de Leygonier y Hubert produced daguerreotypes in Seville, although none of his portraits using this method have survived. In 1843, he set up what may have been the first commercial studio in that city. Several years later, Eugenio Lorichon moved to Seville, combining his business there with his work in Málaga and his regular visits to other Andalusian cities. Gairoard and Count Lippa worked fairly extensively in Málaga in lively competition with each other until the arrival of Lorichon in 1853.

The work of these pioneers of photography – along with that of so many obscure and forgotten itinerant portraitists, who were the travelling companions of pedlars, alms collectors, preachers, tooth-pullers, vendors of dispensations and

LORICHON. Daguerreotype, ca. 1850.
(Museu de la Ciència i la Tècnica de Catalunya.)

salves and so many other members of the migratory legions of the time – was not particularly outstanding and does little more than merely bear witness to the likeness of our ancestors as they sat serious and defenceless before the cold gaze of the lens. Most of these photographers set up their improvised studios in the most unlikely places, from the street itself to patios or bull rings. Daguerreotypists would even take their cameras from their studios to make "house call" portraits, or to take views of streets and monuments, none of which have survived, unfortunately. This early mobility also made possible one of the most shocking photographic specialities, that of photographing cadavers at home. This practise is a constant reference in the long-winded advertisements of the time and, bolstered by the high rate of infant mortality and the special sensitivity to death that were characteristic of the century, it endured for many years, until the authorities found it necessary to take action to suppress this morbid custom.

An impressive number of this sort of daguerreotypes are still to be found in Spain. In contrast only a very few examples of scenic daguerreotypes have survived, in spite of the documentary evidence to the effect that hundreds of them were taken. On the other hand, the poor quality the daguerreotypes that have come down to us makes it clear that the technique was not practised in Spain with any degree of skill, a situation that can be attributed to a number of causes. Firstly, there was the lack of vision and the absence of any sort of initiative on the part of the country's politicians and officials in promoting Daguerre's invention and the industry that grew up around it. Secondly, there was Spain's cultural and scientific backwardness, which stemmed from the disproportionate influence of the Church and the monarchy in the country's affairs. Lastly, there was the rapid transition to other techniques on the part of professionals of the stature of Leygonier, Clifford and Count Lippa, whose work has only survived in the form of paper and glass negatives.

The Reproducible Image: Calotypes

The birth and development of photography, coinciding with other technological innovations such as the railroad, the steam engine and the telegraph, was contemporary with the economic development that transformed Spanish culture and society in the 19th century. It is therefore not in the least surprising that the liberal and progressive bourgeoisie soon felt the need to exploit it as saleable merchandise on the pretext of responding to the cultural demand of ample sectors of society. What was at stake was the birth of an industry based on a new means of depicting reality, one that would supersede the cosmoramas, dioramas, engravings and lithographs that had brought images of the farthest and most picturesque corners of the world to the European public.

From the beginning, the daguerreotype's potential for faithfully reproducing views of documents, cities and works of art was apparent. Lithographic copies taken from daguerreotype originals soon became popular, making photography a privileged competitor of manual drawing. On 19 August 1839, a French magazine published a lithograph taken from a daguerreotype, and this became a common practice over the next few years. Noël-Marie Lerebours achieved the most outstanding results in this area with his renowned *Excursions daguerriennes: vues et monuments les plus remarquables du globe*, published between 1840 and 1844. The daguerreotypes taken by Lerebours' team were printed in the form of engravings in very large editions. Three had been taken in Spain, two of them in Granada – the inevitable Alhambra – and one of the Alcázar at Segovia. Towards the end of 1839, Francisco Javier Parcerissa y Boada began publishing the monumental work *Recuerdos y Bellezas de España* ("A Work Dedicated to Divulging the Country's Monuments, Antiquities and Picturesque Vistas, with Plates Drawn From Life or Taken by Daguerreotype by D.F.J. Parcerissa and Texts by D.P. de Madrazo"), with views of monuments in 28 Spanish provinces. Another similar work appeared in 1842, with the title *España* ("A Picturesque Work with Plates Taken by Daguerreotype or Drawn from Life and Engraved on Steel or Boxwood Plates by Messrs Luis Rigalt, José Puiggari, Antonio Roca and Ramón Alabern). This volume included texts by Francisco Pi y Maragall, who, along with Pablo Piferrer, Pedro de Madrazo and José María Quadrado, had also contributed to Parcerissa's work.[15]

It was a time that saw the images captured by cameras converted into a valuable resource for publishers, who, by mid-century, had made their first timid attempts at publishing images. Works with a more general scope were soon joined by others of a regional nature, such as the Blanch e Illa's *Guía de Gerona Artística y Monumental* (1851), and *Panorama Óptico-Histórico de las Islas Baleares*, with its lithographs drawn from daguerreotypes and attributed to Francisco Montaner "thanks

JAMES MOFFAT. *William Henry Fox Talbot*, 1864. *(Fox Talbot Museum.)*

PRINCE SEBASTIAN. *Unknown subject. Calotype, ca. 1855. (Carlos Morenés Collection.)*

to the assistance of various compatriots who imported a daguerreotype device from Paris and generously allowed us to use it to compose the vistas offered here".[16]

Nevertheless, the daguerreotype – a unique image fixed on sensitised metal – did not provide an ideal means for multiplying the image of reality. The use of the daguerreotype on voyages presented almost insuperable difficulties, but it had one even greater drawback, and that was its absolute unsuitability for what Lacan defined as "our century's great need", in other words the reproduction of photographic views in large editions. From the end of the 1840s onwards the challenge tackled by pioneers in the field was precisely the reproduction of photographic images with the goal of bringing them to a much wider public.

Thus, following a number of attempts by people such as J.F.W. Herschel, Friedrich Gerber and H. Bayard and two years after Daguerre had made his invention public, the British scientist William Henry Fox Talbot presented the talbotype or calotype, the culmination of his earlier *photogenic drawings*, which were obtained by placing objects on paper treated with an emulsion of gold chloride and silver nitrate. Although the image was not as sharp as that provided by the daguerreotype, the calotype offered the possibility of producing multiple photographic images us-

CH. CLIFFORD. View of Carrera San Jerónimo and the Parliament building.
Calotype, Madrid, 1853. (Museo Municipal de Madrid.)

ing a paper negative. This potential for obtaining thousands of copies of a single photographic shot – which would eventually become one of the defining characteristics of photography – facilitated the birth of an incipient industry, in spite of the enormous logistic problems still faced by photographers. While the technique was not a particularly difficult one to learn, the transportation of the paraphernalia required for the photographic tours undertaken by the pioneers in the field was anything but simple. Maxime du Camps, who took dozens of calotypes in Egypt while visiting that country with Gustave Flaubert in 1849, wrote "Learning to take photographs is simplicity itself, but carrying the equipment from place on mules, camels or even human porters is a truly complex problem." Charles Clifford, who took up residence in Spain in 1850, commented on the difficulties that he had encountered in his numerous professional voyages around the country "The photographer faces not a few problems in his work when travelling in a country like

Spain, where the conveniences of transportation are unknown, where the temperature commonly reaches 105 degrees in the shade, where water is as difficult to find as in the Sahara Desert itself, and where, owing to the extreme dryness of the soil, dust is the rule rather than the exception. In addition to all of this there is the fact that, owing to the considerable size of the photographs [Clifford was working by then with glass negatives measuring over 30 × 40 cm], the equipment must necessarily be bulky and can weigh up to 650 lbs. With such impedimenta duly balanced and strapped to the back of a mule and we ourselves enthusiastically mounted in a likewise manner, we set off on our daily expeditions at four o'clock in the morning. You may imagine our desperation and anxiety each time one of these long-eared beasts stumbles, threatening our fragile lenses, plates and trays."[17]

Talbot's invention opened an immense range of applications for photography by allowing the multiplication and democratisation of images. It was the paper negative – especially following the innovations introduced by Baldus and Le Gray – that permitted the definitive development of photography and provided impetus for the birth of an incipient industry centred on the marketing and popularisation of the shots taken by pioneers in the field. "Photography", wrote Lacan in 1856, "has moved from portraitist's terrace into the painter's studio, the man of the world's study and the boudoir of our elegant folk. Photography has crossed oceans, mountain ranges and continents. There are photographers in Bombay, Madagascar and Valparaíso. Since it may be used by each individual according to their taste and needs, it has accompanied the artist and the tourist to museums, cathedrals and the lofty peaks of the Alps and Pyrenees. Just open any photographic album and the whole world (the Nile, Jerusalem, Thebes, Palestine, Egypt, Nubia) unfolds itself before your very eyes as in a tale of fantasy. And the wizards are Maxime du Camps and M. Thénard."[18]

During the years that saw the birth of photography as a business, dozens of European photographers, particularly British and French, followed the example set by Du Camp and Thénard and set their artistic and professional sights on countries in the Far East, and even Spain. One of these photographic travellers was the Briton Claudius G. Wheelhouse, who took a great number of calotypes in Portugal, Spain and Italy on his way to Egypt. His *Photographic Sketches of the Mediterranean* is an album of albumen prints taken from paper negatives. In this work, along with some admirable vistas of cities such as Seville and Cádiz, he included some highly revealing anecdotes on the nature of his work and that of his fellow pioneers in the photography business, who were taken as magicians, sorcerers or spies by a populace who had no previous experience of photographic images. Referring to his work in Cádiz, he writes "In order to take the photograph I unwittingly entered the city's fortifications and when I was congratulating myself on my success, I found myself surrounded by an officer and a dozen soldiers who promptly arrested me, thinking I was a spy who was making a map of those fortifications. (...) Lord Lincoln contacted the English consul and although he had never heard of photography in his life, he did his best to explain that I was in fact no spy and that I was merely practising a recently discovered art consisting of obtaining images with the help of sunlight."[19]

Wheelhouse was not the only foreign traveller who encountered such difficulties. George Borrows came close to being arrested when he was taking notes on some Roman ruins. T. Gautier himself had serious problems with customs officials at Vitoria when he startled them by trying to take their picture with his daguerreotype camera. Years later, Gautier recounted the incident to George Sand, stressing that reaction born of surprise and distrust that they "inspired" in the Spaniards of the time.

Some years later, the Viscount of Dax, E.K. Tenison and the Viscount of Vigier travelled in Spain and took several series of calotypes that attained substantial popularity. "Would you like to visit Spain?" wrote E. Lacan in 1856. "Here you have Toledo, set on its hilltop as if on a marble pedestal; cross the river, climb up to the city and stop a moment before the Alcázar, then go to straightaway to the church of San Juan de los Reyes and observe the chains hung symmetrically on the walls. These are the chains worn in their Moorish prisons by the Christian captives liberated by Ferdinand and Isabella. (...) Observe this patio with its Moorish arches and orange trees as tall as oaks: it is the patio of the mosque at Córdoba. But it is undoubtedly the Alhambra that you are seeking to gaze upon in this magical voyage where your imagination only need wish it to see it appear before your eyes, the Alhambra whose praises are sung by all poets and the mere mention of whose name is sufficient to evoke all of the Earth's delights. You can visit Spain in photographs and rest your gaze where you please. The Viscount of Vigier, Tenison and the Viscount of Dax will be your guides."[20]

In 1851, the Viscount of Vigier published his album of calotypes of Seville, taken in 1850-1851 at the request of the Duke of Montpensier, who used such

E.K. TENISON. The Segovia aqueduct. Calotype, 1852. (Bibliothèque Nationale, Paris.)

distractions as a means of consoling himself for his failures in the political arena. Tenison published his work, *Memories of Spain*, in 1854, including forty calotypes taken between 1852 and 1854 in cities such as Toledo, Seville, Madrid, Segovia, Granada, Córdoba, Montserrat, Burgos and Valladolid. It is one of the most complete sets of photographs taken in Spain at such an early date.

In 1850, Charles Clifford, a skilful English photographer, arrived in Spain and quickly became a favourite of Queen Isabella II. His first documented "Spanish" work is an album entitled *Copia talbotípica de los monumentos erigidos en conmemoración del restablecimiento de S.M. y la presentación de S.S.R. la Princesa de Asturias, en el templo de Atocha*. Although it is merely a reproduction of drawings, plans and models, its importance lies in the technique that was used (calotype or talbotype), in its date (19 February 1852), and in the fact that it may well have been the first professional work commissioned by the queen to the "little English photographer". Besides this album, Clifford took dozens of calotypes in different parts of Spain, including some frankly excellent views of Madrid, Salamanca, Granada, Segovia, El

Escorial and Seville. Like most British photographers, he must have stopped working with paper negatives by 1855 and had by then begun using collodion-emulsion glass negatives.[21]

Another traveller who took an important series of calotypes was the archaeologist Louis de Clercq, who visited Spain during the winter of 1859 on his way to Syria and Asia Minor. De Clercq took 50 photographs on waxed paper negatives, later collected in his work *Voyages en Espagne, Villes, Monuments et Vues Pittoresques* and including views of Granada, Cádiz, Seville, Madrid, Aranjuez and El Escorial.

Unfortunately, these pioneers of photography displayed barely any interest at all in portraying human subjects, unlike the writers and graphic artists – Borrow, Doré, Gautier, Chapuy, Andersen, Guesdon, Richard Ford, Davillier, among others – who visited the country around the same time. In this way, they responded to the demands of the first publishers of photographic images, who were more interested in selling the physical appearance of exotic countries, a category that, for the Romantic and Postromantic generations, included Spain, than in the "breath of their soul" or the nature and customs of their people. Wheelhouse wrote of how he had to wait for hours on end for people to go away, out of range of his cameras. One notable exception is found in J.J. Heilmann's photograph *Spanish Refugees*, taken in Pau in 1854, showing four enigmatic-looking Basques, who may well have been smugglers of the French borderlands. One year later, William Lake Price took another photograph with a Spanish subject – although in this case with a collodion negative – that became very well known. This was the famous *Don Quijote in his Study*, depicting a discreetly stereotypical Alonso Quijano in a setting that was very much in keeping with the Victorian taste for reconstructing interiors crowded with antiques. As late as 1858, the German J.A. Lorent took a number of calotypes in the Alhambra when he passed through Granada on his way to North Africa.[22]

Aside from these photographers' work with paper negatives, most of the daguerreotypists who had established themselves in Spanish cities, such as Lorichon, *Franck*, Pérez Rodríguez, Leygonier, Ducloux, Marchetti, Herrero, and others, alternated their use of the daguerreotype technique with what was known at the time as "paper photography". By 1849 it was in general use among photographers working in Spain. Pascual Pérez Rodríguez, the first Valencian professional photographer and one of the first Spaniards to use paper negatives, wrote that year on the advantages offered by the calotype: "The first proof is a sort of master or mould that can be used to make millions of copies, with the outstanding advantage that the master does not deteriorate and after a thousand copies the results are just as clear and perfect as in the first copy." Two years earlier, Pérez Rodríguez had published his *Álbum del Cabañal*, illustrated with calotypes, making him one of the earliest Spanish photographers to exploit this process commercially.[23] Francisco de Leygonier and Luis L. Masson did a great deal of work with the calotype process in Seville around the middle of the 1850s. Masson took excellent calotypes of bullfighting subjects that are probably the first of their kind. Alejandro Massari probably also used paper negatives after establishing himself in that city in 1855. Particularly worthy of note is the recent discovery of a sizeable collection of paper negatives taken by the infante Sebastian during the years that he lived in Italy and showing his considerable skill as a portraitist.

Although we know that many of the photographers working in Spain used paper negatives, very little of any importance remains of their production with this technique. The calotype was not of great significance in this country and was used mostly by foreign photographers such as Tenison, Masson, Wheelhouse, Vigier, Lorent, de Clercq and Clifford, already mentioned above. Nevertheless, the image that these pioneers left us of our country is considerably richer than that produced by the daguerreotypists, who dedicated themselves almost exclusively to taking portraits. It is important to bear in mind that with the daguerreotype, photography remained in the realm of a mere invention, while the calotype succeeded in creating its own distinctive aesthetic. In this sense, some of the calotypes taken in Spain are extraordinarily beautiful and although they may not be on a level with the quality of better known works by H. Bayard, Hill and Adamson or Calvet R. Jones, they are certainly worthy of a place in the history of the European calotype.

The Ascendancy of Photography

From the end of the 1840s onwards, the major challenge faced by the pioneers of photography was the reproduction of photographic images in large editions in order to make them accessible to the public at large. The faltering initial advances made with daguerreotypes and calotypes were followed by feverish activity aimed at creating an ample market for photography that would be capable of meeting the growing demand on the part of the rising middle class. What was at stake was not only the ultimate improvement of a new technique, but also the consolidation of the industry that was growing up around that technique. In spite of the progress achieved from 1848 onwards by Blanquart Evrard and Niepce de Saint Victor, photography was still not in a position to take off definitively as an industry. While the albumen glass negative introduced by Niepce de Saint Victor provided a much clearer image than the paper negative, the technical difficulties involved in using it, including exposure times of up to 15 minutes, meant that the older techniques introduced by Daguerre, Talbot and Le Gray continued to be the most widely-used ones. In 1851, Scott Archer made huge progress when he succeeded in replacing albumen with collodion, thereby bringing exposure time down to two seconds. One of the classic manuals in the history of photography, published in 1862, puts it in the followings terms: "The use of collodion has effectively dealt the final blow to metal plate photography. When it is well-saturated with the silver components it reacts to light rays with marvellous rapidity. Thanks to collodion, the movement of waves ever agitated by the wind, the coach racing down the road, the horse lunging forward, and the ship driven by steam may all be captured instantaneously and reproduced."[24]

The collodion process finally overcame the technical limitations that characterised of the daguerreotype and the calotype, although these two techniques were still in use around the middle of the century for purposes such as portraiture. Lacan, as editor of the magazine *La Lumière*, was in a privileged position to observe the development of photography and he described the methods most commonly used in 1856: the daguerreotype, the wet paper negative or calotype, the waxed-paper calotype, the albumen negative and collodion negative. The daguerreotype was used almost exclusively for portraits; the calotype had fallen into almost total disuse, owing to its lack of clarity, and the albumen negative, owing to the long exposures required, was limited almost totally to depiction of monuments and works of art. Only collodion was suitable for all these application, since it "combined all of the advantages offered by the other processes".[25] With the introduction of dry collodion, Lacan had already foreseen in 1856 that the future task of photographers would be to document the whole world in al-

Tent used as a laboratory and darkroom, from the wet plate collodion period, ca. 1870.

bums and photographic "museums", laying the groundwork for a considerable productive speculation. Two years earlier, Disdéri had already pointed out that the future industrial development of photography would depend on its ability to reach ample sectors of the public, including not only the middle classes but also the working classes. In 1861, he wrote "The time has come to gather together all of the little-known artistic riches scattered around the world and bring them to the public at large in the form of inexpensive reproductions in small and medium-sized formats."[26]

Photography began to occupy a privileged position that would allow it to develop into a genuine intermediary between reality and the growing masses that were gaining access to an incipient visual culture. André Rouillé writes "Photography then took on a new social dimension and moved closer to fulfilling its vocation as a medium for mass communication. In order to do so, photography had to adapt to market requirements, or, in other words, its successive transformations were to depend on the specific conditions of capitalist society, which was then industrialising.[27]

With the improvement of the collodion process and the incipient techniques of photomechanical printing, photography was starting to fulfil the basic conditions for industrial development, namely speed, clarity and reproducibility, although the major challenge was still that of increasing production and lowering the price, both of them preconditions for becoming an article of trade. A contemporary report states "In general, the price of photographs is still very high; manufacturers have not yet realised that if they were to lower their prices they would sell considerably more products and that the popularisation of photography would increase their total profit."[28]

By the beginning of the 1860s, photographers were offering all types of images – celebrity portraits, art reproductions, landscapes and views of exotic cities, war scenes – in response to the growing demand generated by a society that was characterised by the cultural values of the liberal and progressive middle class. With the introduction of the photomechanical printing methods pioneered by Alphonse Poitevin, photography began its transformation into a genuine article of commerce, thereby allowing capital investment on a level with other industries. According to Mayer and Pierson, the 207 working studios in Paris in 1862 had "very sizeable staffs who were much better paid than factory workers", while a number of London's 200 studios employed over 100 technicians and many had staffs of more than 50. Already in 1855, Disdéri was running a workshop with 77 employees and selling up to one thousand five hundred portraits daily. In 1862, over one hundred and five million photographs were taken, most of them in the *carte de visite* format. Ten years earlier, when the paper negative was beginning to compete seriously with the daguerreotype, one hundred and thirty tonnes of glass plates had been sold in France. These figures grew spectacularly over the following years. According to G. Freund, in 1891 there were over one thousand studios in France, the photographic industry employed over half a million workers and overall production in the industry was valued at thirty million gold francs. Although figures for Spain were not on a level with those for France, England or the United States, with only 39 studios recorded for Madrid, it was a time of prosperity for photographers, who, according to *Káulak*, "were accumulating capital of up to 200,000 *duros*".[29]

The development of means of transport had a significant impact on the work of the early photographers who compiled the photographic image of Spain at a

Portable darkroom used by William Atkinson for his series of images of the Isabella II Railway, ca. 1855. (Patrimonio Nacional.)

time when new ideas were beginning to make headway in this country in spite of the persistence of the secular "traditional obstacles". Road-building activity had increased notably around the beginning of the century. On the eve of the Regency there were two thousand kilometres of roads in the country and this had increased to four thousand kilometres by 1856. In 1868, when the *Glorious Revolution* brought the reign of Isabella II to an end, there were eighteen thousand kilometres of roads and highways. However, it was the railroad that truly revolutionised transport. In 1848, the first railroad was inaugurated between Barcelona and Mataró, followed three years later by the Madrid-Aranjuez line. During the reign of Isabella II railroads experienced spectacular growth. In 1858 there were 158 kilometres of railway lines, and by 1861 this had grown to over five thousand kilometres.

This revolution in transport brought with it a revolution in the work of the travelling photographers who, on their own initiative or commissioned by the large publishers of images, visited the cities of Spain to complete their photographic *Museums*. One of the most appropriate forms for the massive distribution of those *Museums* was the stereograph. This procedure, introduced by Charles Wheatstone in 1839 and perfected ten years later by David Brewster, did not come into general

Binocular device for viewing stereographs, end of the 19th century.

use until the Great Exhibition in 1851. Within seven years the London Stereo-scopic Company had over 100 views on offer to the public and in 1862 they sold one million stereograph cards. These cards were produced using two superim-posed images taken by a camera with two lenses and a single negative, creating a full sensation of depth on viewing through a binocular stereoscope. Beginning around 1860, stereoscopic photography was marketed on a massive scale in the form of vistas of cities and landscapes and mythological or lightly erotic scenes that were viewed enthusiastically in the drawing rooms of aristocratic and middle class homes alike. These series of photographs attained such spectacular success that photographers as prestigious as Roger Fenton, Robert Howlett, Francis Frith and the Gaudin brothers began working in this format and their works soon edged out of the market the large-format views by Clifford, the Bisson brothers, Baldus and Le Gray. In 1857, Alexis Gaudin's company, which published *La Lumière*, ad-vertised hundreds of views of "all of the countries in the world", as did the British London Stereoscopic Company. This was the golden age of stereoscopic photog-raphy and of the Photographic Museums, which soon became a common presence in all western countries.

A number of anonymous photographers in the employ of the leading pub-lishers of stereoscopic views worked in Spain's cities and are to thank for most of the photographic images of this country dating from that time. Among them

ANONYMOUS. Port of Alicante. Stereograph, ca. 1870. (José Huguet Collection.)

were the staff members of the Gaudin and London companies mentioned earlier, and particularly the Englishman F. Frith. As with Wheelhouse, Frith's goal was not Spain, but rather the Middle East. On his way to Syria, Egypt and Palestine between 1856 and 1859, he must have made stopovers in the cities of Andalusia, although his known "Spanish" photographs – of Málaga, Toledo, Gibraltar, Seville, Burgos and Barcelona – must have been taken after he opened his studio in Surrey in 1859.[30] One of the best photographers to work for Frith was R.P. Napper, who, after leaving his former employer, travelled to Spain where he took one of the most surprising and magnificent series of photographs of the era, compiled in the album *Views in Andalusia*. This work is truly extraordinary, owing less to its excellent technical quality than to the vigour of its composition and the author's interest in depicting, with no artifice other than that imposed by the technique itself, personal subjects, including gypsies, shepherds, servants, muleteers, that are practically absent from the work of his contemporaries. Ten years later, and with an entirely different approach, the British engineer William Atkinson completed a noteworthy report on the so-called "Isabella II Railroad", built between 1853 and 1857.[31] In 1868, Thurston Thompson photographed Santiago de Compostela and several years later the country was visited by W.J. Sawyer, Maurice Gourdon and J. David, the latter an unexceptional portraitist who produced various series with military themes. Worthy

L. LEVY. *Departure of the diligence under the Segovia aqueduct,
ca. 1895. (Monasor Collection.)*

R.P. NAPPER. Group of gypsies in Andalusia, ca. 1863. (Ignacio Medina Collection.)

of special mention is the Pole Count Lippa who set up in 1844 in Málaga and later worked in different cities in Andalusia, Extremadura, Valencia and Madrid. He was an active promoter of the technique and a skilful salesman of cameras and other photographic equipment, and hundreds of his portraits and views, of admirable quality, have survived.

As late as the end of the 19th century Spain drew the attention of such important photographers as Lucien Levy and Paul Nadar. Levy produced a splendid series of views of nearly every city in Spain in which he captured not only their monuments but also social aspects, popular neighbourhoods and the daily lives of their inhabitants. Paul Nadar's work is particularly noteworthy, consisting of a series of excellent views of the northern part of the country, including several portraits of ordinary people.[32]

Two Foreigners in Isabella II's Court: Clifford and Laurent

Nevertheless, the most important foreign photographers established in Spain and the ones who had the strongest influence on Spanish photography in the 19th century were Charles Clifford and Jean Laurent. Our knowledge of Clifford's work goes as far back as his use of paper negatives, which may have been the basis of his introduction into the court of Isabella II. Up until that time he had also worked as a daguerreotype portraitist while simultaneously beginning a "vast publication on the monuments of Spain", which he sold by subscription or directly from his Madrid studio. For this purpose he travelled constantly around the country, covering two objectives at once: to photograph cities and monuments and to procure new subscribers for his publication. In July 1855, the press reported on "the magnificent collection that Mr Clifford has compiled in the course of his extended visit to Andalusia" and announced his forthcoming voyage to Paris to promote that collection. Three years later, El Museo Universal stated that the English photographer had by then "copied" over eight hundred outstanding monuments on his numerous voyages through Spain.

By that time Clifford was a well-known and highly respected photographer at court. In 1858, when the royal councillors decided that the queen should make a series of voyages around the country, he was commissioned to make a graphic chronicle of Spain as a monumental and modernised country to be presented to the world as proof of the monarchy's virtues. His photographs were subsequently used in that royal propaganda campaign, comprising multitudinous receptions, fervent royal audiences, solemn inaugurations and expressions of a loyalty that was somewhat less unswerving than the queen of two continents might have wished for.[33] Between the time when Isabella II began her series of official visits, on 21 July 1858, and the photographer's death in 1863, he took hundreds of photographs, compiled in various albums: Viaje a Valladolid (1858), Viaje a Alicante, Baleares y Barcelona (1860), Viaje a las provincias de Toledo y Extremadura (1858) and Viaje a Andalucía y Murcia (1862). Although Clifford's immediate aim was to provide publicity in favour of the Crown at a time when Isabella was not an especially well-loved figure among Spaniards, he produced work of estimable quality that provides eloquent graphic testimony of the Spain of his day.

CH. CLIFFORD. The Guadalquivir River and the Gold Tower. Seville, 1862. (Private Collection.)

Clifford's fame extended well beyond Spain's national boundaries. He travelled to London in 1861 to take Queen Victoria's portrait and she commissioned him produce a complete collection of 600 photographs of Spain's monuments and cities. One year later he carried out another commission from the crowned heads of Spain and other European countries comprising an album of 171 views taken during his ten years in Spain. This album constituted a genuine anthology of his work and was accompanied by a brochure with very revealing information on the vicissitudes of his travels on photographic expeditions, transporting his unwieldy equipment on muleback, in diligences or in the memorable trains of the time.[34] He had taken two official portraits of Isabella II in 1861, opening the next phase in his career with new photographic equipment – "the largest device built to date", according to the press of the time – with which he took a number of his most celebrated works, such as the ones published in his excellent album on Andalusia. The Danish writer Hans Christian Andersen mentions him working in Granada, in one of the rare written testimonies to the labour of the pioneers of photography. "The Court of the Lions and the Hall of the Two Sisters were being photographed at the behest of Her Majesty the

Queen by a famous English photographer [whose name Andersen does not mention and probably did not know] and no one was allowed to enter lest they disturb him. Through the arches I recognised the whole tribe of gypsies that we had seen climbing the hill earlier; they had been summoned to enliven the photographs with their human presence. (...) In no time at all the photograph had been taken."[35]

Aside from shots such as the ones mentioned above and others of regional types taken in the course of the royal voyages, Clifford only took portraits of popular types or characters, similar to those taken by Thomson, Nègre, Beato, Napper and Laurent, on rare occasions, and when he did so they lacked intensity and vigour and were excessively distant and cold. In this sense, the results that he achieved in recording the work on the Isabella II Canal (1855-1856) are particularly interesting, showing as they do an exceptional professional capacity for capturing the sea of toiling workers and equipment in images taken *d'après nature*, a proposition that constituted an immense technical challenge and a true desideratum for the photographers of the time. With the album of the Isabella II Canal and other equally memorable photographs, such as the ones of the original Puerta del Sol in Madrid and of construction of the Puente de los Franceses, and those taken in Andalusia, Clifford, whose motives were predominantly scientific and commercial, became one of the photographers who best portrayed the monumental, artistic and technological facets of Spain under Isabella II.[36]

Jean Laurent Minier was the most active promoter of photography in Spain in the 19th century and its most representative and emblematic figure. He moved to Spain in 1843 and took his first known "Spanish" photographs in 1857. On 21 May 1858, *La Época* published an ample commentary on his album on the Madrid-Alicante railroad. Over the course of half a century, Laurent and the members of his company took thousands of photographs in all of the genres of the time, from reports on public works or street scenes to series on monuments, bullfights, popular types, works of art and celebrity portrait galleries. He sold these photographs in all formats from his shops in Madrid and Paris and through an extensive network of correspondents and agents. In this way, he succeed in promoting his image of Spain to excellent financial advantage, to the extent that we can safely say that Laurent y Cía. was the leading Spanish photographic company of the 19th century, on a level with the companies set up in the rest of Europe by Frith, Gaudin, Braun, Alinari, Wilson and Levy.

J. LAURENT. View of Murcia, ca. 1870. (Olmedilla Collection.)

It is not an easy task to pass judgement on the quality of Laurent's huge body of work, although many of his images stand up very well in comparison with those of the best photographers of the time, which he clearly surpasses in his shots of streets scenes and human subjects. While they are not entirely free of the folkloric and picturesque clichés to which many of the French travellers that had preceded him, such as Gautier and Mérimée, were so prone, his portraits of popular types are, as a rule, excellent and invaluable for their contribution to our knowledge of the Spaniards of the time. Laurent's work, reproduced in thousands of collections distributed throughout the country, became the best known and the most emblematic and popular photographs of 19th-century Spain. His archives, expanded by the work of his successors, including Lacoste, Dosch, Roig, Portugal and Ruiz Vernacci, came to contain the respectable number of fifty thousand large-format negatives, of which up to twenty thousand may have been taken by Laurent himself.[37] This gives us an idea of the vast contribution made by this extraordinary photographer and businessman, a contribution that is central to any understanding of the history of Spanish photography in the 19th century.

The First Spanish Masters

Around 1860, dozens of Spanish photographers, the more talented pupils of Leygonier, Count Lippa and Laurent himself, began taking over the field from the foreigners, both in the area of portraits and in the reproduction of works of art or travel photography. Worth mentioning among them are Pascual Pérez Rodríguez, Julián Martínez de Hebert, José Martínez Sánchez, Hermenegildo Otero, José Rodrigo, Santos Pego, E. Martí, Amadeo Courbon, Alfredo Truán, Mariano Júdez, Francisco Zagala, Andrés Cisneros, Pablo Bausac, Casiano Alguacil, José Spreafico, J.G. Ayola, Rafael Garzón, Enrique Facio, Antonio García, Pau Audouard, Emilio Beauchay, Antonio Esplugas, Eduardo Otero, Juan José Muñoz and Rafael Rocafull.

Martínez Sánchez and Antonio Cosmes made one of the earliest photographic reports on the occasion of the arrival of Isabella II at the port of Valencia. Martínez Sánchez was one of the most outstanding members of the first generation of Madrid-based professionals and produced a number of works with an industrial theme during the 1860s. He formed a partnership with Laurent in 1865 and together they patented and marketed a type of paper known as "leptographic", which came close to replacing albumen paper. Martínez Sánchez's excellent photographs of public works, the Puente del Diablo at Martorell and the construction of the Tarragona railroad station all date from this period. This accomplished photographer was overshadowed for several years by Laurent but his work stands up very well to comparison with the French master's. Antonio Cosmes is known to have been one of the first Mexican daguerreotypists and after working in various cities he established himself in Valencia.

José María Sánchez was a prominent portraitist and produced a number of views of Madrid in the 1850s that were published in a *Museum* sold for a price 6 silver reales in the capital and 7 in the rest of the country. J. Suárez's *Museo Fotográfico* was a similar work containing an excellent urban report on the capital in the aftermath of the 1868 revolution. Around the same time, Casiano Alguacil began publishing an album of views of his birthplace, Toledo, along with a "gallery of illustrious

J. MARTÍNEZ SÁNCHEZ. La Baña Lighthouse. Tarragona, ca. 1865. (Universidad de Navarra.)

J. SPREAFICO. Railway workers at Córdoba Station, 1867. (Patrimonio Nacional.)

men in the fields of science, literature, arms and the arts". However, this extraordinary photographer's most memorable work is his collection of portraits of Toledan
popular types, such as beggars, labourers, barbers and hatters, which are comparable
to the portraits taken by Eugène Atget in Paris around the end of the 19th century.
Similar work is also found in the sizeable gallery of portraits taken by José Rodrigo
in the Lorca area. Having established himself there in 1863, Rodrigo was the author
of notable photographic reports on public construction works and a collection of
views of Cartagena during the period of the Cantonalist revolt in 1873.

José Spreafico established himself in Málaga in 1861 and in 1867 he produced
one of the greatest monographic works of Spanish industrial photography of the
19th century, in the form of a report on the construction of the Córdoba-Málaga railroad, containing a dozen excellent images. The quality of his second known work,
Recuerdo histórico de la Rábida, places him among the best photographers of his
time. Alfonso Begué was one of the first Spanish professionals to sell stereoscopic
views, around the end of the 1850s. His images of the "public and neighbourhood

HEBERT. View of Salamanca, ca. 1870. (Filmoteca de Castilla y León.)

fountains of the city of Madrid", taken in 1864, are particularly noteworthy. Six years later, Martínez de Hebert took a magnificent collection of views of Salamanca, which includes some of the best photographs of the time. Antonio García took numerous images of Valencia and was quite successful in selling them during the 1860s. Although of lesser quality, worth mentioning is the work of photographers in other parts of Spain who portrayed their cities during this same period, including Martí and Mariezcurrena in Barcelona, Bernardo Maeso and Francisco Sancho Vidal in Valladolid, Mariano Júdez in Zaragoza, Santos Pego in Las Palmas, Juan José Muñoz in Ciudad Real, Hermenegildo Otero in San Sebastián, and Manuel Baroja in Murcia. Some of them, such as Mariezcurrena and Hermenegildo Otero, took shots of a number of different Spanish cities, following in the footsteps their foreign traveller predecessors. However, the moment when photography "in Spain" could be considered to be truly and properly Spanish arrived with the definitive spread of portraiture following the popularisation of the *carte de visite*, just prior to the 1868 revolution.

Democratisation of the Portrait

Along with travel photography and reproductions of works of art, the portrait became the most representative embodiment of photography. The portrait's apotheosis came about at a time when profound and parallel changes were taking place in society. The determined rise of the 19th-century liberal middle class was gradually displacing the traditional political classes and aristocracy and the resulting democratisation brought in its wake art forms that were more accessible to the newly ascendant social classes. Having one's portrait made was becoming a sign of social advancement and there was no better means than photography – the most democratic and revolutionary technique of representation available – to place this aspiration within the reach of ample strata of society. G. and P. Francastel write "Since the middle classes wanted above all to possess what had formerly been the privilege of the dominant classes, they also wished to be able to contemplate their own likenesses and pass them on to their children. At this moment, around 1850, a new means of capturing images emerged: photography. This possibility of recording the individual's features by mechanical means led, in a sense, to the obsolescence of a class of artisans whose function was midway between art and craft."[38]

In its stubborn competition with the miniature, the daguerreotype had to its advantage its faithful mirroring of the model – in effect the burnished metal made the daguerreotype a sort of mirror – at a time when the goal consisted of the greatest possible accuracy of representation. In this respect, the daguerreotype was clearly superior to the miniature and at the same time its substantially lower cost made it accessible to the members of the emerging middle class. Colouring provided it with all of the chromatic qualities of miniatures and its format and presentation in the same kind of case created a pictorial illusion for this middle class public, which was to become its principal clientele. Claudet wrote in 1865 "We must admit that certain arts are now disappearing, since photography has finished them off. Why are there no more miniaturists? For the simple reason that, in place of portraits offering a greater or lesser likeness, photography offers an exactitude that, at very least, pleases the heart and fills the memory with satisfaction." In fact, the true victim of photography was neither landscape nor genre painting, but the miniature portrait, which had been one of the most lucrative specialities practised by painters. Although they continued to produce miniatures until the end of the century, it was an art form that was irrevocably displaced with the introduction of the daguerreotype and the *carte de visite*, with the result that most second-rate painters ended up becoming photographers, a profession in which they were to combine their supposed artistic aptitudes with the craftsman's skills involved in this new means of depicting reality, which everyone seemed determined to refuse to recognise as art. It is precisely to this prior training as craftsmen that we can attribute the high quality and sophistication of the photographic portraits produced in the pre-industrial years. According to A. Scharf, of the 59 daguerreotypists established in Berlin and Hamburg before 1859, at least 29 had previously been painters, and this same circumstance was repeated in other countries, such as France and Great Britain. In Spain, Antonio Cosmes, Martínez Hebert, Octavio Codecasa, Rafael Rocafull, Gerónimo Muñoz, Manuel Moliné and Ángel Díez-Pinés were among the painters who took up photography in those early years.

However, as photography was hemmed in by the costly nature of the daguerreotype – a unique item, impossible to reproduce and made of metal – it was accessible only to more prosperous sectors of the middle class and therefore offered little scope for industrial development. It was the introduction of the *carte de visite*, the renowned calling card-sized portraits patented by Adolphe Disdéri in 1854 and popularised after 1858, that finally democratised the photographic portrait. *Cartes de visite* were produced using cameras with four or six lenses that could be mounted on moving chassis, allowing up to six different portraits to be taken in a single shot. For the same cost and effort and with the same exposure and development time, it was possible to obtain different portraits in the *carte de visite* format, 6 × 9 cm, that were much less expensive and easier to handle than previous formats. The daguerreotype had become obsolete. At the Photographic Society's exhibition in London in 1856, over six hundred images were shown, of which only three were daguerreotypes, and this circumstance was repeated at the 1855 Universal Exposition in Paris. Although the daguerreotype survived somewhat longer in the United States – in 1860 there were still 300 daguerreotype studios in that country – the profession of daguerreotypist had disappeared by 1865. In Spain, the daguerreotype lived on until the end of the decade and it is not unusual to find advertisements for "daguerreotype portraitists" in the press of the time. In fact, from 1860 onwards, the daguerreotype became a sign of social distinction as opposed to the "vulgarity" of the *carte de visite* portrait.

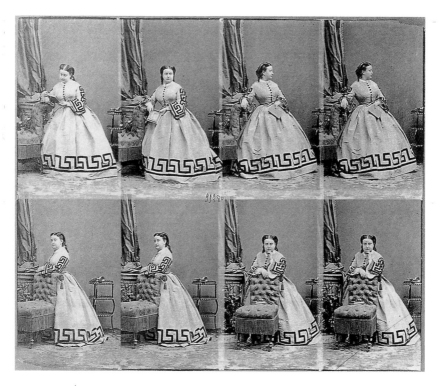

DISDÉRI. Multiple portrait of Princess Gabrielle Bonaparte. Uncut carte de visite, 1862. (Gernsheim Collection. University of Texas, Austin.)

With the introduction of the glass negative, a new technique was developed that, for a number of years, became a sort of substitute daguerreotype. This was the ambrotype, consisting of an underexposed glass negative that, when placed on a dark backing, provided a surprising similarity to a daguerreotype. Although they lacked the brilliance and intensity of daguerreotypes, ambrotypes were much cheaper and easier to make and from the end of the 1850s and throughout the following decade it became one of the most widespread techniques used by portraitists, particularly in the United States. It was never excessively popular in Spain, although such well-known photographers as Antonio Cosmes, Enrique Godínez, Moliné and Alvareda took ambrotypes. It was soon superseded by the truly popular photograph of the 19th century – the tintype. This technique's low cost was due not only to the paltry quality of the materials employed – merely thin iron sheets – but also the duplicate images obtained by the use of multiple lenses, similar to the process used for producing *carte de visite* portraits. Tintypes became popular in the United States after 1860 but did not attain prevalence in Europe until ten years later, when the technique was used as an "American" speciality by itinerant photographers. Once the use of silver bromide-gelatin plates became widespread, the tintype process gradually disappeared. It was hardly used at all in Spain until the final decades of the century, when it became the most obvious forerunner of today's photo booths.[39]

However, ambrotypes and tintypes were also unique objects, ones that could not be reproduced, and like the daguerreotype they could not provide a solution to the great challenge facing the incipient photographic industry, which required a means of multiplying images in large editions, thereby lowering costs. Disdéri had sensed that the future of the portraiture business depended on its ability to reach a much larger clientele. In order to do so, the cost of the large-format portraits popular in 1850s had to be reduced. Thus, a dozen portraits in the new *carte de visite* format cost between 50 and 100 francs. In Spain, the price of a daguerreotype in 1860 ranged from 30 to 60 reales, while *carte de visite* portraits were available at a price 8 or even 4 reales, with extra copies costing only 2 reales.

Photography, then, was set to become an art that was within the reach of ever larger sectors of society. In this sense, the *carte de visite* constituted a veritable revelation and provided undreamed of opportunities for the photographic business. It not only awakened the need of the humbler segments of the middle classes for possession of their own or their families' and friends' portraits, but also this new clientele's demand for likenesses of the leading personalities of the time. Lacan had already clearly foreseen this phenomenon in 1856 when he wrote "The photographer is more than a mere technician who does their work with greater or lesser professional care; he also becomes nothing less than the indispensable mediator between the great figures of history and posterity. Any photographer who gathers together a large number of portraits of celebrities and has them published by an intelligent publisher will do excellent business and at the same time create a work of exceptional interest for the present and a genuine iconographic monument for the future."[40]

ALONSO MARTÍNEZ.
Isabella II, ca. 1860.
(Patrimonio Nacional.)

CH. MONNEY. Soldiers of the Liberal
Army at the Plaza de Bilbao. *1874.*
(Private Collection.)

Photography came to reproduce in astonishing numbers the likenesses of public figures, at a time when photomechanical techniques were not yet in a position to provide this capacity through the press. By 1860, Mayer and Pierson had compiled a gallery of over one thousand celebrities and Disdéri sold tens of thousands of portraits of Napoleon III in 1850. In 1860, John E. Mayall sold over one hundred thousand portraits of Queen Victoria and in the spring of 1869 the Carlist propaganda services distributed some seventy thousand portraits of the pretender Don Carlos. In the early part of the 1860s, the leading studios – those of José Albiñana, Enrique Godínez, Alonso Martínez, Laurent and Gumersindo Ortiz – produced thousands of portraits of Isabella II, allowing the Spaniards of the time to take home a likeness of their queen, along with those of the other more or less prominent members of her court. Politicians, members of the royal family, actors, writers, musicians and bullfighters all posed for photographers and swelled their "celebrity galleries", which replaced the old collections of lithographs published prior to the photographic revolution. Antonio Flores wrote in 1860 "Nowadays, we do not miss a detail and everyone has an album, or two or three albums, or as many as they need to hold portraits of their friends and our friends in turn have our portraits. Very few people do not take part in this type of exchange. And the people who do not have friends, since they cannot do without their portrait album, buy whatever portraits they want or whatever portraits they can, because we are now all up for auction. This is how we can own the portrait of every king, every sage, every artist and every phenomenon in the world. No one can avoid being portrayed and sold."[41]

At that time every self-respecting photographer offered their customers an abundant sample collection of celebrity portraits. Eusebio Juliá, one of Madrid's most talented portraitists, produced large editions of his famous album "of all of the eminent figures who have now long occupied the leading positions in our country", which he sold in different formats, ranging from *carte de visite* to "life-size", as had Camille Silvy with *Beauties of England* and Disdéri with his *Gallery of Contemporaries*. Rovira offered a *Gallery of the Country's Representatives* at the provisional parliament of 1868, and similar albums were sold by Charles Monney, Alonso Martínez, Hébert, the Debas brothers and Laurent. Photographers such as Antonio García, Pau Audouard, J. Beauchy and Antonio Esplugas kept this practice up until the end of the century and, particularly Esplugas, produced interesting collections of portraits of actors, musicians, singers and bullfighters. A photographer's standing came to be judged not by the quality but rather by the quantity of such portraits, which he exhibited in his studio windows, thus providing a further attraction for the hundreds of sightseers strolling the streets of city centres. Mesonero Romanos wrote in 1861 "Many spend five or six hours scrutinising the progress of work on the Puerta del Sol, while others will instead spend their time examining, one by one, the thousands of *carte de visite* portraits on show outside photographers' studios."[42]

The 1860s were decisive for the development of photography in Spain. Most of the century's leading portraitists opened their studios in the course of that decade, taking advantage of the enormous demand for *carte de visite* portraits. Outstanding among the myriad of professionals who established themselves during the 1850s and the first part of 1860s were Jules Beauchy, Gumersindo Ortiz and Enrique Godínez in Sevilla, Alfredo Truán in Gijón, Mariano Júdez in Zaragoza,

J. RODRIGO. Little girl lying against a dog, 1873. (Lorca Municipal Archives.)

Cisneros in Santiago de Compostela, Julio Virenque in Mallorca, Valentín Pla, Jules Derrey and Antonio García in Valencia, José Spreafico in Málaga, Zenón Quintana in Santander, Otero and Marín in San Sebastián, Anselmo María Coyne in Zaragoza, and Casiano Alguacil in Toledo. The list is completed by Eusebio Juliá, Martínez Hebert, Ángel Alonso Martínez, José María Sánchez, Martínez Sánchez and Antonio Selfa in Madrid, and Rovira, Moliné and Albareda, E. Martí, Cantó and Durán Rovira, in Barcelona.

Around this time the situation of the provinces as photographic colonies of the major cities began to ease somewhat, although dozens of itinerant photographers continued travelling from town to town and city to city to meet the increasing demand throughout the whole country. Among the most active of these travelling photographers were Heraclio Gautier, Terraillón, Juan José Muñoz, Alfredo Esperón, Charles Monney, the self-styled Count Vernay and, particularly, J. Poujade and the ubiquitous Count Lippa, who worked ceaselessly for over a decade. Santiago Ramón y Cajal remembered them in one of the very few written testimonies to these pioneers' memorable wanderings: "I was first truly impressed by photography somewhat later, in 1868, as I recall, in the city of Huesca. Of course, years earlier I had already encountered this or that itinerant photographer, of the breed who, armed with tents and fairground booths, box cameras and gigantic lenses, and taking things more or less as they came, practised Daguerre's primitive art."[43]

The Spread of Photography

The prospect of financial gain attracted many young people from circles linked to artistic creativity, such as painters, engravers, lithographers and a varied range of members of the counter-culture of the time, who saw in the new profession of photography an opportunity to obtain instant profit and even to make a name for themselves in artistic spheres. We have already mentioned the case of miniaturists who turned to photography. Carlos Brambilla, Martínez Hebert, Luis Sellier, Rafael Rocafull, Rafael Castro and Julián Campomanes were among the first artists to establish themselves as photographers. Others became the privileged collaborators of portraitists when it became fashionable to have portraits retouched and tinted. As Claudet himself admitted in 1860, photography attracted a great number of second-rate painters who eventually became mere retouchers. Ignacio Codecasa worked from 1849 onward with Pascual Pérez Rodríguez; Manuel Moliné went into partnership with the daguerreotypist Rafael Albareda in 1856; Laurent hired Gaumain in 1861 to retouch and tint portraits with washes; Francisco Geloso worked for Eusebio Juliá and Enrique Rumoroso for the Debas brothers, while Joaquín Sorolla began as a tinter in Antonio García's studio. The continued prestige of hand-drawn portraits led photographers of the time to extol their painter-photographer status as a guarantee of the quality of their work. The title of "painter" was frequently stamped on the back of photographers' cards, often accompanied by symbolic elements, such as suns, paintbrushes and palettes, as a means of aggrandising their professional image.[44]

Not all of these new photographers had artistic backgrounds, however. Anyone with a touch of boldness could feel themselves qualified to take up the new trade. Adolphe wrote in 1861 "While it is true that among the pioneer photographers there were genuine artists, most of those now practising the technique are mere photograph merchants." The golden age of the photographic portrait was over, having given way to the eminence of mere handymen. From seamsters such as Idelmón and ushers such as J. Mon, to cobblers such as Alliet and watch-makers such as Díaz Ponce, dozens of professionals with only a rudimentary command of the technique set up studios in cities and towns around the country. With only a very few exceptions, their main intent was not to take good portraits – assuming that they were capable of doing so – but rather to produce many and sell even more. Ramón y Cajal himself expressed his puzzlement at how the photographers of his time went about their work. He wrote "And yet, these modest photographers worked such miracles without the least emotion, completely lacking in any intellectual curiosity whatsoever. From their replies to eager questions I deduced that they had not the slightest interest in the theory of latent images."[45]

The rate at which the portrait trade grew is comparable only to the degree to which the quality of the portraits produced declined. There had been an abrupt move, almost without transition, from interminable sittings in painters' studios to the quick and easy pose at photographers' studios. The technical simplicity of the operation led to real stagnation in artistic terms and the imposition of an irritating routine. Disdéri had not only reduced the cost and the size of portraits, in spite of his claim of capturing the subject's "personal likeness", but also their quality. This becomes particularly evident upon comparison of his work and that of his hundreds of followers with that of Hill and Adamson, Nadar, Carjat, Pierson and others who worked with large formats during the 1850s. In effect, the best Spanish photographic portraits of the 19th century date from that period, which saw the initiation of the first generation of photographers to work mainly with the new collodion techniques, even if many of them were hold-overs from the daguerreotype era.

In spite of the official neglect that permitted the destruction of most of the portraits taken by those pioneering figures, some have survived, thanks to the providential foresight of collectors such as José Amador Ríos, Eugenio Hartzenbusch and the painter Manuel Castellano. Castellano's collection, amassed between 1850 and 1875, is a particularly important one and contains around twenty thousand photographs of a wide range of Madrid's citizens of the time, including a number of photographers, such Juliá, Martínez Sánchez, José María Sánchez, Arandes, the brothers José and Salvador Albiñana, Rodríguez Sánchez, Godínez, Antonio Cosmes and the infante Sebastián. They must have been the authors of the earliest portraits in the collection, which are precisely the best and most interesting ones, as well as the ones in the largest formats, as is to be expected from the period prior to the massive spread of photography. Many of these images were probably used by Castellano and other painters of the time for their own works, a practice shared by Ingres, Delacroix, Courbet, Cézanne, Manet and Dégas, thus making photography, as expressed by Baudelaire, into the "humblest" servant of the arts and sciences.[46] It is important to bear in mind that photography provided 19th-century painters with an ideal means of obtaining a comprehensive catalogue of objects, apparel, faces, hands and other features that allowed both artists and models to avoid lengthy and tiring poses in the studio.

With its vulgarisation, photography suffered a profound setback and regressed to a stage that had already been altogether surpassed by painted portraits. In contrast with the starkness and absence of any sort of contrived artifice of the best portraits of the pre-industrial period, the new portraitists soon crammed their studios with every imaginable type of contraption that, in their comic pretentiousness, were meant to emphasise their subjects' social standing and disguise their own lack of talent. Scores of ridiculous props, such as backdrops, theatre boxes, boats, fake pianos and even cardboard lap-dogs, replaced the simple headrests, columns and curtains of the early days. Although a few voices were raised against such absurdities, these contraptions multiplied, converting studios into genuine scenery storerooms, midway between, in Benjamin's words, execution and performance, torture chamber and throne.

In the portraits of this period, condemned to the frigid setting of pretentious mother-of-pearl covered albums, barely even the smallest hint of personality shines through. The subjects follow one another in anxious succession, like replicas of themselves. Nevertheless, over and above their vulgarity, we are left with the fascination of their permanence, the testimony of their visages, gestures, clothing and the pulse of insistent and lasting life that lingers on in these old and yellowed cards. The technical limitations of the time, requiring lengthy sittings, obliged the subject to live and experience the very moment that the camera captured their likeness for posterity. Subjects grew and defined themselves in their own effigies and the power of photography to synthesise infuses these portraits, in spite of their lack of refinement, with an intensity not to be found in later snapshots.

ANONYMOUS. Young woman on a balcony. Madrid, ca. 1860.
(Castellano Collection, Biblioteca Nacional.)

THOMAS LE CLAIR. Children in the photographer's studio. Oil on canvas.
(Courtesy of Hirschl and Adler Galleries.)

The Proliferation of Studios

Portrait fever proved not to be a passing fad and so provided studios with the opportunity for a long and prosperous existence. In addition, Spain's social, economic and political circumstances had changed drastically since the daguerreotype years. The population had grown from 11,962,767 in 1833 to 16,662,000 in 1877. Cities such as Madrid and Barcelona had tripled their populations as a result of the migratory movements that had begun emptying the country's towns and villages. At mid-century, Madrid had 160,000 inhabitants and Barcelona had 175,000. By 1880 these figures had grown to 346,000 in Barcelona and 398,000 in Madrid, a practically uniform growth rate that made these cities the focal point of Spanish life, along with Zaragoza, Valencia, Santander, Cádiz, Málaga, Oviedo and Bilbao. On the eve of the 1868 revolution Spanish society remained predominantly agrarian, with a working population of 26,000 miners, 150,000 industrial workers, 600,000 craftsmen, 1,818,000 servants and no fewer than 2,390,000 farmers and farm hands. In spite of the transformations undergone by Spanish society, in fact merely 1 per cent of the population – comprising the middle class, the aristoc-

A. GARCÍA. *Julio Cebrián Mezquita painting*
a self-portrait, ca. 1870. (José Huguet.)

E. JULIA. *Ruperto Chapi, ca. 1875.*
(Monasor Collection.)

racy and the military – dominated the remaining 99 per cent, by means of restric-
tive electoral laws and the exercise of power. These social inequalities were heightened towards the end of Isabella II's reign. At a different level, the economic slump
of 1866 led to a severe shortage of consumer goods that helped to spur on the revolutionary process that brought the monarchy to an end two years later.

In spite of industrial progress in regions such as Asturias, the Basque Country
and Catalonia, workers continued to earn between 3 and 5 pesetas while a kilogram of meat cost 1.50 pesetas and a kilogram of bread cost 35 centimos. The
Restoration brought this unequal and inequitable economic growth to a head,
while the most conservative sectors of the middle class took economic and political control of the country. As in the past, the state's cultural policy remained
non-existent. In 1859 there were only 56 public libraries and from 1875 to
1904 the yearly budget for scientific material amounted to the ridiculous sum of
35,000 pesetas. It is not surprising, then, that in 1887 the illiteracy rate still stood
at 71.5 per cent and that industry was still controlled by foreign companies.

J. LAURENT. Salvador Sánchez "Frascuelo",
1879. (Elena de Diego Collection.)

E. OTERO. Rafael Molina "Lagartijo",
ca. 1880. (Álvarez Barrios Collection.)

This cultural, economic and social reality decisively shaped the activity of Spanish photographers, who, in only a very few cases, succeeded in gaining entry into the country's cultural élite. With notable exceptions, most of the professionals destined for the profession under the Restoration barely surpassed the technical and cultural background of their predecessors. Antonio Cánovas de Castillo (*Káulak*) gave an eloquent description of the theoretical artistic training received by that generation of photographers: "There before the sign reading 'Apprentice Wanted' would appear a boy who would make as good a photographer as he would a shoemaker, shop assistant or coachman. Once accepted, the apprentice would be shown how to sweep the gallery and wash down the darkroom. During his second year, the boy would learn how to pronounce hyposulfite, albumen, silver nitrate and other technical terms. (...) By his third year, curiosity would have led him to focus and adjust apertures and open and close cameras. In his third year, the master would show him how to avoid cutting his fingers on glass plates. And this is how boys twelve or fifteen years old learned and learn the photographic profession. Many do not know how to read, but they focus, shoot and develop and, in short, they are photographers."[47]

In the 1870s and 1880s the number of photographic studios mushroomed. From the beginnings of the popularisation brought about by *carte de visite*, prices dropped continuously, allowing the industry to diversify its offer substantially. Although the *carte de visite* remained in use until the end of the century, portraitists introduced new, larger formats that soon gained popularity. In 1868 the *Cabinet* portrait (10 × 15 cm) appeared on the market, followed in 1870 by the *Victoria* (7.5 × 11 cm), and in 1875 by the *Promenade* (10 × 18 cm), *Boudoir* (12.4 × 19.3 cm) and *Imperial* (16.8 × 21.7 cm). Although the impact of these novelties on the Spanish photographic industry was less spectacular than in other European countries, the considerable increase in clientele opened a veritable golden age of gallery portraiture. The legendary names – Laurent, *Napoleón*, Hébert, Spreafico, Antonio García, Juliá, Godínez, Martín Sánchez – were soon joined by others who left their imprint on the splendour of the portrait industry of the end of the 19th century. Memorable among them were Antonio Esplugas and Pau Audouard, in Barcelona, Manuel Alviach, Valentín Gómez, E. Otero, the Debas brothers and Manuel Company, in Madrid, S. Muchart, in Málaga, Emilio Beauchy, in Seville, Marcos Baeza, in Tenerife, Otero and Aguirre, in San Sebastián, Ignacio Coyne, in Zaragoza, Juan and Ricardo Almagro, in Murcia, Emilio Pliego, in Pamplona, José Truyol, in Palma de Mallorca, Luis Sellier, in La Coruña, Manuel Cantos, in Alicante, and Jules Derrey, in Valencia.

The photographic industry grew considerably, although not to the same extent as in London or Paris. While official statistics show the existence of 17 studios in Madrid in 1862, this figure had grown to 58 by 1897, while there were 57 in Barcelona. By the end of the century, Barcelona outdid Madrid in the number of studios – 73 in comparison with 57 – although they produced less work. These cities were followed, in order of importance, by Valencia, with 32 studios, Jaén, with 26, La Coruña, with 19, Zaragoza and Oviedo, with 14, Seville, with 13, Málaga and Murcia, with 12, and Santander, with 10. In total, there were 239 legally registered photographic establishments in Spain, which paid over sixty-five thousand pesetas yearly to the Treasury.[48]

Although towards the end of the century every town worthy of the name had its own photographic studio, photographers still travelled from place to place plying their trade, just as in the memorable daguerreotype and *carte de visite* years. Some even extended their travels overseas, such as the Madrid photographers

Mouton and Villar who, during the 1870s, announced their stopover in the Canary Islands en route to Havana. Other professionals, such as Juan Buil, Hermenegildo Méndez and J. Pumariega, had already embarked on such adventures to the colonies of emigrants who were driven by misfortune to cross the seas. In any case, the golden age of photographic portraiture came to an end with the century, owing to the widespread ownership of cameras by amateurs, a growing tax burden and an ever more demanding public. *Káulak* wrote "One of the many industries now undergoing a severe and disturbing crisis is that of professional photography. Photography in Spain is one of those activities that will never make anyone rich. Today, Spanish photographers either live frugally or in absolute penury."[49]

Uses of Photography

The photographic portrait, however, was not the only speciality or use found for photography in the 19th century. Already at that stage in its short history it had found other directions to take in consolidating its development, stemming from its nature as a faithful mirror of reality and its inexhaustible potential for recording, description and portrayal. This potential quickly made it the ideal instrument for taxonomy or the analysis or surveying of human or animal types. Both Daguerre and Talbot had succeeded in taking photographs using solar microscopes and Alfred Donné published a series of drawings in 1844 based on microscopic daguerreotypes. In spite of the serious technical difficulties caused by unfavourable atmospheric conditions, astronomic photography was commonplace from the 1840s onward, thanks to the use of infrared emulsions. The astronomer Janssen wrote that "the photographic plate is the scientist's true retina" and as early as 1839 François Arago had foreseen the possibilities offered by the daguerreotype for mapping the Moon photographically, although this was not actually accomplished until 1862, in the work of Lewis Rutherfurd. Celestial photographs showed surprising astronomical phenomena, such as those taken by the British astronomer Warren de la Rue in the 1850s and 1860s showing parallel stripes on Jupiter. Some years later, Emilio Rocafull produced images of the moon at the San Fernando Observatory. In July 1860, José Montserrat was able to overcome the difficulties caused by high temperatures, which dried the wet collodion emulsion that he used

In 1874, E. MUYBRIDGE devised a battery of 24 lenses and used them to capture that number of images of the human body in motion.

on his glass plates, and succeeded in taking several shots of a solar eclipse. Warren de la Rue travelled to Álava the same year to photograph the eclipse, and John Spiller and William Crookes took part in the scientific expedition to Cádiz in 1870 to study the lunar transit of Venus for the first time. In addition, photographs were soon taken of plants and insects and biological and entomological studies received new impetus from the vast potential of photographic records.

By 1870, photography had been definitively adopted by most areas of scientific research. Notable work in this connection was done by A. Quinsac, who took a microscopic photograph of the brain of a fly larva and by the Spaniard L. Moratalla, who took microscopic photographs of insects for Madrid's Municipal Laboratory. Étienne-Jules Marey and E. Muybridge made particularly important contributions to the knowledge and depiction of movement based on multiple shots. In 1874, Muybridge devised a battery of 24 lenses and used them to capture that number of images of bodies in motion. Four years later, Marey invented a "photographic gun" capable of capturing images at the then unheard-of speed of 720 thousandths of a second. With their photographs, Marey and Muybridge revealed aspects of motion that were imperceptible to the human eye and that contradicted many of the scientific and artistic observations current at the time. Appearances did not always coincide with reality and reality was not always apparent, and these experiments added to the recognised merits of photography above and beyond its faithful representation of nature. With these developments, photography moved on to occupy a new sphere, midway between magic and science, leading certain scientists, such as Charles Darwin, to adopt it as a means for supporting their physiological theory of emotional expression.

Progressive technical refinement heightened scientists' interest in photography, as was the case in other European countries. One of the members of the Pacific Scientific Expedition to South America in 1862 was the draftsman and photographer Rafael Castro, who was responsible for producing a graphic record of the expedition and all of its zoological, botanical and anthropological discoveries, for study at the Natural Science Museum. Photography also played an important role at the Ebro Observatory, where the astronomer José Joaquín Landerer placed this task in the hands of the bacteriologist Jaume Ferrán, who later took a decisive part in the battle against cholera in 1885. In 1897, Ferrán published the results of his work in collaboration with Inocencio Pauli in the book *Instantaneidad en fotografía*, which included a description of a system that was very similar to the silver bromide-gelatin process and much more manageable and logical than the old collodion-based system. Many of his photographs were strictly utilitarian and dealt with microscopic studies of his ophthalmological and dermatological patients. Doctor Joan Soler introduced the use of photography at the Hospital de la Santa Creu in Barcelona for the purpose of studying venereal disease. César Comas, one of the pioneers of radiology in Spain, also used photography to study leprosy, tuberculosis and venereal disease.

In spite of these and other applications of photography in graphic publishing and in the nascent field of photojournalism, the portrait continued to be the technique's most emblematic embodiment at the close of the century. To the old celebrity galleries, photographers added series of photo-caricatures and mosaic portraits, popularised by Disdéri in 1863, which, after a brief period of popularity, were soon abandoned. The portraits used for identity or records of delinquents or convicts met with more lasting success. This type of image had been used in countries such as France, Germany and Great Britain since 1860 and first

R. CASTRO. The photographer (with pencil and drawing pad), posing with Azazola, Jiménez Espada and other members of the Pacific Scientific Expedition, 1862. (Museo de Ciencias Naturales, Madrid.)

J. LAURENT. *Spanish senators. Carte
de visite mosaic portrait, 1865.
(Monasor Collection.)*

gained currency in Spain on the eve of the 1868 revolution, as witnessed by a
number of photographs of pickpockets in Manuel Castellano's famous collection. However, the most significant precedent for this new application of the
photographic image – one with considerable financial importance, if we are to
judge by the attention that it received in the first congresses held by Spain's
professionals – was the series of portraits of criminals and suspects commissioned by governor Julián de Zugasti in 1870 for use in his relentless persecution
of banditry.[50]

Another speciality practised by 19th-century professionals were photographs
of the deceased. In the words of Agustín García Calvo, "It is the desire to hold onto
the dead that promotes and sells photographs." And so, this desire to possess the
past, both one's own and that of the persons near and dear to one, fostered this industry, at a time when not everyone had the opportunity to have their portrait
taken before setting out on the final journey. Those rigid and bedizened infantes
and infantas of Spain painted by Madrazo before the last blush of life had disap-

*J. RODRIGO. Father and dead son. Lorca,
ca. 1870. (Lorca Municipal Archives.)*

peared from their visages were succeeded by the children of the upper middle class captured in identical poses by the daguerreotypist's camera. With the development of photography death became an even more egalitarian occurrence, as it allowed the ritual art of portraying the deceased to take on new forms of popular representation. With the spread of the *carte de visite*, these old and yellowed cards became a manner of certifying what was not to be, preserving in their coats of albumen the testimony of rigid little corpses converted by the prodigy of the technique into an illusion of life that somehow escaped the certainty of death. Photography is always at odds with metaphor, except in these portraits of cadavers. Here it takes on a contradictory and horrific quality, in showing the deceased as something still caught up in the flow of life, making them, as Barthes put it, into the living image of something dead.

Living images of dead circumstances are also found in *ex voto* portraits, one of the most moving popular manifestations of photography. During the final years of the 19th century, when photographers set up shop in the more remote

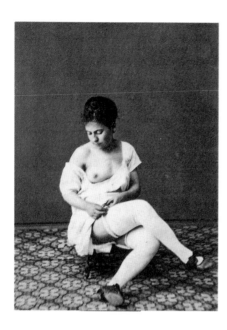

A. ESPLUGAS. *Female nude,*
ca. 1885. (Private Collection.)

towns of Spain, large numbers of photographic *ex votos* were left as offerings,
alongside wax figures, blonde lace and embroidery. The photographers of the
time exploited the technical potential of their trade to recreate diseases or acci-
dents in crude photomontages and desolate settings. Especially common are
scenes of sick people surrounded by attentive and distressed family members,
patients with fatal illnesses on their deathbeds, accident victims or other unfor-
tunates. Photographic *ex votos* were produced until well into the 20th century and
this type of work is still commonly found in chapels and shrines around the
country.

Another speciality of the photographic industry from the daguerreotype period onwards was the nude. In the beginning, owing to the medium's crude realism,
photographs of nudes were seen as true obscenities. Disdéri himself complained in
1862 of the profusion of obscene images "that are keeping the courts so constantly busy". Nevertheless, in spite of the opposition of the authorities and the forces
of law and order, this type of image found an extensive market in Europe from the
1850s onwards. In Spain, in contrast with the abundance of portraits of the dead,
there are almost no examples of photographs of nudes, as might be expected from

a country that had been dominated by the pulpit and the barracks for centuries. In any case, until the apotheosis of the nude in works of such painters as Sorolla and Romero de Torres, a number of painter-photographers, including Anglada Camarasa, Mariano Fortuny, Casas Abarca and José Luis Pellicer, took large numbers of this type of photograph and almost certainly used them in creating their paintings. The series of nudes taken by Antonio Esplugas in the 1880s were probably used for similar purposes. Although this genre was not widely practised by Spanish photographers, there was a sizeable market for risqué photographs imported, for the most part, from the Parisian erotica market. Our grandfathers were very keen on contemplating these "nudes in relief", which they viewed with great attention in their stereoscopes, while our grandmothers went about their daily task of earning their place in heaven by organising charity balls and attending triduums and novenas.

Amateur Photography

There have been amateur photographers since the very beginning and in Spain the majority of the pioneers in the field took up the new technique as a hobby. Among them were Ramón Alabern, Felipe Monláu, José Roura, Pedro Mata, Joaquín Hysern, Mariano de la Paz Graells, the Duke of Veragua, Alejandro Oliván and the Marquis of Valmar, who played a decisive role in introducing the daguerreotype, in the face of the lack of vision displayed by Spain's cultural authorities, who failed to grasp photography's cultural, social and economic import. We owe the earliest daguerreotype views of Spanish cities to the efforts of these enthusiasts. Leopoldo Augusto de Cueto, Marquis of Valmar, left valuable written testimony of the tribulations of these early amateurs and their working methods, following the instructions given in Daguerre's manual, which, as mentioned earlier, was soon translated into Spanish: "We started out full of eagerness and enthusiasm, but to our bitter disappointment, everything turned out badly. We failed to follow Daguerre's written instructions to the letter. (...) We spoiled the five dozen metal plates that had been included in the price of the camera. We hastily ordered more plates from Paris, along with further technical instructions. Our subsequent experiments were somewhat less of

J. COLLADO. The Slaughter Ball. *Albacete, ca. 1900. (Collado Collection.)*

a failure than the initial ones and we soon made so bold as to work out of doors."[51]

Photography was considered a respectable pastime by the aristocracy and the upper middle class and soon became an embellishment to the education of the members of those classes. Daguerre had already written in 1840 "The well-to-do classes will find in the daguerreotype a highly agreeable pursuit. (...) The minor amount of work that it requires will make it especially attractive to ladies." Woelker's advertising in 1844 claims "Ladies of distinction will take up photography for entertainment and recreation." The infante Sebastián was one of those early amateurs who, along with the pharmacist Juan de Álava, became members of the Société Française de Photographie from the mid-1850s onwards. Other aristocrats, such as the Asturian Count of Campo Giro and the Viscount of San Javier, were active photographers from the 1860s onwards. The Viscount of San Javier produced an interesting report on Fernando Po and Corisco in conjunction with colonel Teodosio Noeli, one of Madrid's most active amateur photographers.

N.P. ZUBIZARRETA. Running of bulls in Morata de Tajuña, ca. 1895.
(María Teresa Zubizarreta Collection.)

In any case, with the exceptions mentioned above, photography in Spain up until 1880 was mainly a professional pursuit and many of the professionals in the field were not Spaniards. In 1880 dry silver bromide-gelatin plates – the celebrated *Jungla, Darwent* and *Universal* brands – and hydroquinone developers became available on the market. This circumstance, along with the appearance of the first Kodak box cameras in 1888, led to a progressive democratisation of the practice of photography that, towards the end of the century, began making itself felt like a sort of fever that rocked the day-to-day routine of the more up-to-the-minute segments of the Spanish middle class. The number of amateur photographers surged. Outstanding among these hobbyists were the pharmacist Francesc d'A i Salarich and the engineer Leopoldo Gil i Llompart in Catalonia, Pedro Barthe, Augusto Pérez Romero, Juan N. de Díaz Custodio and L.E. Escacena in Andalusia, and Mauro Ibáñez and Julio Altadill in Navarre. In Aragon, amateur photographic activity was centred around the figure of José Antonio Dosset Monzón, who actively promoted what was to become the Sociedad Fotográfica.

By the turn of the century, amateur photography had taken on considerable proportions. The magazine *La Fotografía* claimed that in 1900 there were over a thousand amateur photographers in Madrid alone, in comparison with the 58 professionals on record. Among the most active were the brothers Máximo and Antonio Cánovas del Castillo, the Count of Polentinos and Manuel Suárez Espada, all of whom contributed decisively to the creation of the future Sociedad Fotográfica de Madrid. However, the amateurs not only outnumbered the professionals, but they also seem to have outdone them in the quality and artistic ambition of their work. In addition, a number of them were also the most enthusiastic researchers into the mysteries of the exposed image. In this connection, worth mentioning is the activity of Ferrán i Clua and Santiago Ramón y Cajal, both of them doctors, who, spurred on by their insatiable curiosity, each devised procedures similar to the silver bromide-gelatin process at a time when this type of emulsion was on the verge of superseding the collodion process. Ramón y Cajal wrote "I went so far in my devotion to the art of photography as to become a manufacturer of silver bromide-gelatin plates and I spent entire nights pouring out photosensitive emulsions by the lantern's red glow and perplexing my curious neighbours, who were convinced that I was some sort of phantasm or necromancer. (...) If I had connected at that time with an intelligent partner in possession of a certain amount of capital, a very substantial and perfectly feasible industry would have been created in Spain."[52] Ramón y Cajal also photographed scenes of everyday life, scantily clad female models, landscapes, and views of cities. Everything was of interest to this untiring, curious and tenacious man. One of the results of his experiments was an outstanding series of theoretical studies published in the magazine *La Fotografía*, beginning in 1901.

The magnitude of the activity of the growing legion of amateurs came had a substantial impact on the Spanish photographic industry and led to creation of specialist publications, whose most illustrious predecessor was *La Fotografía*, published in Seville by José Sierra Payba in 1864. In 1886 *La Fotografía* appeared in Barcelona and *La Revista Fotográfica* was published in that same city from 1891 to 1893. In 1891, Carlos Shomberg created *Novedades Fotográficas* in Bilbao in 1891, and José Baltá de Cela founded *La Fotografía Práctica* in 1893. Three years later, the first issue of *Arte Fotográfico* was published in Seville, promoted by Luis E. Escacena and in 1901 Antonio Cánovas del Castillo (*Káulak*) created *La Fotografía* in

S. RAMÓN Y CAJAL. Self-portrait, ca. 1900. (Instituto Cajal, Madrid.)

Madrid. For a number of years this last publication was the official review of the Sociedad Fotográfica de Madrid and was highly influential among Spanish amateurs of the time.

As a rule, these publications attempted to respond to the interests and technical needs of amateurs who, towards the end of the century, began forming associations such as the aforementioned Sociedad Fotográfica de Madrid, founded in 1900 as an offshoot of that city's Círculo de Bellas Artes. The Sociedad published its first list of members that year; of the 55 names on the list, 10 were titled. Six years later, the Club Fotográfico Barcelonés was founded with the aim of organising photographic excursions and publishing albums of the images obtained on those outings. This type of activity was very much in line with the cultural precepts of a certain sector of the regionalist middle class that also found expression in the creation of naturalist and ramblers associations, such as the historical Centro Excursionista de Cataluña, founded in 1876, whose more illustrious members included Soler i Santaló, Gaspar Sala, Frederic Bordas, Carles Fargas and Josep Maria Co de Triola. These societies and the ones founded later in Catalonia, Valencia and Aragon, soon became genuine factions supporting late Spanish pictorialism and whose pervasive influence, exercised through yearbooks, salons and reviews, was felt until well into the new century.

Journalistic Photography

The progressive development of amateur photography significantly eroded the activity of photographic studios and placed professionals in a delicate position, a problem that they attempted to solve in common-sense councils held in Madrid and Valencia in the opening years of the 20th century. With very few exceptions, the studios went into decline and photographers were forced to seek new professional directions if they were to continue making a living at their trade. A new era in the photographic business was about to begin, which, with Christian Franzen, Manuel Company, Laureano, the Debas brothers, Manuel Asenjo, Cantos, Antonio Esplugas, Pau Audouard, Zagala, Otero and Aguirre, J. Femenias, Joaritzi and Heribert Mariezcurrena, most of them prestigious portraitists, was to be characterised by work done outside the realm of the studios. The future was to belong to those who were able to adapt to the demands of the new times, a period marked by the unstoppable rise of journalistic photography, the origins of which date back to the middle of the 18th century.

The birth of photographic reports was closely linked to the development of the collodion process, which permitted shorter exposures and even made instantaneity conceivable. However, during those early years, so-called "historical photographs" had no immediate practical use, since the press had as yet no means of reproducing them on a mass scale, and it was the photographers themselves who undertook their work in the hope of procuring an adequate return on the images obtained. The first armed conflicts to be photographed were the war between Mexico and the United States (1846-1847) and the siege of Rome (1849), but it was the Crimean War (1853-1855) that marked the true beginning of graphic journalism, thanks to the systematic work of photographers of the stature of James Robertson and Roger Fenton, who took some two hundred images of the siege of Sebastopol. The admirable photographic records of the American Civil War (1862-1865) by Matthew Brady, Alexander Gardner and Timothy O'Sullivan were somewhat more advanced. Several years earlier, in 1860, Robertson and Felice A. Beato had taken horrific photographs in China during the Opium War.

While this incipient journalistic photography was developing, the first illustrated magazines were making their appearance. One of the most notable forerunners in this area was The *Illustrated London News*, first published in 1842. Its success was so spectacular that between 1855 and 1860 its print run increased from two hundred thousand to three hundred thousand. Its example was followed in France by *L'Illustration* (1843) and in the United States by *Harpers Weekly* (1875), which employed dozens of draughtsmen and illustrators. Their work was becoming increasingly dependent on images taken by photographers, which served as the basis for the engravings that illustrated these publications. Lacan had already written in 1856 "Photography has truly become history's helping hand. By merely having recorded recent events, after narrating the grand scenes of war, photography has made a place for itself in the halls where international congresses and peace conferences are held. (...) Yesterday it was the pitiful scenes of a flood, today the baptismal ceremonies of an imperial prince. Photography is everywhere and it records the memorable events of our collective lives."[53] However, when Lacan wrote this visionary text, photography was not as yet in a position to compete with the dexterity of engravers. Plates were extremely slow to produce and the equipment un-wieldy to handle. Many years would pass before the technique would catch up with the advances made in the area of printed images. The silver bromide-gelatin dry emulsion became available in 1871 and the first anastigmat lenses were pro-duced in 1884. In 1878, Charles Harper Bennet created an emulsion that could be kept for several days and had an exposure time of 25 hundredths of a second. In 1882, E.J. Marey designed the photographic gun, which had been previously con-ceived by Herchel and, in 1880, *The Daily Graphic* produced halftone photome-chanical copies. Seven years later, magnesium flash powder was introduced, allowing photographers to capture images in places where this had previously been impossible. With these advances, graphic journalism underwent spectacular de-velopment and paved the way for a new photographic speciality.

In Spain, the first photographs destined specifically for the press were taken in the 1860s, although illustrated magazines had regularly been using photographs as the basis for engravings since the previous decade. The most notable precursor of this use is to be found in an illustration published in 1852 by the Valencia news-paper *Diario Mercantil* and drawn from a daguerreotype taken by Pérez Rodríguez. In 1858, *El Museo Universal* advertised the regular collaboration of Charles Clifford and that same year Laurent began working with *La Crónica*, while dozens of other professionals submitted their photographs to newspapers, which were placing ever more emphasis on graphic information. Photographers began accompanying draughtsmen and reporters on their tasks of documenting important events, such as the Moroccan War of 1859. During that conflict, Enrique Facio, along with the writer Pedro Antonio Alarcón and the painter Mariano Fortuny, was assigned by General O'Donnell's propaganda services to record "the most memorable occur-rences of the titanic struggle" between the Spanish and Moroccan armies.

The Carlist Wars provided a further occasion for the work of photographers such as Charles Monney, Luciano Carrouche, Otero and Aguirre, and Mauro Ibáñez. Monney was the author of the most complete series of views of the siege of Bilbao, in the early months of 1874. These are excellent photographs and they depict the popular and military aspects of one of the most dramatic and memo-rable episodes of the Third Carlist War. Worthy of note on the Legitimist side are the work of José de Lejarreta, in the streets of Durango in 1873, the Pole Ladislas Kornarzewski, who followed several of the factions led by the priest Santa Cruz,

*A. GARCÍA. Carlist partisans
in prison. Valencia, 1869.
(José Huguet Collection.)*

J. Parada, a veteran of the Carlist militias who had settled in Bordeaux and who photographed outstanding political and military leaders in his studio there, Otero and Aguirre, who depicted the bombardment of Durango and San Sebastian, Guiard, in whose studio in Santiago Compostela the Galician rebels posed, and Antonio García, who photographed Carlist captives in Valencia in 1869. Most of the images captured by these photographers lack any discernible journalistic qualities and centre their attention instead on an iconographic testimony of the gestures, uniforms and impedimenta of these dedicated "crusaders for the cause". In this sense they are comparable to the work of José Lorente Gallego, who portrayed the members of the popular militias in Cartagena during the Cantonalist revolt in 1873. All that remains to be added to these sparse examples are the occasional and unremarkable report, such as those produced by Amadeo Courbón in Santander during the revolutionary incidents of 1868, by José Rodrigo during the Cantonalist revolt in Cartagena, and by Manuel Company during the Moroccan campaign of 1893.

As mentioned earlier, many of these reports were published in the press in the form of engravings before the rotary presses of *Blanco y Negro* and *Nuevo Mundo* had the capability of producing halftones. By then, Spanish graphic journalism had come a long way since José María Carnecero published the first illustrations in *Cartas Españolas* in 1831. A number of publications subsequently used engravings and lithographs with varying success, including *El Artista*, founded in 1835 by Federico de Madrazo, and *El Semanario Pintoresco Español*, created two years later by Mesonero Romanos and a veritable school of engravers of the stature of Calixto Ortega, Vicente Castillo and Bernardo Rico. Nevertheless, *El Semanario* used engravings more for their ornamental qualities than as illustrations. Graphic illustration was not yet considered an informative element that could complement news and reports on current events, although already in *El Museo de las Familias* (1843) and *El Museo Universal* (1856) graphic reporting was practised by such accomplished figures as Francisco Ortego, Valeriano Bécquer and Daniel Perea. However, it was *La Ilustración Española y Americana*, founded in 1869 by Abelardo de Carlos, that opened up in Spain a field that had already been pioneered twenty years earlier elsewhere in Europe. *La Ilustración* was a personal undertaking by its founder, who had already given considerable impetus to printing in Spain with the creation of the Rybadeneyra works.

For many years photography and engraving co-existed in illustrated magazines.[54] Photography gradually evolved to the point where it appropriated the space dedicated by the press to reporting on current events, while engravings were relegated to the reproduction of famous paintings, buildings and monuments. Illustrated magazines increasingly used photographers' work and built up extensive networks of correspondents who submitted their reports from all regions of Spain. In 1884, the professionals collaborating with *La Ilustración Española y Americana* included Zenón Quintana, from Santander, José Oliván, from Salamanca, Patricio Gal, from Irún, Francisco Zagala, from Pontevedra, Casiano Alguacil, from Toledo, Antonio Barcia, from Santiago de Compostela, Marcos Sala and Laureano, from Barcelona, and Hébert, Company and the Debas brothers from Madrid. Among the most outstanding contributors was Juan Comba, one of the magazine's leading illustrators who began basing his work on his own photographs in 1880. Comba is considered one of the fathers of graphic journalism in Spain and he produced major photographic reports on

E. FACIO. Military encampment during the war with Morocco.
Ceuta, 1860. (Patrimonio Nacional.)

CHARLES MONNEY. Defense of Bilbao under siege by Carlist troops.
1874. (Olmedilla Collection.)

subjects such as the fire in the Alcázar at Toledo in 1887 and Queen Victoria's visit to Spain in 1889. Heribert Mariezcurrena, known for his research in the area of photomechanical printing, produced important reports for the Barcelona edition of *La Ilustración*, such as the one published serially in the February 1885 editions on the earthquakes that had devastated the provinces of Córdoba and Málaga.[55]

However, photography did not become an integral part of the Spanish press until the appearance of the influential graphic magazines *Blanco y Negro*, *Nuevo Mundo* and *La Revista Moderna*. The first issue of *Blanco y Negro* was published on 10 May 1891, with a print run of 20,000 copies. Conceived as a true "illustrated magazine" in the style of the German *Flagender Blatter*, it began to include photography, although to a much lesser extent than drawings and engravings. From 1895 onwards, photographs began to occupy a much more prominent position on its pages with the publication of Christian Franzen's excellent reports on Madrid's beau monde and nightlife. Over the following years other photographers of the stature of Manuel Company, García Rufiño, Pedro Calvet, Hauser y Menet, *Napoleón*, Avrillón and Manuel Novoa also became contributors. *Nuevo Mundo* appeared on 18 March 1894 and soon became *Blanco y Negro*'s main competitor, so much so that four years later it was being published in print runs of 49,317 copies. Originally called *El Nuevo Mundo*, the initial issues did not contain so much as a single photograph, owing to the atrocious quality of the photomechanical processes of the time. In 1896 it began publishing systematically the work of its first photographic contributors, including Franzen, Company, Fernando Debas, Amador, Luis Alonso and Alfonso Sánchez García (*Alfonso*). During the first few years of the new century the number of its reporters grew considerably, to include José Demaria López (*Campúa*), Alejandro Merletti, Venancio Gombáu, Francisco Goñi, Vicente Barberá, Julio Duque and Gómez Durán, and *Nuevo Mundo* definitively displaced the competing graphic magazines. *La Revista Moderna* was first published in 1897, edited by Eduardo Sánchez de Castilla. It published its first mainly photographic report in its issue number eight and began using colour covers in 1898, with trichrome photographs by Matéu inside.

These were not particularly prosperous times for the press and even less so for the graphic weeklies, which, due to their high production costs, were sold at prices that were prohibitive for the public at large. In 1900, a periodical cost 5 centimos, an exorbitant sum for an ordinary family, bearing in mind that a kilogram of bread cost 50 centimos and that the average daily wage was under 3 pesetas. Add to this the high rate of illiteracy – 64 per cent at the end of the 19th century – and we have a basic idea of the social and cultural context in which the Spanish press had to carry out its activity. It is not surprising, then, that journalists' working conditions were compared on occasion with those of the proletariat. The situation of graphic editors was even worse, given the fact that there were practically none on the staffs of Spanish publications until the appearance of the first illustrated dailies at the turn of the century.

Before photomechanical techniques had advanced sufficiently to allow the faithful reproduction of photographs, some reporters disseminated their work through the sale of albums and numbered series of views. The old "photographic museums" produced by photographers in their own workshops were followed by the first series produced using photolithography and phototypy, thanks to the technical progress made by pioneers such as R.J. Lemercier and Alphonse Poitevin in the 1850s. These processes were introduced gradually in Spain by photographers such as Antonio Selfa, who set up a workshop for making zincographic reproductions in Madrid in 1863. Ten years later, Heribert Mariezcurrena, Miguel Joaritzi, Joan Serra and Josep Thomas created the Sociedad Heliográfica Española in Barcelona.[56] That company was dissolved in 1879, the same year that Thomas founded the celebrated Fototipia Thomas, which, along with the analogous enterprises set up by Joaritzi, Mariezcurrena, Rivas Castiñeira, Álvarez, Laurent, and Hauser and Menet, produced postcards and posters. By the turn of the century this had become a lucrative business. In 1900, Hauser and Menet declared a yearly production of 500,000 postcards and two years later *Káulak* claimed to have sold 180,000 copies of his series *Las Doloras*, based on the poem of the same name by the prodigious Campoamor.

These series of images marketed by these historical phototypy businesses were soon joined by snapshots of more or less memorable events sold by the photographers themselves as a professional sideline. A good example of this sort of activity is Antonio Esplugas, one of the most emblematic portraitists of the Catalan middle class, who sold aerial views of Barcelona as well as images of military manoeuvres, mass demonstrations and even public executions, such as that of the famous Isidre Montpart, garrotted in the Patio dels Corders in the old Barcelona

J. BEAUCHY. "El Burrero" cabaret. Seville, ca. 1890. (Carlos Teixidor Collection.)

prison in 1892. Manuel Company also produced various photographic editions of his best images of the Moroccan campaign, while Edmundo and Fernando Debas did the same with their shots of sports subjects, Julio Beauchy marketed complete series of his bullfighting shots and Amador sold thousands of copies of his celebrated portrait of the miraculously preserved body of San Isidro Labrador. Another system for disseminating photographic images was the publication of collectible series such as the celebrated *Panorama Nacional*, the most illustrious predecessor of our present-day fascicles. Published in 1896 by the lithographer Hermenegildo Miralles, the *Panorama Nacional* was not the only publication of its kind around the end of the century. Also worth mentioning in this category are, among others, *España Artística*, *Barcelona a la vista*, *Portafolio Fotográfico de España* and *Galicia Pintoresca*, which contained the work of dozens of photographers, including Marqueríe, from Gijón, Plá, from Alicante, Ayola, from Granada, Pallejá, from Tarragona, San Miguel, from Bilbao, Luareano, from Barcelona, and Company and Fernando Debas, from Madrid.

A. ESPLUGAS. Execution of Isidro Montpar. Barcelona, 1892.
(Private Collection.)

PART TWO

P. AUDOUARD. Quadruplets in a four-place pushchair.
ca. 1905. (Biblioteca Nacional.)

Spain in 1900

After long years marked by coup attempts, civil strife, and bitter struggles between the past and future, between freedom and chains, Spain finished the 19th century with the brutal trauma of the loss of its last colonies. The Treaty of Paris ceded Cuba, the Philippines, Puerto Rico and Guam to the United States and plunged Spain into a severe crisis that undermined its economic and social structure and even the political system created under the Restoration engineered by Cánovas. Tuñón de Lara writes "The crisis was diverse and multifaceted; there was a structural crisis because the empire had disappeared, an economic crisis because this substantial source of income had been cut off, a political crisis because the liberal and conservative parties that took turns in office, supported by a network of local political bosses, were debilitated and discredited, and a social crisis because the development of industry in some regions strengthened the working class, which was in confrontation with intransigent employers."[57]

In the crucial year of 1898 – the year that, in many opinions, marked the end of the 19th century in Spain – over 60 per cent of the almost nineteen million Spaniards were illiterate, 63 per cent were seasonal farm labourers and landless peasants and only 16 per cent worked in industry. In 1900, approximately ten thousand families owned over half of the registered property in the country, and 42 per cent of all privately owned land was in the hands of just 1 per cent of landowners. Urban workers earned wretched wages, ranging from 2.5 pesetas for a building labourer to 4 pesetas for a carpenter, but no farmhands earned more than 1.25 pesetas daily and women were paid half that rate, not to mention the thousands of seasonal hands who earned under a peseta and children who worked merely for their keep.

This pre-industrial Spain, an agrarian country dominated by political bosses, dedicated a negligible portion of its budget to science and culture – 35,000 pesetas annually from 1875 to 1904 – while the army maintained a staff of 561 generals, 582 colonels and 19,790 officers, and in 1921 alone the astronomical sum of two hundred million pesetas was spent on the unpopular war with Morocco. The situation was therefore just as desperate in areas such as education. Unamuno wrote "We live in a poor country and where there is no food there can only be despair. Our financial poverty explains our intellectual poverty."

Higher education continued to be a privilege of the well-to-do classes, whose interest in learning was on a level with their arrogant and secular ignorance. Chamberlain wrote "This lack of culture on the part of the classes that pass for erudite is necessarily reflected in the life of the nation. (...) In the midst of such ignorance and backwardness any type of effort at regeneration is faced with enormous difficulties."[58] Like many intellectuals of the time, Chamberlain proposed a solution originating with the political establishment, very much along the lines of the regenerationist positions of Lucas Mallada, Joaquín Costa and Macías Picavea, who argued in favour of a "providential man", a "surgeon of steel", in the words of Costa, who could lead the country to redemption. This solution differed little from the one advocated by certain sectors of the industrial middle class and ultimately taken up even by the leaders of the Conservative Union. Nevertheless, as early as 1836, Mariano José de Larra, a regenerationist before his time, had pointed out "All of the difficulties that must be overcome in carrying out a regeneration project have to do with involving the masses." This was precisely the great challenge facing Spanish regenerationists and their great failure, both in terms of the economy and politics, and in photography as well, with late pictorialist precepts that were totally caught up in the ethical and aesthetic ideas of the middle class regenerationism prevailing at the beginning of the 20th century. This explains why the ordinary people failed to take up this movement with any interest or enthusiasm whatsoever and why it failed so roundly in its attempt to reform the country's public life and bring culture and education to an impoverished population, one that suffered from profound and centuries-old deficiencies, not only in respect of schooling, but also of the basic necessities of life.

Economic underdevelopment, political corruption, the disgraceful African adventure that led to the sacrifice of thousands of young lives on the desolate Moroccan fronts, and the persistence of 19th-century structures in industry all spurred the emerging urban proletariat on to a growing radicalisation channelled by socialist and anarchist movements that focussed their protests on miserable working conditions, exploitation, and endless conscription for the war in Morocco.[59] Meanwhile, the generation of young intellectuals who had grown up during the years of the colonial disaster began experiencing Spain's circumstances with a certain degree of intensity – "My Spain hurts", as Unamuno so concisely put it – and looking favourably on the militant proletariat that had been growing constantly since the time of Anselmo Lorenzo. In spite of their differences, those intellectuals of the Generation of '98 seemed to be united in their shared rejection of the political structures of the Restoration. From Azorín to Valle-Inclán, Pío Baroja, Ramiro de Maeztu and Jacinto Benavente, all of them coincided in their militant opposition to the vices of political power. This militancy even affected some of the successors to the Generation of '98 and made a lasting impression on their future intellectual development.

Spain's political and social circumstances are barely reflected in photography, which maintained its traditional distance from artistic currency and was dismissed or ignored by cultural élites, who still considered it to be a mere accessory of the arts or a hobby of no particular import. Unlike poets, novelists and painters, Spain's photographic artists, most of whom followed the pictorialist trends that were imported rather late into Europe, were unable to depict the reality that surrounded them and showed no interest whatsoever in the intense social upheaval that followed upon the final collapse of the archaic political framework of the Restoration. In contrast with Spanish literature, thought and art, "artistic" photography in Spain at this time was, quite simply, pathetic.

Let Others Invent!

Spain's political and economic situation had a substantial impact on the industrial and commercial structures of photography, which, at the turn of the century, found itself still afflicted by the lingering 19th-century crisis in portraiture. This crisis was repeatedly condemned by leading figures of the time, such as Antonio Cánovas del Castillo (*Káulak*), who continually deplored the disquieting depression that Spanish professional photography had been unable to shake off since the closing years of the 19th century. Faced with this situation, photographers sought solutions in the form of associations along the lines of trade unions, such as the Unión Fotográfica de Valencia, founded in 1903 under the leadership of the prestigious figure of Antonio García. This association held a National Assembly of Professional Photographers in 1908, three years after a similar congress in Madrid, in an attempt to solve its problems through the creation of co-operatives, mutual funds and discount shops.[60]

The crisis undergone by Spanish photography at the beginning of the 20th century also led to acute technical dependency on the European industry. Spain kept to the precept expressed by Unamuno to the effect that others should be left to take the lead in technological advances. In 1902, the magazine *La Fotografía* provided a list of the technical innovations available at the time, such as telephoto lenses, Kodak stereoscopes and other "optical marvels" produced by Goerz, Zeiss, Steinbel and Voigtländer, as well a flood of gum bichromates and carbons, three-colour processes, and so on, while deploring the fact that they were all imports. "As for the manufacture of plates, no one has yet decided to compete with Lumière in this business. All manner of companies are set up in this country, but none has ever been formed that could make a substantial return on a modest investment, as would be the case with the manufacture of photosensitive plates and accessories."[61]

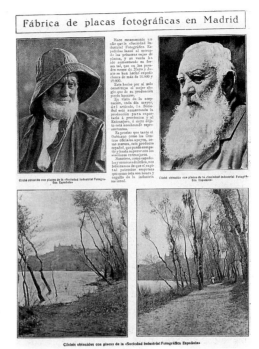

The Sociedad Industrial Española was the leading Spanish manufacturer of glass negatives. Mundo Gráfico, 16 August 1922.

According to this magazine's figures, yearly consumption of glass negatives in Spain amounted to 164,000 (4,000 in the 18×24 cm format and larger, 25,000 in the 13×18 cm format, 75,000 in formats of between 6×9 cm and 9×12, and 60,000 in other formats), most of which were imported from foreign producers. Not only plates were imported, but also cameras and papers, which were supplied by Lumière, Agfa, Perutz, Kodak and Schleussner.[62] The few Spanish companies that tried to compete with them did so on a small scale and did not last long, as they were unable to contend with the tough foreign competition. The company Manufactura General Española de Productos Fotográficos S.A. was founded in Murcia in 1893 and produced silver bromide-gelatin *Victoria* plates and marketed a type of paper called "aristotype" – the famous citrate paper – produced to formulas imported from Germany. Following upon this unpretentious industrial undertaking, the company Manufacturas de Papeles Fotográficos was formed in Barcelona in 1916 and absorbed in 1923 by Editorial Fotográfica, which was to become in 1924 the historic firm Negra y Tort, forerunner of the later Negra Industrial. This was the only Spanish producer of photographic products that was able to contend successfully with the relentless foreign competition. All of the others did erratic and ephemeral business. In 1922, Rafael Garriga, editor-in-chief of the magazine *El Progreso Fotográfico*, founded Fotoquímica Garriga, which produced bromide papers and continued to manufacture citrate papers, although these had already gone into a steep decline. This company lasted only a few years, and the existence of Papeles Fotográficos Llimona, also founded in 1922, was even briefer. One year earlier, the Sociedad Industrial Fotográfica Española, unquestionably the most ambitious Spanish enterprise in the manufacture of glass negatives, had been formed in Madrid. This factory, the only one of its kind in Spain and with an entirely Spanish staff, as it stressed in its publicity, succeeded in selling the respectable number of 10,000 and 20,000 plates in May and June of 1922, although there is no evidence that it went on to consolidate its business definitively.[63]

Spanish photography was also technically dependent on imports in the field of colour photography, which was developed by L. Ducos de Hauron, Niepce de Saint Victor, F.E. Ives, John Joli, Gabriel Lippman and the Lumière brothers. Ducos de Hauron had been the first to make practical use of the known principle of breaking down chromatic light into the three primary colours (blue, green and red), but the French physicist Gabriel Lippman was the first to produce colour photographs, using his celebrated interferential method (1891), for which we was awarded the Nobel Prize 1908. Nevertheless, it was the Lumière brothers who popularised colour photography with their Autochrome plates, first demonstrated in Paris in June 1907 in the offices of *L'Illustration*. This process remained prevalent for over twenty years, until the appearance in 1935 of the Kodachrome film still in use today.

Colour photography's most active advocate in Spain was Santiago Ramón y Cajal, whose interest in the Lippman method led him to publish his book *Fotografía de los Colores* in 1912. As indicated by its subtitle, *Bases teóricas y reglas técnicas* ("Fundamentals of Theory and Technical Considerations"), Ramón y Cajal's intent was "exclusively to provide a clear and methodical explanation of the theoretical basis and practical procedures of colour photography, following in the footsteps and taking advantage of the teachings of such eminent foreign experts as Ducos de Hauron, Lippman, Lumière, Namias, Valenta, Ives, Quentin, and so on." The ubiquitous Antonio Cánovas del Castillo (*Káulak*), for his part, included an extensive chapter on Autochrome plates in his manual *La Fotografía Moderna*, also

BARBER-PEREFERRER (Foto Lux). *Shop assistants at the "Lux" photo shop.*
Gerona, ca. 1920. (Gerona Municipal Archives.)

published in 1912. Unlike Ramón y Cajal, *Káulak* did not analyse the process from a scientific standpoint, but simply gave a very straightforward and basic explanation of its use.[64]

There were no outstanding practitioners of colour photography in Spain and very few works of any merit were produced with this technique, which was used from 1910 onwards by amateurs such as Ramón y Cajal himself, Fungairiño, Amós Salvador, Emili Vilá, Eduardo Retola, Luis Sanjurjo, Joan Massó and Aurelio Grasa, and by professionals such as Jaime Pacheco and Ciriaco Nieto (*Linker*). The most noteworthy of these were Aurelio Grasa, who took some admirable autochromes of bullfighting subjects, Fungairiño, who took the first colour photograph to be published in a Spanish weekly, and Joan Massó, who produced a series of excellent autochromes in the early 1920s.

Photographic Circles

The latest advances in photography had led to spectacular growth in the number of amateurs, who began joining together in photographic societies from the beginning of the century onwards with objectives that bore little resemblance to those of the nascent professional associations. In Madrid, *La Ilustración Española y Americana* reported in its issue of 30 December 1899 on the constitution of the Sociedad Fotográfica, whose membership grew to 400 by June 1901. The background of the members of this new association, renamed the Real Sociedad Fotográfica de Madrid in 1907, clearly reflects the social context of amateur photography of the times, which was restricted to the aristocracy and the upper middle class. Of the first 140 members, 20 were titled and the rest belonged to the city's political, military and financial élites, including the brothers Máximo and Antonio Cánovas del Castillo, General Noeli, Santiago Ramón y Cajal, Carlos Iñigo, Francisco Cabrerizo and Suárez Espada, who was, if only briefly, its first president.[65]

In Catalonia, the Club Fotográfico Barcelonés had been founded in 1894 for the purpose of organising photographic excursions and publishing albums with the resulting images. Nevertheless, in spite of the presence of some three thousand amateur photographers in Barcelona alone and in spite of their ongoing efforts in the area of publishing and their precocious business ventures, Catalonia's photog-

KÁULAK. Amateur photographers at the Alameda Palace at Osuna. Madrid, 1900. (Private Collection.)

raphers were unable to create a stable association until 15 June 1923, when the Agrupación Fotográfica de Cataluña was founded by Josep Demestres, Joaquín Pla Janini, Salvador Lluch and Claudio Carbonell. The Agrupación Fotográfica de Cataluña was enormously influential among photographers in Catalonia and in effect served as a model for other similar cultural and ramblers' groups, which included photographic sections.[66] In Aragon, the earliest attempts at founding an association were made in 1900 by amateur photographers in Zaragoza, with the aim of creating an "independent centre" that could organise photographic excursions, competitions and exhibitions. These associational efforts culminated in the foundation of the Sociedad Fotográfica de Zaragoza in May 1923. Among the more outstanding members of this society were Lorenzo Pardo, Francisco Samperio, the Faci brother, Julio Requejo and García Carril. With somewhat different aims, a group of enthusiasts including Lisardo Arlandis, Vicente Peydró, José Gil and Bernardo Ferrer formed the Photo-Club in Valencia in 1928.

The formation of these photographic societies was of central importance to the associational activities of Spanish amateur photographers and provided the foundation on which the phenomenon of the salon movement eventually developed, a circumstance to which other associations, such as the workers' section of the Ateneo de Gijón, the Centro Excursionista de San Andrés, the Sociedad Peñalara and the Centro Excursionista de Barcelona also contributed. Given the almost total lack of any commercial and exhibition circuits, these societies provided the only means of disseminating and promoting photography, and the only school of style available to Spanish enthusiasts of the time. They also served to promote the other major vehicle for dissemination of new photographic techniques and trends, the specialist magazines.

La Fotografía was founded by Káulak in October 1901 and was the official publication of the Sociedad Fotográfica de Madrid until the latter began publishing its own newsletter in January 1906. La Fotografía attained print runs of 3,000 copies in 1904 and was the most influential publication of its time, surviving until 1914 after a second phase with Antonio Prats as editor-in-chief. In 1906, this magazine published a list of the specialist reviews then existing in Spain: Daguerre, Avante, Agua, azucarillos y aguardiente, La Fotografía and Gomas o nada. None of them were particularly influential in Spanish photographic circles, owing to the lack of commercial drive on the part of their editors, most of whom were, first and foremost, enthusiasts. Professional photographers only participated to any extent in Daguerre, and even they were unable to overcome the difficulties involved in a publication of this sort.

The magazine Photos appeared in Zaragoza in 1904 and published photographs by Alberto Muro, Eduardo Cativiela and other Aragonese photographers, along with the work of eminent pictorialists such as Julio García de la Puente, J. Peinado and Vicente Gómez Novella. Two years later, the first issue of Graphos Ilustrado, a monthly edited by Antonio Escobar, was published in Madrid, with works by the leading "artistic" photographers of the day, including Káulak, Vicente Gómez Novella, Carlos Iñigo, Gerardo Bustillo and the first Ortiz Echagüe. With Graphos and La Fotografía, Madrid was able to maintain its dominant position for several years in the face of the growing prominence of Catalonia, where the most influential and dynamic photographic magazines of the first third of the century were published: Lux (1915-1922), El Progreso Fotográfico (1920-1936), Cri-

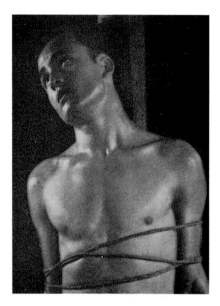 

ARISSA. The Slave. Published in 1933 in Art de la Llum.

PLA JANINI. Neptune. Published in 1933 in Art de la Llum.

terium (1921-1923), *La Revista Fotográfica* (1923-1926), the newsletter of the Agrupación Fotográfica de Cataluña (beginning in 1923), *Radium* (1924-1928), *Arte Fotográfico* (1927-1928), *La fotografía para todos* (1926), *Art de la llum* (1933-1936) and *24 × 36* (1934-1936).

Criterium was edited by Miguel Huertas and regularly published photographs by Joan Vilatobá, *Linker* and Rafael Areñas. Its spirit was later kept alive in *El Progreso Fotográfico*, the pages of which carried the work of Ortiz Echagüe, Antonio Arissa, Claudio Carbonell, Miguel Goicoechea, R.P. Noguera, Francisco Mora Carbonell and other eminent pictorialists. *Foto* was directed by José Pérez Noguera and was impeccably printed on top quality paper. It followed the same pictorialist line as the others, as might be expected in view of its editor's "artistic" bent. *Art de la llum* was launched at the height of the struggle for Catalonia's Statute of Autonomy. With the significant subtitle "Revista Fotogràfica de Catalunya", this magazine was written entirely in Catalan and from its first issue, published in June 1933, stressed its dedication to "the restitution of the personality of Catalonia in the field of photography, held to be cultural reality". *Art de la llum* was the most authentic expression of decidedly Catalan nationalist and pictorialist political and photographic militancy and the result of an unprecedented effort with the participation of 23 regional, local and provincial photographic societies and 18 trading firms. Edited by Andreu Mir Escudé, *Art de la llum* printed photographs by Thorez, L. Missonne, Nuemuller, J. Parsons, Keighley and other leading proponents of the declining European photographic impressionism, and by some of its more outstanding Spanish figures, such as Pla Janini, Arissa, A. Campañá, Carbonell, Joan Porqueras, Casals Ariet, Josep Masana, R. Batlles and Francisco Andrada.

Aside from the ones already mentioned, other technical and professional magazines were published in Catalonia, and it is in these publications that we find the first traces of modernity in Spanish photography of the time. Worth mentioning among them are *El Mirador* (1933), *D'Ací i D'Allà* (1918) and the newsletter *AC* ("Notes on Contemporary Activity"), the official publication of GATEPAC (Association of Spanish Architects and Technicians for Progress in Architecture). *El Mirador* published works by Pere Catalá Pic, Mario de Bocovich, M. Cifreda and Joan Sac that were highly critical of pictorialism. Photography was an important presence in *D'Ací i D'Allà*, particularly after Josep Sala took over its artistic direction in 1932. This magazine printed photographs by J. Artigas, J.M. Llovet, Josep Masana, Ramón Batlles, Adolf Zerkowitz and Sala himself. Sala's works also appeared in *AC*, which printed a number of his photograms and overprints that bordered on abstraction. The surprising magazine *Ford* was also published in Barcelona with a different set of aims, and with the collaboration of Pere Catalá Pic, Emili Vilá, Ramón Batlles, Josep María de Sagarra, Josep Sala and other leading proponents of the photographic modernity of the day. The pages of this magazine published one of Catalá Pic's most interesting works on the photographic avant-garde and introduced Man Ray on the occasion of the 1935 show in Barcelona.

So-called "artistic" photography was also published regularly in periodicals such as *Mundo Gráfico*, *Nuevo Mundo*, *Blanco y Negro* and particularly *La Esfera*, all of which reported assiduously on exhibitions and salons organised by photographic societies. Lastly, mention must be made of the magazines linked directly to trading firms and equipment manufacturers. *El Fotógrafo profesional* (1914-1922) was Kodak's in-house publication and offered with each issue a photographic print on its famous *Nikko*, *Kodura* and *Bromide Velour* papers. *Agfa* (1926-1931) was published by the company of the same name, while *Unión Fotográfica* (1919-1930) was the official publication of the Spanish Professional Photographers' Society.[67]

Denial of Reality – Pictorialist Photography

During the last few decades of the 19th century photography was the object of an intense controversy as to its nature. In contrast with the faithful representation of reality characteristic of this medium, from mid-century onward so-called "artistic" photography went about exhaustively repeating the same contrived, allegorical formulas found in the worst academic painting of the time. Even then there was a tendency to want to seclude photography in the frigid, inaccessible realms of Art and Beauty and to keep it free of any taint or caprice of accurately reflecting reality, as suggested by the British critic Cornelius J. Hughes. In this fallacious dichotomy between Truth and Beauty – as if the two were necessarily at odds – "artistic" photographers opted unswervingly for the latter and did not hesitate to banish reality, which they did not consider to be artistic material worthy of their work. This gave rise to so-called pictorialist photography, which stemmed from a lack of humility on the part of its creators and from the exaggerated artistic pretensions of photography itself.

Pictorialist photographers, most of them members of the aristocracy and the cultured upper middle class and heavily influenced by the Pre-Raphaelites, the Viennese Symbolists, Art Nouveau and the earliest French proponents of Art Deco, were determined to severe any connection between Truth and photography as a necessary precondition for making this technique into a true art form. In their drive to preserve photography from the ravages of vulgarisation and extension facilitated by technical advances, the pictorialists attempted to shut it away in shrines inaccessible not only to the legions of enthusiast newcomers but also to the professionals who made a living from the self-sacrificing practice of their trade. The aim pursued from these elitist photographic ivory towers of the time, including the Linked Ring Brotherhood in London, the Photo-Club de Paris, the Vienna Camera Club, the Association Belge de Photographie and the New York Camera Club, was not only for photography to imitate painting but also that it should be integrated into the conventional market for art. In short, the idea was to tame photog-

KÁULAK. Plagiarism of Velázquez. *1904.*
(Real Sociedad Fotográfica.)

raphy and make it conform to the narrow limits of aesthetic forms already defined in the world of painting. This was tantamount to denying outright photography's essential characteristics, which were none other than its clarity, low cost and reproducibility.

Pictorialist photography did not come into existence overnight, but instead had its origins in the narrative and allegorical academicism of certain pioneers, such as E.J. Mayall, who, as early as 1845, had produced a rendering of the *Lord's Prayer* in a series of ten daguerreotypes, with the stated aim of "illustrating poetry and movement". In spite of the severe criticism directed against this type of photography from the start, Mayall soon had followers in W. Lake Price, Oscar Gustave Rejlander and Henry Peach Robinson, on whose work the pictorialist movement was based, with its definitive enshrinement in Robinson's manual *Pictorial Effect in Photography* (1869), in which the author attempted to "define the laws governing the composition of a photograph to achieve the greatest possible pictorial effect". Robinson's work was translated into numerous languages and became a veritable style book for such prestigious photographers as Julia M. Cameron or D.O. Hill himself, who were attempting to develop the field of "artistic" photography by staging subjects with literary, historical, allegorical or mythological themes. These ear-

C. IÑIGO. Allegory of sainthood. ca. 1905.
(Real Sociedad Fotográfica.)

ly pictorialist photographers, highly acclaimed at the time in the cultural circles of the Victorian aristocracy, displayed, as pointed out by Gersheim, an unfortunate tendency to "construct" photographs rather than taking them. The authors of such photographs found no better means of achieving their ends than to choose supposedly artistic, meaningful or edifying themes, find the most appropriate models to personify their characters, arrange them theatrically in a pompous, overelaborate setting and have them strike the most convincing and appropriate pose for the moral of their sublime creations.[68]

In the face of this extreme affectation, Peter Henry Emerson advocated a return to Nature a source of inspiration and as a way of rising above the "artistic anachronisms and fallacies" of Victorian pictorialism. His book, *Naturalistic Photography for Students of Art* (1889) had a considerable influence on figures such as George Davison, Benjamin G. Wilkinson, Lyddell Sawyer and Franck M. Sutcliffe, whose work marked the beginning of a second wave of pictorialists, this time indebted to Impressionism, with its most outstanding proponents in the Britons Alfred Maskell and Alexander Keighley, the Frenchmen Robert Demachy and Constant Puyo, the Belgian Leonard Misonne, the Austrian H. Kühn and the Americans Clarence White, Alfred Stieglitz and Edward Steichen. Although they abandoned once and for all the historicist and allegorical pomposity of the original pictorialists, this new breed inherited their "artistic" pretensions and the same rejection of reality as photographic material. To this end they adopted the appropriate techniques, including extreme *flous*, pronounced fuzziness in copies, rough papers, soft focus and haloes achieved using so-called "artist's lenses", to infuse their works with the pictorial effect that they sought. For this purpose, the new pictorialists did not hesitate to destroy the very nature of the medium in which they were working, once again burying reality and playing the game of disguising the origin. In the words of Marc Melon "It is not a matter, then, of photography finding inspiration in the images created by painting and taking from them what it cannot provide itself, but rather of contending with those images, wagering the price of its own specific nature, even at the risk of being reduced to an appearance that would conceal its very identity."[69] The new pigmentation techniques introduced between 1894 and 1907 – gum bichromates, greasy inks, *fressons* – eventually allowed photographers to conceal the "photographic" qualities of their works and give them a pictorial finish and appearance and the aura of a unique work spoken of by Barthes. Robert Demachy stated in 1906 "It does not matter to me in the least whether the photographer uses oil and gum or platinum, whether they smear their negative or attack it with a scraper, as long as they can show me an image that their neighbour is unable to achieve. (...) We may then be accused of doing away with the *photographic character* of photography. This is precisely what we wish to do." This was an unmitigated negation of photography as an autonomous mode of expression and a veritable exercise in submission to painting and the rules of the conventional art market. Paul Strand wrote "These pictorialists' main error is that they have failed to discover the basic qualities of photography. They are ignorant of and scorn its own tradition. (...) All of which demonstrates their lack of faith in the dignity of the very medium that they use, and use badly, and at the same time the absurdity of their pretension that they too are artists."[70]

The echo of pictorialism reached Spain many years later, in a cultural and historical context marked by the crisis of the Restoration. Spanish photographers finally adopted this new photographic aesthetic well into the 20th century, with the intention, formulated by *Káulak*, of "stimulating the senses and providing a pleasing sight for the eye, in the same way as the most renowned painted works." This late reflection of the pictorialist aesthetic in Spanish "artistic" photography of the

J. VILATOBÁ. Where Will I Find You in Heaven? ca. 1915. (Museu d'Art de Sabadell.)

early 20th century was simply a consequence of the consideration given this medium of expression at the time in the country's cultural spheres. Spanish art of this period was permeated by the aesthetic, ideological and moral values of a decadent and declining aristocracy and an ascendant agrarian and industrial middle class. In addition, the commercial, pedagogical and promotional infrastructure of Spanish art as a whole had been defined in the previous century and in general functioned as a faithful executor of what Jaime Brihuega has defined as the "dictates of the ruling ideology". Furthermore, the new market circles barely offered any opportunities for Spanish artists. With the exception of a half dozen galleries in Madrid and Barcelona, only a few such establishments organised exhibitions and direct sales to private customers were next to impossible, as those customers were almost exclusively restricted to a middle class that was firmly anchored in the bureaucratic officialism that dominated the artistic production of the time.

Photography, scorned insistently by the cultural elite, was in an even more unenviable position. Lacking a solid tradition on which to base its development and in the absence of masters to show the way in the midst of such confusion, it was unable even to follow the guidelines laid down by the existing officialist middle class and remain mired in the stale, outdated aesthetic values of the vestigial, degraded and idle aristocracy described by Machado, a class that was firmly entrenched in the past and contemplated the future with terror in a world that it found increasingly immense, incomprehensible and alien. As late as 1926, Moreno Villa wrote "In this country one only trusts in what is old." More than in what was old, photography trusted only in what was archaic, in the obsolete, pompous and absurd allegorical compositions of Victorian pictorialism that had by then been definitively interred by breakaway movements in American and European photography.

As in the case of all poor imitations, all that the earliest Spanish pictorialists succeeded in emulating were the outward appearances of a movement that had been born at a time and in a place and culture that had nothing in common with the changing reality of Spain at that time. What the first Spanish pictorialists imitated so uncritically and mechanically were not even the forms and aesthetic precepts of photographic impressionism of the end of the 19th century but rather the academicist and moralising narrative tendencies of Victorian pictorialism, which Robinson himself had abandoned by 1893. Antonio Cánovas del Castillo (*Káulak*), Luis de Ocharán, Gerado Bustillo, Joan Vilatobá, Antonio Prats, Nebot and even Masana in the 1920s were closer to the motley, anachronistic iconography of early Victorian pictorialism than to the aesthetic and conceptual innovations of late 19th century impressionism. Carl S. King writes "The Spanish pictorialists quickly adopted many of the techniques of photographic impressionism but they were much more conservative in the area of stylistic and thematic treatment than their European and American counterparts."[71]

The earliest Spanish pictorialist photography, or at least a substantial and highly representative part of it, adopted the same characteristics listed by Amador de los Ríos to define decadent historical painting: it was heroic and dramatic, anecdotal and epigrammatic, bucolic and descriptive. It was also allegoric, mythologic, pretentious and cloyingly pompous. A perfect synthesis of these qualities is found in Casas Abarca, whose celebrated series, *Bucólicas*, *Místicas*, *Modernistas*, *Fantasías*, *Orientales*, *Sensuales*, and so on, published in 1907, make up a veritable thematic index of Spanish pictorialism of the time. Another example of the bookish and narrative element that defined this movement was the photographic re-creation of *Don*

MASANA. Salomé. ca. 1920. (Museu d'Art de Sabadell.)

Quijote de la Mancha (1905), by the Cantabrian aristocrat Luis de Ocharán, fifty years after Lake Price's famous work *Don Quixote in his Study* (1855). However, the best illustration of the symbiosis of aristocratic pretensions and "artistic" photography is found in the work the Marquis of Valdeiglesias's work *Tres fiestas galantes* (1904), illustrated with photographs by Christian Franzen and *Káulak*, who were the preferred portraitists of the social élite of Madrid at the time. These photographs were stagings of historical themes, embarrassing imitations of the old Victorian tableaux vivants, that provided the photographers with the opportunity to create memorable compositions, such as *Káulak*'s famous *Plagiarism of Velázquez*. A plagiarism that prefigured others, which *Káulak* successfully exploited in the popular series of "artistic" photogravures that he published in the opening years of the 20th century.[72]

Other well-known photographers of the time produced similar works, whose titles eloquently express their "artistic" intentions: *Dusk on Calvary* (1907), by F. Nogués, *Solemn Moment* (1907), by Lamberto Lacasa, *The Hero* (1907), by V.C.

Novella, *The Favourite* (1920), by Josep Masana, *Glory of the Vanquished* (1914), by A. Calvache, *Mens sana in corpore sano* (1903), by Christian Franzen, *Cleopatra* (1903), by M. Company, *Ego Sum* (1903), by Manuel Portela, *Dying Mystic* (1904), by *Káulak, Spring Tears* (1906), by Joan Vilatobá, and *The Sultana's Garden* (1913), by Antonio Prats. This excessively pretentious and anachronistic range of themes was merely a reflection of contemporary painting, particularly of the works given the highest awards at National Exhibitions held between 1900 and 1936.[73] The subject of Don Quixote had already been used by Moreno Carbonero in 1878 and once again inspired other painters, such as Carlos Vázquez; *Salutatio matutina* (1910), by Antonio Prats was identical to a painting by Bompiani; *Las Parcas* (1922), by Joaquín Pla Janini, was based on *O Charon!* by the American Percy Newman; and *La Maja*, by Masana, was an obvious plagiarism of Arturo Moreno y Calvo's work of the same name, not to mention *Káulak's* plagiarisms of Velázquez and Goya, portraits by Franzen copied from M. Vigée Lebrun, and *La Madre de la Gioconda* (1915), by Doctor Ferrán, an imitation of Leonardo da Vinci's famous painting.

The Real Sociedad Fotográfica de Madrid and the unflagging propaganda of magazines such as *La Fotografía* and *Graphos Ilustrado* played a crucial role in the first wave of Spanish pictorialist photography. Along with the very prolific circle of enthusiasts in Madrid, including *Káulak*, Carlos Iñigo and Luis de Ocharán, there was considerable activity on the part other amateurs in Barcelona, Valencia, Zaragoza, Pamplona, Bilbao, Gijón and La Coruña. Worthy of note among them were Joan Vilatobá, Albert Rifá, Miguel Renom, C. Nieto (*Linker*), Emilio Massó, Francisco Nogués, Vicente Gómez Novella, Agustín Pisaca, Sebastián Castedo, Bernardino Rolandi and Lamberto Lacasa.

Most of the members of this generation of pictorialists worked with pigment techniques, which were introduced in Spain around 1900. Gum bichromate, used by Demachy since 1894, was taken up by Pisaca, Rabadán, Fungairiño, Gerardo Bustillo, Hernández Briz and Carlos Iñigo from 1903 onwards. A much-talked-about exhibition of gum prints was held at Audouard's studio in 1905, although only two years later its detractors were announcing the technique's "interment" from the pages of *La Fotografía*. Oils and greasy inks, introduced by G.E.H. Rawling in 1904, also found rapid acceptance in Spain and soon replaced gum bichromate. Other processes, such as *Artigue* carbon and *fresson*, also gained widespread popularity, although their use only became generalised among members of the following generation, including Goicoechea, Pla Janini and Ortiz Echagüe, who acquired a dominion of these techniques seldom surpassed outside Spain.

Artists, Patriots and Other Excesses

The irreversible decline of photographic Impressionism in Europe and America was consummated in 1914, simultaneously with the commencement of a second wave of pictorialism in Spain, which was to reach its height in the historical period between the terminal crisis of the Restoration and the political turmoil that led to the Civil War. The classicist, mythological and allegorical excesses of the earlier style gave way to new themes of more clearly folkloric, picturesque and purist inspiration. Although the former aesthetic precepts were maintained to a great extent in the work of Pla Janini, Lladó, Arissa and Masana, the majority of the more notable members of the new generation had in common their determined pursuit of a new, supposedly documentary style of photography, seen as a means of extolling Spanish types, costumes, peoples and customs.

Although this new style of photography inherited the obsolescence, artistic pretension and, to a certain extent, the formal and conceptual pomposity of its predecessor, it was different in many technical and, particularly, thematic aspects. While the earlier pictorialists might consider the technique, the new generation saw the documentary component as much more important.[74] However, it is safe to say that the best photographers of this generation were unquestionably experts in the use of pigmentation processes, particularly bromoil, carbon and *fresson*. The Count de la Ventosa wrote in 1914 "I cannot help but reject bromide, with its sour tones that produce a frighteningly cold impression. Proofs made on carbon transfer or Artigue papers, *fresson* or gum bichromate are the ones that most faithfully reflect the photographer's personal style." In fact, these techniques continued in use as late as the 1960s, although by 1930 most Spanish photographers were using the scorned bromide and chlorobromide papers.[75]

However, what truly differentiates these photographers' work from that of their predecessors are its formal and thematic aspects. The new Spanish "artistic" photography replaced the ethical and aesthetic ideology of the vestigial Span-

F. ANDRADA. Cowhand. Bromoil,
1931. (Real Sociedad Fotográfica.)

ish aristocracy with the regenerationism of the dominant middle class. The disintegration of Spain's empire had triggered a search for national and regional essences, in contrast to the 19th-century patriotism that had languished and died with the loss of the colonies. According to the most vocal regenerationists, what was needed was profound introspection into the very soul of the Homeland in search of a new national spirit that could once again make Spaniards proud of being Spanish. In this way, the middle-class regenerationism that already foreshadowed the rise of the nationalism that was to follow looked to the unknown regions, to penetrate into these "inviolable bosoms and impenetrable corners" where, in the words of Macías Picavea, the "Homeland's indigenous vestiges and the deepest soul of the people" still survived. In short, the aim was to revive the past, faced with the uncertainty of a future that was marked by the terminal crisis of the spent and dying two-party system of the Restoration and the irresistible rise of the political prominence of the working and lower middle classes. This circumstance had already been clearly expressed by Joaquín Costa and understood by the leading political representatives of the middle classes and by the most char-

PLA JANINI. The Hunter. *Bromoil,*
1929. (Plá i Guarro Collection.)

acteristic later proponents of pictorialism, whose works aptly fit the words of Valeriano Bozal, referring to a certain regionalist style of painting: "It sings the praises of tradition in all its aspects: the traditional productive activity of agriculture, caciquism, mythology, racial purity, sobriety, restraint, the past. (...) Everything that was repudiated by the 19th intellectual is ritually exalted here, since the objective is to leave everything just as it is."[76]

Middle-class regenerationism looked to tradition and the past and ended up accentuating folkloric and picturesque elements as a category of popular culture. This explains the exaltation of everything old, wizened and rusty that is one of the essential characteristics of the new "artistic photography". Like the worst brand of regionalist painting, which it took for its model, late Spanish pictorialism extolled the reactionary village, sang the foolish praises of the national hamlet and of the fertile lands of Valencia, Murcia, Aragon and Castile. Particularly Castile. Alongside the best and most vigorous photography of the time, as practised by Stieglitz, E. Atget, Paul Strand, E. Weston and the revolutionary avant-garde movements, late Spanish pictorialism was a sort of photographic musical comedy and as such por-

A. CAMPAÑÁ. Horsepower. *Bromoil, 1923. (Campañá Collection.)*

trayed a coarse, grandiloquent and stagey Spain. While Machado, Baroja and Valle-Inclán were producing a literary, lucid and committed chronicle of the changing, convulsive Spanish reality, the country's masters of the photographic image were reinventing it in reverse and ended up praising the ancestral Spain, fixated on the provinces, mystical and martial, as noble and gentlemanly as it was forgotten, neglected and wretched. This was already noticeable in a certain trend to ethnographic *costumbrismo*, the origins of which are to be found in the precocious pictorialism of Laurent, who used some of the elements that most clearly defined this movement's aesthetic – immobility, theatricality, artificiality – in his celebrated series of popular types, taken between 1860 and 1880. However, what was merely picturesqueness in Laurent's work became, in the photographs of some of the leading pictorialists, a wilful exaltation of the chauvinistic, racial and spiritual aspects of a tradition, seen as a means of guaranteeing the continuity of the middle-class order that was by then beginning to be questioned.

JOSÉ ORTIZ-ECHAGÜE. Back to the City. Fresson, 1916.
(Ortiz-Echagüe Bequest. Universidad de Navarra.)

The most eminent representative of this new breed of photographer was certainly José Ortiz Echagüe, whose monumental tetralogy – *España, tipos y trajes* (1933), *España, pueblos y paisajes* (1938), *España mística* (1943) and *Castillos y alcázares* (1956) – is in itself a programmatic statement of principles. José María Salaverría wrote, on the subject of *Pueblos y paisajes*, "Since Echagüe is above all a Spaniard through and through, he has placed his talent and skill deliberately and almost exclusively at the service of Spain. (...) Spain is treated with an artist and patriot's fervour." This "Spanish" spirit led these photographers to catalogue the Spanish soul, stressing its most emblematic symbols, such as costumes, traditions, rituals, castles and alcazars and what was defined in the rhetoric of the time as the "indigenous and untainted vestiges of the Homeland". And when these symbols were no longer to be found, they simply re-created or invented them. Compairé, Pla Janini, the Count de la Ventosa, Benito de Frutos and especially Ortiz Echagüe did not hesitate to dress their models in old costumes no longer used or made especially for the shot, leaving them surprised at themselves, as Ortega y Gasset observed so precisely in 1933.[77]

Ortiz Echagüe brought all of his enormous skill as a photographer to bear in re-creating a Spain that existed not so much in its people, its unknown and impoverished villages, its moving efforts to overcome the ravages of its history, or its cities then beginning to move towards modernisation, as in his own preconceptions about a Homeland that he imagined as mystical, martial, united, great and the scourge of heretics, liberals and masonic scoundrels. As he was deeply concerned with the verisimilitude of stereotypes, he largely channelled his efforts towards making his cold, schematic, solemn, perfect, boring photographs believable. Among the different painters whose influence may be seen in his work, including Díaz Olano, Zubiaurre, Zurbarán, Sorolla and Zuloaga, it is Zuloaga that stands out the most clearly, in the emulation of his excess, his formal theatricality, his pomposity, his schematism, his deliberate literariness and his exaltation of types, settings and situations. Ortiz Echagüe, and by extension a substantial sector of the late Spanish pictorialists that were his contemporaries, idealised Spanish tradition and its racial essence, spirituality, mysticism and sobriety, all of the qualities that were habitually extolled in the nationalist rhetoric, from Picavea's *Arriba España* to the verbal excesses of fascism in the 1930s.

Ortiz Echagüe was an active photographer for over sixty years and his imposing presence overshadowed the work of the other members of his generation, the most outstanding of which were Pla Janini, José Tinoco, the Count de la Ventosa, Eduardo Susanna, Francisco Andrada, Antonio Arissa, Vicente Peydró, José Bernia, Mora Carbonell, Miguel Goicoechea, Aurelio Grasa, Joan Porqueras, Antoni Campañá, J. Gil Marraco, Vicente Martínez Sanz, Ramón Batlles, Francesc Serra, and Julio Matutano. Among them, it was the Madrid group – Tinoco, Susanna and Andrada – that was influenced most directly by his work and his aesthetics. Mora Carbonell was the most widely known and highly respected outside Spain. He was a master of the bromoil and *fresson* techniques and produced genre scenes, landscapes and compositions with arcadian and pastoral themes. Particularly worth noting is the work of Miguel Goicoechea, from Navarre, with its documentarist slant and avoidance of artificiality and regionalist clichés.[78]

However, it was the Catalan photographers who made up the most numerous and active and homogeneous group in late Spanish pictorialism. Among them,

M. GOICOECHEA. Three pious women from the Valley of Esteríbar. Triple gum print, ca. 1928. (Fernando Goñi Goicoechea Collection.)

Joaquín Pla Janini was the most representative figure and also the most impassioned advocate of a fundamentalist attitude to intervention and pigmentation, taking up the cause of noble emulsions as the only means of ensuring the artistic qualities of photography. His obsession with disguising and concealing the "photographic" appearance of his images made a profound impression on his work in both formal and conceptual terms. He was unquestionably the one who most obstinately maintained the classicist, mythological and allegorical excesses of early pictorialism and to a certain extent acted as a bridge between the two generations of Spanish pictorialists. Some of his best known works, such as *The Fates*, *Neptune*, *The Final Moment* and the *Twilight of Life*, provide a clear example of obsolescence and pomposity, more characteristic of Victorian narrative photography – there is a clear resemblance between these works and some of Robinson's, such as *Dawn and Dusk* (1885), for example – than of the breakaway photographic movements of the end of the 19th century. However, Pla Janini's work is not monolithic and offers different facets, from the ingenuous ruralism of his youth, to unequivocal impressionism and landscapes, by way of a certain nationalist folklorism, as seen in his *Municipal Guard* (1931).[79]

Claudi Carbonell was skilled at all pigmentation techniques and particularly bromoil, of which he was an acknowledged master. He produced landscapes, still-lifes and genre subjects with exquisite delicacy and formal perfection. Antoni Campañá was another of the great masters of the bromoil technique, which he learned from Carbonell and later perfected in Germany with W. Zielke. The technical foundation of his work is in sharp contrast with its formal treatment, which was directly influenced by the avant-garde movements of the period between the wars. This might be explained by the fact that the pigmentarist aesthetic survived longer in Spain than elsewhere – Campañá himself did not stop using bromoil until 1946 – and remained current until well into the 1950s. This creative dual personality is also found in Josep Masana. An accomplished portraitist with a strong technical command and gifted with a powerful imagination and protean capabilities, Masana was one of the Spanish photographers who made the greatest contributions in the areas of advertising and creative photography. He was also one of the most recalcitrant practitioners of narrative pictorialism with biblical and mythological themes and as late as the mid-1920s was the author of some of the most extravagant works of Spanish pictorialism.

Another current of photography, one that was more openly *costumbrista*, folkloric and ethnographic, developed in the shadow of pictorialism and under the direct influence of the aesthetic precepts of the middle-class regenerationism of the time. Dozens of photographers worked in this style, including Ricardo Compairé, Jaime Belda, José Mañas, Tomás Camarillo, Pons Frau, Luis Ksado, Pedro Ferrer, Pons Gribau, *Foto Lux* (Barber and Pereferrer) and Josep Esquirol, whose works may be situated midway between a frankly documentary, anthropological and landscapist approach and a sort of pre-touristic focus, as seen in the work of the Marquis of Santa María del Villar, who took thousands of photographs of middling quality that are difficult to classify.

This, then, was the "artistic" panorama of Spanish photography during the first third of the 20th century, a panorama that had already been defined by Hernández Briz in 1907 in the magazine *Graphos Ilustrado*. This influential Madrid amateur

J. ESQUIROL. Portrait of a fisherman. L'Escala, ca. 1900. (Fundación Joan Miró.)

saw photography in Spain at the time as divided into three categories: scientific photography, practised by naturalists and doctors, documentary photography, practised by the pioneers of graphic journalism, and lastly, "true artistic photography", practised by amateurs (a term that Briz uses as a category), painters and sculptors. He neglected to mention the professionals, who, by that time, were mostly studio portraitists "living in penury" through the heroic and daily exercise of their trade.

The Decline of Portraiture

Professional photography in Spain at the beginning of the 20th century consisted basically of portraiture. When specialist magazines of the time deplored the "serious and worrying" crisis in the photographic business, what they were in fact deploring was the crisis suffered by traditional gallery portraiture. Portraitists were beginning to find themselves more dependent than ever on the taste and whims of a changeable and irregular clientele and simultaneously at the mercy of a growing and intensifying competition that eventually drove prices down to previously unthinkable levels.[80] In 1907 there were 439 officially registered photographers in Spain, practically the same number as in 1880. Of these, 71 were established in Barcelona, 57 in Madrid, 32 in Valencia, 19 in La Coruña, 14 in Zaragoza, 14 in Gerona, 13 in Seville, 12 in Cádiz, 12 in Murcia, 12 in Málaga, 10 in Santander and 7 in Alicante. Between them they paid a total of sixty thousand pesetas in taxes yearly. In 1915 the number of studios had barely changed, with only minor growth in a few cities, such as Madrid.[81] However, the crisis was not only evident in the number of professionals but also in the quality of their work, which had been in constant decline since the revolution of the *carte de visite*. The cultural and technical training of photographers at the beginning of the 20th century was non-existent and with few exceptions still went no further than experience gained in the studio, where they started out as apprentices and assistants. The studio photographers listed in handbooks and industrial yearbooks were little more than handymen for whom photography was merely a means of earning their daily bread honestly. Mediocrity and vulgarity were the most common characteristics of their work, with the rare exception of the few who were able to break out of the routine imposed by their trade. Worthy of mention among these were Audouard, Franzen, *Káulak*, Areñas, Vilatobá, *Alfonso*, Masana, Garzón, V. Gombáu, Esplugas, Antonio García, Novella and Renom.

Some of the most prestigious portraitists of the early years of the 20th century had already made a name for themselves towards the end of the 19th century, such as Esplugas, Audouard and Areñas, in Barcelona, Amador, Company and Franzen, in Madrid, Sellier and Avrillon, in La Coruña, Venancio Gombáu, in Salamanca, the Garays, in Valladolid, Logroño and Bilbao, José Reymundo and M. Pol, in Cádiz, Julio Beauchy, in Seville, Montilla, in Córdoba, Garzón and Ayola, in Granada, the Coynes, in Zaragoza, M. Lohr, in Tenerife, Duomarco and Zenón Quintana, in Santander, Antonio García and Valentín Pla, in Valencia, Díaz Custodio, in Écija, and Félix Mena, in Pamplona. Others set up their studios at the turn of the century, such as *Káulak*, *Alfonso* and Biedma, in Madrid, Miralles, in Murcia, W. Kock, in San Sebastián, Schommer, in Vitoria, Joaquín Pintos, in Vigo, Juan Barrera, in Seville, Samot, in Santander, Vicente Gómez Novella, in Valencia, and Luis Brito, in Santa Cruz de la Palma. In spite of the crisis, the studio portrait was still the article preferred by the middle classes, although evolving tastes forced the professionals to make substantial changes to their products. The older formats, including the *Cabinet*, *Boudoir*, *Imperial* and particularly the *carte de visite*, gradually gave way to other, larger formats printed on the famous *Mimosa* or *Kodura* papers. In addition, photographers centred their attention increasingly on their subjects faces and abandoned the old style of full-length portraiture characteristic of *cartes de visite*.

The changing times also brought about a profound transformation in the appearance of studios. Nevertheless, while they were commonly considered unconvincing and overblown, the congenial old 19th-century backdrops were still an indispensable element for creating the illusion of historical settings in tune with customers' expectations. The best backdrops were those that provided an impersonal, evocative and remote ground that suggested rather than showed atmospheres, whether aristocratic, maritime, biblical or tropical. In 1906, *Káulak* publicised his acquisition of eight new backdrops that, "combined with the nine that he already had, form a first-class ensemble". Alfonso Sánchez García (*Alfonso*) had over ten different backdrops in 1920 and Audouard's de luxe salons held up to twenty with varied subjects.

Christian Franzen in his studio on Calle del Príncipe. Madrid, 1905. (Private Collection.)

Around 1910, studio decoration underwent extensive changes. Columns, pedestals and Second Empire décors began clearly to lose their popularity, along with papier maché staircases, boulders and waterfalls. In 1908, Franzen announced that he had remodelled his gallery to furnish it "with a beautiful glasshouse, a real column with different orders on either side, a pond with a glass surface in place of water, two real trees complete with branches, leaves and roots, a park corner, and a German Renaissance bench, stuffed swans, banks of lilies, rushes and reeds, and a garden with thousands of flowers." In 1920, *Alfonso*'s studio had a number of different settings, including a Renaissance office, a Louis XV sitting room, a sitting room with a Seville ceramic fireplace and an altar to Our Lady of Mount Carmel, ideal for weddings and christenings. Photographers also improvised different décors using damask curtains, panoplies, suits of armour, paintings, carpets, statuettes, artificial flowers, and neo-classical details, a veritable papier maché universe where portraitists constructed what Gisèle Freund has defined as the subjects' masks. A gallery's success depended to a great extent on the variety of its settings and décors and on the skill of its studio hands and retouch-

CHRISTIAN FRANZEN. Portrait of the Queen Mother María Cristina de Habsburgo and Alfonso XIII. ca. 1900. (Adrián Olmedilla Collection.)

ers at straightening overly generous curves, disguising unattractive features, and covering up protuberances and other excesses. Portraits still lacked any expression of individuality whatsoever, since the photographers' overriding aim was to give their subjects an upper-class appearance and they abandoned all aesthetic principles when producing their works.

The old studios began modernising. The traditional skylights were soon replaced by artificial lighting installations, following the example set by the most flamboyant European galleries. Electricity was the great novelty of the century and did away with the booming magnesium flashes previously in use. The first electric arc facilities were installed in Spain around 1905. Pau Audouard, whose studio was considered the most de luxe of the time, opened a sumptuous gallery in the Art Nouveau Lleó Morera building, complete with different stages equipped with artificial lighting. Other successful portraitists followed his example. Artificial lighting, using the famed *Moore-Artigas* lamps and electric arcs, became common after 1910 and soon became an indispensable item in portrait studios. Pau Barceló, former assistant to Masana, observed "The most important thing were the lights, mercury-arc lamps that were not bulky at all but very powerful. They produced a most disagreeable appearance in the flesh but gave excellent results with the negatives used then, which were flat film, matt finished and orthochromatic."[82]

The studios of the time were worlds in themselves, with numerous employees, including studio hands, retouchers, tinters, assistants and darkroom staff, hairdressers and makeup artists. In 1920, Franzen's studio had a staff of over twenty employees, as did *Alfonso*'s, where photographers such as López Renuncio, José Bárcenas and Domingo González acquired their first professional experience. The most important employees in these establishments were the retouchers, studio hands and tinters, who always occupied a privileged place in the professional hierarchy of the trade. Although not all photographic studios had such large staffs, it was normal for any establishment having achieved a certain level of artistic and social prestige to have at least one cameraman and one or two retouchers. However, in most studios outside the larger cities it was usually the owner himself who performed all the necessary tasks with the assistance of his female family members, who were normally in charge of tinting portraits and keeping the accounts of these memorable establishments.[83]

*KÁULAK. Infanta Isabel de Borbón, "La Chata".
ca. 1910. (Alejandro Montiel Collection.)*

By 1920 the predictions of the more pessimistic observers were coming true. In spite of its innovations, studio portraiture appeared to have entered a terminal crisis brought about by the continual drop in prices caused by the increasing democratisation of photography. In the face of repeated campaigns in the specialist press, portraitists attempted to keep their businesses afloat by lowering their prices to levels that were extremely disconcerting for the leading advocates of photographic corporatism of the time. An article published in the May 1914 issue of *El Fotógrafo Profesional* reads "Whoever hopes to make a name for themselves or increase their profits by lowering their prices below established levels is not only sadly mistaken but also degrades themselves and debases their work. Dignity and immediate gain are not the only reasons for maintaining prices. There is also the more weighty consideration of ensuring the future." Traditional portraiture, caught between the alarming drop in prices and popular tastes that were moving ever farther away from the old illusions created by papier maché settings, was on the verge of disappearing and there was nothing to be done to avoid its demise. This apparently irreversible decline of the most representative branch of the photographic industry had important repercussions that directly affected the hundreds of workers

ALFONSO SÁNCHEZ GARCÍA. *Benito Pérez Galdós. ca. 1910.*
(Zamora Lobboch Collection.)

MORENO. Ramón del Valle-Inclán. Madrid, ca. 1920.
(Instituto de Restauración y Conservación de Bienes Culturales.)

employed in the studios. Retouchers, tinters and studio hands were forced to find other work or go into business for themselves, swelling the ranks of competitors to their former employers. Photographers had to look for new professional activities, taking advantage of progress in the area of motion pictures – some, such as Brito, Gaspar, Godes, Calvach and Aguayo, ended up going into filmmaking – or in photographic supplies and printing techniques, a circumstance that led to the birth of modern graphic magazines and the popular collections of fascicles and postcards of Spanish cities, towns and people.

Popular Photography

Not all Spanish portraitists shared the pretensions of the eminent society photographers. Most of them worked in small towns scattered around the country, with few means and little technical background, practising a sort of naive portraiture that had nothing in common with the works produced by the more prominent studios, whose pomposity was matched only by their cloying vulgarity. In comparison with the crude, run-of-the-mill products produced by the majority of famous photographers, some of these professionals took very touching photographs with no trace of pretentiousness. It is precisely this lack of pretension that provides a part of the candour of these images of those normal people in their Sunday best, posing surprised and defenceless before the camera's unblinking gaze. Many of the best portraits of time, the most moving, most surprising and most worthy of preservation, were taken by those modest popular artists who, either as professionals or as a sideline along with some other trade or occupation, succeeded in capturing the image of the people of those memorable years. The passing years, which have piled up so many gravestones on these old portraits, have imbued them with a profoundly evocative air, with an aura of life that transcends their age and the cold, objective portrayal of their subjects, something that brings these yellowing photographs within the uncertain and undefinable boundaries of artistic creation. Susan Sontag writes "Time eventually elevates even the clumsiest of these photographs to the category of art."[84]

This candid style of portraiture occupied many years of the professional careers of Spain's provincial photographers, who responded to the growing demand among the country's inhabitants for these portraits – of themselves and those closest to them – with which they sought to reconstitute the emotional geography of their family circles, which were constantly at the mercy of illness, disappearance, death and separation. The old houses of Spain's villages still contain vestiges of these images, which, appropriately enlarged, retouched and tinted, decorated their whitewashed walls in sentimental homage to absent children, friends, parents and grandparents. There is something enigmatic and evocative in the images taken by that legion of modest, anonymous and now-forgotten photographers, residing in the almost total lack of intervention by the artist, whose elemental rusticity left mainly to chance the ultimate responsibility for capturing the image of their subjects through the miracle of exposed plates. It was a form of vitality with which those simple craftsmen were able to imbue their subjects, to allow them to survive the indignities of Time. Compared with the artificiality, mimicry and supposed style of some self-proclaimed photographic artists, the value of these portraits resides in their very coarseness, their naivety, and their artlessness. Carlos Maside wrote "This is how the normal folk like to see their image captured, this is how they like to preserve the appearance of their childhood, their lost youth, this is how they like to pass it on to their loved ones, to save it from death. Only a petty mind could see as ridiculous these serious, hieratic figures, figures that are full of taut life, perfumed by the mist, wind and sun, tattooed by time, in contact with the earth where, with devotion and concern, they gain their daily bread. (...) How puerile, mannered and affected those photographs adapted to the middle-class tastes of a more fashionable clientele seem alongside their simple village counterparts!"[85]

In parallel to this naive style of portraiture practised by Spain's anonymous and forgotten provincial photographers, a type of popular documentary photography developed whose ability to surprise and amaze us is based, paradoxically, on the very lack of sophistication on the part of its creators. It is enough to peruse the work of the Albacete native Julian Collado (for example, his unforgettable *The Slaughter Ball*), worlds away from the artificiality of the pictorialist photography of the time, to understand the profound evocativeness and emotional content of some of the work of these spontaneous reporters. Of course, not all of them were great photographers. Most of them merely sought to obtain whatever income they could in those years of penury. However, some did possess a true photographic instinct and a touching love for their work, and were gifted with an extraordinary capacity for accurately depicting their subjects. We might say of them what Paul Strand said of Lewis Hine: "He was a modest man who did not consider himself an artist. He did not have the look of an artist, but he was one. He had an astonishing eye." These photographers, perhaps unintentionally, were among the best artists of the time, ones who, like Riis, Atget, Thomson, Fernando Paillet, Martín Chambi, Romualdo García, or Hine himself, were best able to capture with their cameras magnificent images that surprise, amaze or move us today. According to Weston, many of the great photographs of the past were taken precisely by photographers who did not feel the least concern for aesthetics nor any worry for the uncertain future importance of their work.[86]

Worth mentioning among this breed of photographer in Spain were Benito Pons, from Cuenca, Jaime Pacheco, Joaquín Pintos and Ramón Caamaño, from Galicia, Francisco Fernández Trujillo, from Cádiz, José Nogales, from Córdoba, Pablo Rodríguez, from Toledo, Julián Collado, Luis Escobar and Nicanor Cañas, from La Mancha, Felipe Manterola, from Vizcaya, the Majorcan priest Tomás Montserrat and, to a certain extent, the *Alfonso* family, Alejandro Merletti, Joaquín Brangulí, Ángel Blanco and Gómez Durán. Luis Escobar was La Mancha's most outstanding photographer of the time. He set up shop in Albacete in 1910 and for over 30 years travelled around the towns and villages of La Manchuela, making a comprehensive record of ordinary life in the region. His work, characterised by excellent compositional values and surprising formal qualities, constitutes an attractive chronicle of the people of La Mancha of the 1920s and 1930s. He worked unceasingly as a studio portraitist, itinerant photographer, tinter, retoucher and reporter. This untiring worker tried his hand at everything, and he was gifted with a prodigious photographic instinct and identified intimately with the people he portrayed.[87] Joaquín Pintos and Jaime Pacheco produced similar work. Pintos was an accomplished portraitist and reporter, although less penetrating and original than Escobar. Pacheco, Prospéri's successor and a successful portraitist in Vigo, produced surprisingly abundant and varied work in the course of a professional career of over thirty years. The Toledans Eugenio and Pablo Rodríguez, Felipe Manterola and Julián Collado show a much more popular sensibility and with their elementary technical skills produced some of the most memorable photographs of their time. Francisco Tru-

T. MONTSERRAT. Portrait of a country woman. Llucmajor, ca. 1920. (Toni Catany Collection.)

L. ESCOBAR. Prostitutes in the Alto de la Villa. *Albacete, 1928. (Escobar Archives.)*

jillo merits special mention, for his extended work in photographing shipbuilding at the Matagorda shipyards.

The *Alfonso* family produced a different sort of work, especially those family members bearing that given name, Alfonso Sánchez García and his son Alfonso Sánchez Portela. The *Alfonsos* were citizens of Madrid to the core and prime examples of the brand of critical enthusiasm for Madrid so admired by their friend *Azorín*. Over the course of two generations, they scrutinised daily life in the capital more assiduously than anyone, from the bitter, tough life of the poor neighbourhoods to the Palace ceremonials, by way of the anonymous dead in desolate morgues, terrible crimes, mealtimes on the street or open-air market stalls selling honey. Many of these street scenes by Alfonso Sánchez Portela were published in the press of the time, in sections entitled *The Madrid Unknown to Madrid*, *Life at the Bottom* or *Picturesque Madrid*. They depict the Madrid of Pérez Galdós and Baroja, which as on the verge of disappearing, to be swept away by uncontrolled progress that was to transform its homely old appearance into that of a sullen, unwelcoming and slum-ridden city. Barcelona, Valencia, Seville and other cities were

FERNÁNDEZ TRUJILLO. Launch of the ocean liner Magallanes. Matagorda, May 1927. (Spanish Shipyards Archives.)

ALFONSO SÁNCHEZ PORTELA. Woman selling turkeys at the Plaza de Santa Cruz. Madrid, 1925. (General Government Archives.)

not fortunate enough to be served by popular reporters of the stature of the *Alfonsos*, although we would know nothing of the more intimate life of these cities if it were not for the work of their most characteristic photographers, such as Alejandro Merletti, the Brangulís, Carlos Pérez de Rozas and Agustín Centelles, in Barcelona, Juan José Serrano, in Seville, Ángel Blanco, in La Coruña, Jaime Pacheco, in Vigo, Miguel Marín-Chivite, in Zaragoza, Pascual Marín and *Photo-Carte*, in San Sebastián, and the Vidals, in Valencia. Madrid was also home to other photographers, such as José *Campúa*, A. Vilaseca, Pepe Díaz Casariego, José Zegrí, Salazar, Francisco Goñi and Albero and Segovia.

José Suárez, the most universal of the Galician photographers of his time, would be situated on the fringe of this group. With an aesthetic midway between that of the more eminent popular photographers and the avant-garde movements of the period between the wars, Suárez shared with the former an unerring instinct, an apparent simplicity and a proximity and identification with the people he portrayed. He had an extensive knowledge of photography that was unusual among the photographers of his time and in his work ingenuous-

J. SUÁREZ. Young woman mariner. Galicia, 1936. (Suárez Collection.)

ness and candour are replaced by reflection and interpretation. This is why we do not find in his work the spontaneous and instinctive reflex of the people, villages and customs of Galicia that he photographed in the 1930s, but rather the representation in those images of that maltreated land, a land with no choice but to take to the sea. In Suárez's work there is the pulse of the ancient sadness spoken of by Celso Emilio Ferreiro, which is none other than the sadness of the artist himself and the ancient and universal sadness of mankind, because the central theme of his work is mankind and the whole of its material, social and emotional framework.

Most popular portraitists were itinerant and this was one of the major photographic specialities of the time, dating back to the 19th-century pioneers of daguerreotype and *carte de visite* portraits. By the beginning of the 20th century this itineracy had become normal and many professionals were itinerant, including Ángel Garrorena, in Extremadura, Félix Mena, in Navarre, Pintos, Pacheco and Caamaño, in Galicia, Inocencio Ruiz, in La Rioja, Pere Mascaró, in Majorca, and Benito Pons and Luis Escobar, in La Mancha. These travelling photographers would set up their portable studios in courtyards, inns, yards or on the street itself. They carried their cameras, backdrops, developers and trays with them, and properties were improvised from whatever happened to be at hand, including flowerpots, chairs, armchairs, pedestals, and so on. Flaws were inevitable and it is common enough to see a whitewashed wall peeking out from behind the backdrop and destroying the illusion created by fountains, battleships, gazebos, swans or myrtles.

In the early years of photography, itineracy was not feasible for all professionals, in view of the serious logistic difficulties involved in moving the weighty equipment and the need to apply emulsions to negatives immediately before exposure. Although dry plates came into use in 1870, they were not generally available in Spain until ten years later. The difficulties were diminished when this type of negative and silver bromide-gelatin papers became widespread, making the practice of photography much easier, at a time when transportation systems were being thoroughly revolutionised. Itinerant photography came into its own with the beginning of the new century. Photographers travelled the country on mules or donkeys, in diligences, or on trains or the quaint omnibuses of the pre-war period, often carrying out other kinds of work and commissions at the same time. Luis Escobar combined his activities as portraitist in the towns and villages of La Manchuela with those of collector of insurance premiums. Jesús Enero took advantage of his travels in the province of Cuenca to carry out police missions and collect taxes, and Félix Mena travelled through Navarre taking photographs of landscapes and reporting on important events. Itinerant photographers became a standard presence at fairs and markets, along with scrap metal dealers, musicians, comics, puppeteers and vendors of love potions.

In the beginning, itinerant photographers took portraits in the *carte de visite* format. From 1910 onwards the commonest format was the so-called postcard, produced as contact prints from 10 × 15 cm glass negatives. These photographs, appropriately sorted and numbered, were then sold in the inns, markets or houses where the photographer was lodged. However, the travelling photographers did not earn their living solely from portraits, either of individuals or groups. While photographing the local inhabitants, they would also collect their family photographs to enlarge or tint them. They also employed agents to carry out this task

A. BLANCO. Baggage for Havana. La Coruña, ca. 1925. (Archivo Blanco.)

of collecting, visiting towns and villages during the winter, when work in the studios dwindled to alarming levels. Other specialities of the travelling photographers were photographs of religious images or the deceased, or images meant for use as *ex votos*.

As already mentioned, photographs of the deceased were an important speciality, owing, in part, to the fact that, as pointed out by Benjamin, the cultural worth of the image is ultimately justified by its fidelity to the memory of distant or deceased loved ones. This explains our forebears' wish to preserve the visage of their dead relatives, with the most appropriate poses and gestures for their perpetuation. Photographers, then, used their skill and experience to capture the countenance and physique of the deceased for posterity, in positions approximating the relaxation of sleep. At first, the dead were brought to the studio, although this practice was curtailed as a result of complaints from the neighbours and of the difficulties caused by the models' rigidity. This led to development of a speciality within the speciality. The photographer was obliged to go to the home of the deceased and set up the shot there. In view of the authenticity of the circumstances, which were not dealt with in the manuals of the time, each photographer had to improvise to find the technical approach best fitting the situation at hand. Some set up their modest backdrops in patios and back yards, while others sought out intense and dramatic back lighting, and the less original simply would simply have the deceased brought out of doors and placed appropriately on rough, improvised catafalques. The deceased's head would be raised and their family members gathered round in the proper attitudes of mourning. Photography thus became not only the means of recording the sorrowful ritual of death, but also one more element of that ritual.[88]

Catholic Spain was much more profligate in the commemoration of death than in the playful praise of the senses. At the beginning of the 20th century, many more photographs of nudes were taken by amateurs than by professionals, who found scarce opportunities to do business in a genre where few of them had any hope of competing with the French market in erotic photographs. Most of the risqué publications of the time were also imported from Paris, although around the turn of the century several of the first Spanish magazines of an immodest nature began making their timid appearance, profusely illustrated with mostly anonymous photographs. Worth mentioning among them are *La Saeta*, *Vida Galante*, *La Hoja de Parra*, *Las mujeres en la intimidad* and *Portafolio del desnudo*, with contributions from Luis Araquistaín, Eduardo Zamacois and the incomparable Gómez Carrillo. Altogether different were the pretentious and embarrassing works of some of the Spanish pictorialists, whose "theme" was no more than a pretext to photograph the female body – never the male body – in a prudish society dominated by the aesthetic and moral values of the very middle class to which those photographers belonged.[89]

Diametrically opposed to these works, we find some images that lack the narrative excesses and the cloying pretentiousness of the pictorialists. Worthy of mention among them are the estimable nudes by Emili Vilá and a number by Masana himself, whose versatility and skill never cease to surprise us. On a more ingenuous and simpler level are the anonymous popular nudes, with their models drawn from the pitiable legions of specialists in love for sale, who posed with a

C. YANGUAS. Portrait. Vitoria, ca. 1915. (Vitoria-Gasteiz Municipal Archives.)

blunt provocativeness appropriate to the places where these mercenary sessions were improvised. The surprising chronicles by Luis Escobar, Emilio Meléndez and Ceferino Yanguas are of an altogether different sort and are reminiscent of the undisguised sensuality found in the photographs taken by E.F. Bellock in 1912 in the Storyville red-light district. Between body and image, photography, which is never entirely ingenuous or objective, here takes the side of the body, with a simple voluptuosity not entirely lacking in candour.

Fascicles and Postcards

Before photography became fully integrated into the graphic press, photographers sought to market their work in the form of series of collotypes and collectible views, such as the *Panorama Nacional* mentioned earlier, which was published towards the end of the 19th century. This fulfilled Lacan's astute prediction, made in 1856, of the future development of the photographic industry on the basis of photomechanical techniques. Around the beginning of the new century new collectible series began appearing, including *Portafolio Fotográfico* and *España Artística*, with contributions from Rafael Garzón, Adolfo Mas, A. Esplugas, Company, and Calvet and Simón. Other fascicles were also published with a regional or provincial focus. There were also well-known series of a more anthropological nature, such as *Estampas de Galicia* (1929), by the Santiago de Compostela native Luis Ksado, which was a continuation of the popular *Portafolio de Galicia*, published at the beginning of the century by Pedro Ferrer.

However, the photographic reproduction industry found its most important outlet in postcards, which reached the peak of their popularity between 1900 and 1925. In the beginning, most were printed with the collotype process, using the emulsion of the photographic copy itself. Of this type of product, the series published by Joaritzi, Mariezcurrena, Hauser and Menet, Laurent, and Thomas were very successful, with thousands of different images of monuments, cities and works of art sold. The technique evolved over the following years, with the use of intaglio, lithography and chromolithography, which became extremely popular towards the end of the 19th century. Chromolithographs produced a surprising effect and up to twelve lithograph stones were used on occasion for a single image. However, postcards were not always coloured using such sophisticated techniques. Much more common was expedient hand-tinting, or simply the direct colouring of silver bromide copies by treatment with anilines, inks or watercolours.

Postcards provide an accurate summary of Spanish photography at the beginning of the 20th century. The dozens of different series constitute a veritable catalogue of the styles and trends of the time, from views and landscapes to portraits and caricatures, by way of bullfighting, sports, the stage or risqué subjects. Postcards multiplied the images of our towns and cities and popularised the faces of cabaret stars, bullfighters, sportsmen and members of royalty. Lastly, there were also series of "artistic" postcards that were clearly indebted to the pictorialism of the time, by photographers such as the Cantabrian Julio García de la Puente, Lucas Escolá, from Aragon, Jaime Belda, from La Mancha, and the ubiquitous *Káulak*.[90]

In the opening years of the new century certain of the specialist companies, such as the historical businesses *Thomas*, Hauser and Menet, Moreno, Mas, and

FRANZEN. Queen Victoria Eugenia
Postcard, 1910. (Monasor Collection.)

ANONYMOUS. La Chelito. Postcard,
ca. 1910. (Monasor Collection.)

Roisin, were highly successful and compiled catalogues with thousands of views from around the country. In 1905, Hauser and Menet had over five thousand different postcards on offer, a number rivalled only by *Thomas* and Roisin, who achieved similar sales figures in 1910. Of particular interest are the series with an ethnological and anthropological slant, such as those by *Foto Lux* (Barber and Pereferrer) in Gerona, or Josep Esquirol, the author of an estimable series entitled *Caps d'Estudi*, in La Escala. Postcards became extraordinarily popular and set off a veritable collection fever among the middle classes of the time. Sending and receiving postcards became a symbol of social and cultural status and the most economical and convenient means of acquiring an image of the world that, thanks to photography and the post, entered the homes of a public that followed in this way the new "fashion of the century", consisting of the practice of the social grace of making gifts of postcards.

The postcard craze attracted a number of foreign photographers to Spain, including the Frenchman Soeur, the Austrian Kühn – no relation to the famous H. Kühn – and Otto Wunderlich. Wunderlich's work, the most abundant and highest quality, bears a certain resemblance to that of the early itinerant photographers of the 19th century. Between 1910 and 1930 he visited most of the regions of Spain, capturing the image of popular types, monuments and works of art in photographs that he later sold in numbered series and published in the press of the time. A selection of these images was published in the book *España* (1929). Of particular importance was the work of the German Kurt Hielscher, one of the pioneers of the modern illustrated book. An inveterate traveller, after having toured various European countries he visited Spain for the first time in 1911, and later returned on the eve of World War I. In the space of five years he travelled over five thousand kilometres around Spain on horseback and on trains and diligences. After the war he returned to Germany, where he published his famous book *Das Unbekannte Spanien* (Unknown Spain), to resounding success.[91]

In a similar vein are the chronicles of various photographers sent to Spain by magazines and publishers, such as Henri Guerlain, author of *Espagne* (1932), Wolfgang Weber, who produced the excellent *Barcelona, Weldstadt im Werdenn* (1928) and Gilbert Grosvenor, Chalmers Adams and Gervais Courtellemont, commissioned by the National Geographic magazine to illustrate a special issue on Spain in 1929. Other photographers, with a different purpose and an aesthetic closer to that of the pictorialists, also visited Spain, including James Craig Annan, Alvin Langdon Coburn and Alexander Keighley. Annan travelled to Spain 1913 and took photographs in Toledo, Ronda, Burgos, Segovia and Granada. Coburn, one of the leading Photo-Secessionists, made a photographic tour of Mediterranean countries, in the course of which he took several photographs with bullfighting subjects, with a slightly out-of-focus treatment that was his only concession to the impressionist aesthetic of the time.[92] The works of Keighley, one of the founders of the mythic Linked Ring and the subject of a special issue of *Art de la llum* in July 1934, are better known. An altogether different approach is found in the work of photographers of the stature of Bill Brandt, who produced estimable views of Barcelona in 1930, and Henri Cartier-Bresson, who took unforgettable images of different Spanish cities in the early 1930s.

The Eyes of History

Advances in photomechanical technology had fostered the growth of the illustrated press in the closing years of the 19th century. We have already seen the importance in this respect of the weeklies *Blanco y Negro* and *Nuevo Mundo*, which served as models for the publications of the time. In Catalonia, *L'Esquella* began publishing photographic reports in 1890, although it was Manuel Roca who consecrated the presence of photography on its pages from 1907 onwards. *La Campana de Gracia* followed a similar course, as did *Cu-Cut*, published by La Lliga (1902), *La Ilustración Catalana* in its second phase (1903-1917), the graphic supplement of *El Diluvio Ilustrado* (published weekly 1904-1907), *La Actualidad* (1906-1912), *La Hormiga de Oro* (1884), and the sports weeklies *Mundo Deportivo* (1906) and *Stadium* (1912). After Mariezcurrena's pioneering work, a new generation of graphic reporters took up the task, including Alejandro Merletti, Josep Moragas, Josep Brangulí Soler, Federico Balell and Josep Domínguez, soon joined by Josep María Co de Triola, Ramón Claret and the Lérida native F. Portela, all of them born in the 1880s, and Lluís Torrents, Carlos Pérez de Rozas and the Tarragona native Hermenegildo Vallvé, all born in the early 1890s.[93]

However, during those early years of Spanish photojournalism, the daily newspapers paid scarcely any attention to photography until the appearance of *ABC*, *El Gráfico*, *La Vanguardia* and *El Imparcial*. *ABC* was launched in 1903 as a weekly and could have been Spain's first important illustrated daily newspaper, except for the fact that it did not become a daily until 1905. On 13 June 1904, Rafael Gasset commenced publishing *El Gráfico*, stealing a march on the historical conservative daily. Gasset placed Julio Burell in charge of the new daily, which soon had print runs of two hundred thousand copies. Francisco Goñi, C. Irigoyen, F. Gómez Durán, Campúa, Amador, Merletti, Barberá and Alfonso Sánchez García all worked for *El Gráfico*, the latter as photographic editor. Unfortunately, *El Gráfico* had a short life. Constant harassment by the Maura government led to its closure in December 1904. *ABC*, definitively transformed into a daily on 1 July 1905, carried on in its stead. In its extensive and carefully planned "illustrated chronicle", the monarchist daily published photographs by Merletti, Barberá, Goñi and Manuel Asenjo. Along with *ABC*, other dailies began gradually introducing photography, including *El Imparcial* (which had been publishing photographs since 1903), *Mundo al*

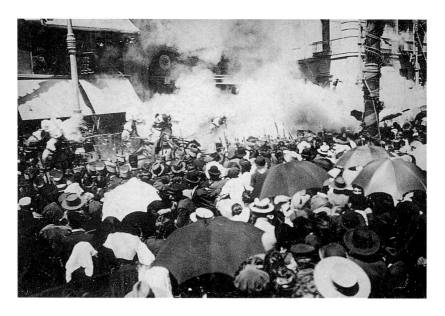

MESONERO ROMANOS. Assassination attempt on Alfonso XIII on his wedding day. Madrid, May 1906. (Private Collection.)

Día, La Vanguardia, El Heraldo de Aragón, and *La Noche* (1911), which also had a short life. *La Vanguardia* began publishing photogravures in 1910, although it was Pich y Pon who transformed it three years later into an important illustrated daily along the lines of the *Daily Mirror* or *ABC*. Several years later, *El Día Gráfico* (1913) began publishing photographs and thus became, along with *La Vanguardia*, the training ground for the first significant generation of Catalan reporters.

Meanwhile, Spain was living through the backwash of its colonial disaster and witnessing the inexorable demise of the farce that was the Restoration. In the year that *ABC* was founded, the country went through four different prime ministers and when *La Vanguardia* began publishing photogravures Barcelona had just undergone the terrible events of the Tragic Week and Ferrer Guardia had been executed by firing squad in the fosse of the sinister Montjuïc fortress. The graphic press was there to reflect these occurrences and it was precisely on the basis of these stories that the first important graphic reporters, such as Merletti, *Alfonso, Campúa*, Gómez Durán, Asenjo, Leopoldo Alonso and José Zegrí, were able to

A. MAS. Desecration of graves at the Magdalenas convent during the Tragic Week. Barcelona, 1909. (Mas Archives.)

consolidate their reputation. Ferrer's trial was covered spectacularly by Merletti, using a miniature camera that he had devised himself, the events of the Tragic Week were reported by Adolf Mas, a very young Sagarra, Josep Brangulí and Enrique Castelló, and the images of the anarchist Mateo Morral's attempt to assassinate Alfonso XIII (1906) spectacularly increased the print runs of the illustrated press of the time.[94]

Spanish graphic journalism definitively achieved popular recognition during the war with Morocco during which, between 1907 and 1914, many of the best graphic reporters of the moment, including Alfonso Sánchez García, José *Campúa*, Leopoldo Alonso, Francisco Goñi, José Zegri, Alba, Serrano Quiles, Quesada, Rectoret, Arnaud, Iglesias and Ricardo del Rivero, were sent to cover the conflict. For years the war was the focal point of the country's political life and the direct or indirect cause of crucial events in Spain's history, such as the radicalisation of workers' protests, the Tragic Week and the 1917 general strike. The war affected thousands of Spanish families – twenty-three thousand young men were massacred

BARTOLOMÉ ROS. General Franco and Lieutenant Colonel Millán Astray during the ceremony of reinstatement of the latter as commander of the Legion. Dar-Riffen, 1926. (Rosa Ros Collection.)

in 1921 at the disastrous Battle of Anwal alone – and the newspapers had to work even harder to provide the public with images reflecting its horrors, albeit timidly. In this way, the Moroccan War became another emblematic episode for Spanish graphic journalism, since it bridged the efforts of two generations of reporters, from the arrival of *Campúa* and the elder *Alfonso* in 1907, to coverage by the younger *Alfonso*, Díaz Casariego and Lázaro of the final military actions, culminating in the landing at Alhucemas in 1925. In a sense, the reports on Morocco also provide us with an idea not only of the capacity of Spain's photographers, but also of the circumstances of the graphic press of the time, which was still in a phase that could be compared to a new-born animal taking its first unsteady steps. The work of Spain's reporters – and not just the photographers – had little of the quality and insight of some of the authors, such as Ramón Sender, Manuel Ciges Aparicio or Arturo Barea, who wrote on the Moroccan War in such excellent novels as *Imán, Del cuartel y de la guerra* and *La forja de un rebelde*. In their defence, it must be admitted that the journalists had to deal with the extreme restrictions imposed by military censorship, which was insistently denounced, even in Parliament, by the

J. DÍAZ CASARIEGO. Peasants under arrest after the Castilblanco uprising.
31 December 1931. (Private Collection.)

socialist leader Pablo Iglesias.[95] In spite of the censorship, several reporters, such as Díaz Casariego and Alfonso Sánchez Portela, succeeding in crossing the Moroccan lines and producing a report on the Rif leader Abd el-Krim and on the prisoners captured at the battles of Anwal and Mount Arruit. This report made a substantial impact, as did similar reports by *Campúa*, Alonso, Iglesias and Alfonso Sánchez García during the 1907-1914 campaign.

Around this time, the Spanish graphic press began taking off definitively. By 1911 *Blanco y Negro* and *Nuevo Mundo* were at their peak and *La Ilustración Española y Americana*, *La Hormiga de Oro* and *L'Esquella de la Torratxa* still maintained a considerable degree of prestige. In those opening years of the 20th century, illustrated magazines, like the old collections of photogravures and lithographs, offered a rare opportunity to discover the image of the world, thanks to the miracle of photography. Many years later, Francisco Ayala recalled "To me, Madrid was the world shown to me in the illustrations of the graphic weeklies. (...) Collections of *Blanco y Negro* or *Nuevo Mundo*, bound into thick yearly volumes dating from before my birth, had revealed to me – as I spelt out the names and learned to recognise the faces of politicians, infamous criminals, bullfighters and actors – this or that place in the Capital of the Realm as they appeared in one photograph or another."[96] A momentous secession occurred in 1911 in the editorial staff of *Nuevo Mundo*, led by Verdugo Landi, Mariano Zavala, *Campúa* and Díaz Casariego, who, just a few weeks later published the first issue of the excellent and even more popular *Mundo Gráfico*, with an initial print run of 80,000 copies. In 1913, Zavala and Verdugo formed the company Prensa Gráfica as part of their determined competition with Prensa Española and particularly *Blanco y Negro*. That same year, the new publishing company, in which Nicolás María de Urgoiti played a decisive role, brought out the first issues of the prestigious magazine *La Esfera*. It was magnificently printed and presented the work of Madrid's best reporters of the time, led by Salazar, *Campúa*, Vilaseca and *Alfonso*. This was the golden age of Spain's emerging graphic journalism. In 1920, no fewer than 11 important illustrated magazines were published, 6 of them in Madrid, and many attained considerable circulations. That year, *Blanco y Negro* printed 100,000 copies, and 115,000 in 1923. *Nuevo Mundo* printed 125,000 in 1913, and *Mundo Gráfico* printed over 125,000 in 1927. The more élitist *La Esfera* printed over 60,000 copies in 1914, although these figures then gradually diminished until the magazine's final closure in 1930. In 1916, Editorial Catalana, publisher of *La Veu de Catalunya*, launched *D'Ací i D'Allà*, initially edited by Josep Carner. During its first phase, up until 1924, *D'Ací i D'Allà* was the first important Catalan graphic magazine, although its public was limited to certain sectors of the upper middle class. *La Unión Ilustrada*, in Málaga, and *La Semana Gráfica*, in Valencia, also attained respectable circulations in the years leading up to the Republic, as did other regional publications, such as *Vida Manchega* and *Vida Gallega*, with reporters including Pintos, Pacheco, Ángel Blanco, Suárez, Pablo Rodríguez, Luis Escobar and Julián Collado.

The exceptional popularity of the graphic press also established the popularity of certain reporters, such as Alfonso Sánchez García and Alfonso Sánchez Portela, both known professionally as *Alfonso*, *Campúa*, Gómez Durán, Martín Vidal, Alonso, Merletti, Branguli, M. Asenjo, Vilaseca, Barberá Massip, L. Torrents, Duque, Salazar, Pacheco, Miguel Marín Chivite, *Photo-Carte*, P. Marín, Díaz Casariego, the Vidal Corella brothers, and many others who contributed to almost three decades of the life of Spanish journalism. Although most of them cov-

BENÍTEZ CASAUS. Street celebration upon proclamation of the Second Republic. Madrid, 14 April 1931. (Private Collection.)

147

ALFONSO SÁNCHEZ PORTELA. Sanjurjo's attempted coup. Madrid, 1932.
(General Government Archives.)

ered all types of news, around 1910 a certain degree of specialisation arose, particularly in areas such as current events, bullfighting, politics and sports. Outstanding in the area of bullfighting were José Irigoyen, Pío, Cortés, Aurelio Grasa, Santiago Losarcos, Torres Molina, Wandel, Sánchez del Pando, *Finezas* and, especially, Baldomero, Pepe Aguayo, Mateo, Serrano, Rodero, *Campúa* and the elder *Alfonso*. Worth mentioning among sports reporters were Co de Triola, Ramón Claret, Ricardo del Rivero, Francisco Goñi, Luis Vidal, Raimundo Álvaro, Luis Sánchez Portela, Albero and Segovia, Joan Bert, Josep Gaspar and Gabriel Casas.[97]

Journalists, and even more so graphic reporters, still found themselves in a precarious position. With the beginning of the Primo de Rivera dictatorship, in 1921, interest in the press and its dissemination dropped off considerably, owing to the tough restrictions imposed by government censorship. Journalists' working conditions improved somewhat after 1926 with the formation of the Press Guilds, which regulated professional working conditions. In 1927, an editor-in-chief in

A. MERLETTI. *Alcalá Zamora, president of the Republic, with Francesc Macià, president of the Catalan autonomous government. 1931. (Institut d'Estudis Fotogràfics de Catalunya.)*

Madrid earned between 500 and 700 pesetas monthly, while a writer would earn between 200 and 300 pesetas. The situation of graphic reporters was even worse since, in most cases, their status hardly went beyond that of mere contributor. In 1930, only *Alfonso* was on record as a writer under contract to the Madrid press, as a staff member at *La Libertad*. Darío Pérez wrote in 1927 "The graphic reporter is an obscure worker, dedicated to his hectic and difficult journalist's tasks. His successes are normally spectacular, but his moral and material benefits are sparse. The image has become indispensable for the press, but the photographic reporter does not seem to be fully a part of the editorial staff; he appears to be something separate. And yet, he integrates and completes that staff."[98]

At the time, the work performed by photographers had barely changed since the early years of *Nuevo Mundo* and *Blanco y Negro*. With rare exceptions, reporters lacked a solid cultural background and did little more than follow the established methods that had been moulded by the improvisation and instinct of the pioneers in the field. Agustín Centelles recalled "When I began working, the normal type of report was static and artificial. The common practice at important events was for the photographers to line up in row and wait for the glare from a magnesium flash to trip their shutters all at once. This routine and the lack of professional ambition produced mediocre and inexpressive results that I found completely unsatisfactory." Under the Primo de Rivera dictatorship, graphic journalism in Spain experienced moments of exasperating monotony. The work of the country's reporters was still highly conditioned by their equipment, which consisted of cameras using large format glass negatives. However, by 1913 the Leitz firm had developed the first *Leica* with a standard picture size (24 × 36 mm). This legendary brand's first cameras appeared on the market in 1925, the same year as the *Ermanox*, using a 4.4x6 picture size. The *Rolleiflex* (another excellent medium-format camera) was introduced in 1929, followed one year later by the *Contax*, which, for many years, was the Leica's true competitor. Meanwhile, great advances were made with celluloid negatives subsequent to the manufacture of *Agfa-Pan* 100 ASA films in 1930. At the same time, the magnesium flash was finally displaced by the battery-powered flash produced by Osram. Although these advances led to a veritable revolution in the field of graphic journalism, they only began appearing in Spain during the first years of the Republic.

For their part, periodicals publishers had no clearly defined editorial policy on how images were to be handled and the final results of photographic editing were generally left to improvisation by those in charge of layout. This situation was in direct contrast to the rigorous approach taken by the new breed of European graphic magazines, particularly in Germany.[99] The influence of these publications was not felt in Spain until the closing years of the dictatorship, when *Estampa* and *Crónica* appeared. Founded by Luis Montiel, printed in a magnificent photogravure, dynamic and with the inexpensive price of 30 centimos, similar to that of *Mundo Gráfico*, *Estampa* was spectacularly successful and within two weeks attained a print run rivalling *Blanco y Negro* and *Mundo Gráfico*. The company Prensa Gráfica responded on 17 November 1929 with the publication of *Crónica*, along much the same lines as *Estampa*. These two periodicals became Spain's leading graphic magazines during the Republic, since *Imatges – Setmanari gràfic d'actualitats*, published in Barcelona beginning in 1930, published barely 25 issues.

However, in spite of the instability, the improvisation and the absence of a modern and rigorous approach to handling photography in Spain's illustrated magazines – with the modest exceptions of *Estampa* and *Crónica* proving the rule – the work done by those "diligent and daring" reporters constitutes an immense graphic record of life in Spain at the time. Photography, as a living projection of past reality – according to the view expressed by Barthes – offers us in these images the complementary value of its nature as certification of what once was, quite aside from its arguable technical or artistic merits. And so, in spite of the stiff poses, the photographers' direct intervention in setting up shots, and the attitude of the subjects themselves, dazzled and defenceless before the camera, the compelling truth of photography obliges us to believe that what has been captured by lens did once exist and that its echoes still sound in the fleeting reality of the present. This is why today, so many years after it was produced, the work of Spain's unsophisticated, diligent and congenial photographers of the beginning of the 20th century takes on special value.

A Certain Avant-garde

Little by little, Spain was leaving behind the 19th century image captured in the unchanging time of photographic plates. In a sense, 1917 was a historical watershed that marked end of one century and the beginning of another, announced by the final collapse of the Restoration. The decline of the old political structures and the increasingly important role of workers organisations culminated in the general strike of that year, while the Moroccan War dragged on dramatically, weakening the successive governments, which dissolved like sugar cubes in the stormy sea of consecutive crises. Between 1902, when Alfonso XIII reached the age of majority, and 1923, when the Primo de Rivera dictatorship suspended the constitution, there were no fewer than 13 different governments, and between 1917 and 1923 there were 13 complete cabinet reshuffles and 30 partial ones. Primo de Rivera and General Damaso Berenguer were the king's final trump cards and the monarchy by then only had the support of the most fundamentalist segments of the armed forces, the church, the aristocracy and the agrarian middle class. It soon became clear that this was not enough to shore up the old dynastic order in the wake of the municipal elections of 1931. The fall of the dictatorship sparked a chain of events that followed one upon another with alarming rapidity: the formation of Berenguer's government, the signing of the Pact of San Sebastian, the military revolts at Jaca and Cuatro Vientos, the Republican Revolutionary Committee's manifesto and the proclamation of the Republic on 14 April 1930. Antonio Machado wrote "With the first leaves of the poplars and the last of the almond blossoms, Spring brought in with it the Republic."

Spain's cultural life was drawn irresistibly into the wave of popular enthusiasm awoken by the political dawning of that Republican spring. The country's new leaders, members of the middle classes, had, for the most part, a rich intellectual background. This circumstance contributed decisively to the flourishing cultural activity of the period 1931-1936. Figures such as Manuel Azaña, Julián Besteiro and Fernando de los Ríos took an active role in politics, while others, including Ortega y Gasset, Gregorio Marañón, Antonio Machado, Valle-Inclán and Pérez de Ayala, were openly committed to the Republic. This new cultural environment was also reflected in the artistic and journalistic activities of the time. Dozens of magazines appeared during the Republic, such as *Cruz y Raya*, *Nueva Cultura*, *Leviatán*, *Gaceta del Arte* and *Caballo verde para la poesía*, promoted by José Bergamín, Rafael Alberti, Guillermo de Torre, Eduardo Westerdahl and Domingo Pérez Munik. This boom in the press – in Madrid alone there were eight morning and ten evening daily papers – provided a definite impulse for the development of graphic journalism, which experienced a situation comparable only to the professional fever that had led to the birth of *Mundo Gráfico* and *La Esfera*. The old illustrated magazines continued to be published in 1931, while *Estampa*, *Crónica* and the illustrated daily *Ahora*, with print runs of over one hundred thousand copies, developed with extraordinary impetus.

This cultural ebullience, however, could not conceal Spain's economic and social situation. The Republic had inherited a country that was still primarily agrarian, in which five thousand members of the minor nobility owned half the arable land, leaving over two million farm labourers dependent upon sporadic employment on the large estates. Seasonal farm workers made up three quarters of the population and received an average wage of between 3 and 3.5 pesetas for working days of up to 12 hours. This almost medieval situation was at the root of the rural unrest that shook the provinces of Andalusia and Extremadura during

N. DE LEKUONA. Photocollage. 1934. (Centro Nacional de Arte Reina Sofía.)

the first few years of the Republic, with Castilblanco, Casas Viejas and Puebla de Don Fadrique as the best-known and most representative instances, an unrest that was violently suppressed by the Civil Guard. Industrial workers, most of them recent arrivals in the large cities from the poorest regions of the country, were no better off. Ehrenburg wrote "Spain is not *Carmen*, or bullfights, or Alfonso XIII or Cambó, or Lerroux's diplomacy, or the novels of Blasco Ibáñez. Spain is twenty million ragged *Quijotes* and vast expanses of stones, suffused with bitter injustice."[100]

Meanwhile, Spanish photography, of the variety that was awarded prizes at the salons and published in specialist magazines, remained firmly anchored in the folkloric and picturesque aesthetic typical of the middle-class regenerationism of the beginning of the 20th century. While Ehrenburg was writing this harsh and passionate text, Ortiz Echagüe was commencing publication of his monumental tetralogy, the first issue of *Art de la llum* was published, and the leading proponents of late Spanish pictorialism were at their productive peak. The Republican politicians were faced with the dramatic circumstances of Spain's popular classes and the nation's self-styled photographic artists were capable only of depicting an arcadian, bucolic, happy country. However, outside the bounds of the officialism of the salons and photographic societies, a certain professional segment – significantly linked to the world of posters and advertising – began introducing timidly a few of the postulates of the avant-garde of the period between the wars, which, in photography, had as their starting point a frontal attack on pictorialism. A chink was gradually opened to modernism, represented at the time by the apotheosis of straight photography and the theoretical principles of New Objectivity put forward by Albert Renger-Pätzch, L. Moholy-Nagy's New Vision, and Emmanuel Sougez's Pure Photography. For the first time, the old principles of pictorialist impressionism were questioned in an articulate and coherent manner. Renger-Pätzch proclaimed "Let us leave art to the artists and let us create photographs using photographic means that speak for themselves, through their very nature as photographs." These postulates were echoed faintly in Spain by individuals such as Pere Catalá Pic, who directly criticised the still dominant photographic officialism. He wrote in 1932 "And now, it is no longer the ridiculous Art Nouveau composition of the nymph draped in tulle beneath the poplars, it is no longer Rembrandt's light or Corot's landscapes, or David's academicism.

J. SALA. Publicity photograph. 1930. (Private Collection.)

(...) The photographer feels strong with the arm of his technique, which he now begins to wield in defence of his creations. Today, photography no longer imitates more or less realistic art, but rather, with pride in its own artistic personality, is conscious of its own worth."[101]

Aside from these comments by Catalá Pic, which make up practically the whole of the theoretical corpus of Spain's supposed photographic avant-garde, there are almost no texts by Spanish authors that might have served as the basis for an articulate avant-garde in Spanish photography of the time. In addition, these overly anecdotal and superficial texts, were written for the most part by authors linked to literary or painting circles, such as Eduardo Westerdahl, Salvador Dalí, Gregorio Prieto, Giménez Caballero and Guillermo de Torre. Dalí, who, like other painters, including Picasso, Benjamín Palencia and Remedios Varó, dabbled in collage, wrote several articles in which he revealed his "esteem for photography" as a "pure creation of the spirit", one that was able to "capture the subtlest and most uncontrollable poetry". Clearly a text with little of the avant-garde about it, and one that is full of clichés.[102] In view of such meagre theoretical backing, it may be overly generous and of doubtful rigour to speak of a photographic avant-garde in Spain, even though a portion of the work, and not in all instances the most representative portion, of some Spanish photographers was produced at the same time as and with similar results to proponents of New Objectivity, New Vision and other avant-garde movements of the period between the wars. Even more doubtful would be any attempt to place the work of these photographers within any of the photographic trends defined by the standard historians of photography. It would also be questionable and "methodologically futile" in the field of painting, as Jaime Brihuega has rightly pointed out.

Worth mentioning among these photographers were a half dozen Catalan professionals who were outstanding practitioners of the so-called applied photography – particularly in the areas of advertising and fashion – that was so widely denigrated much later by the self-styled avant-garde of the 1970s and 80s. These photographers' work was a pale reflection of the work done around the same time in the more industrially advanced countries of Europe and in the United States, where photography was eventually incorporated into the process of promoting the new and expanding industries. Photography had changed its clientele; the former middle-class public that had collected postcards and visited portrait studios were succeeded by the new captains of industry, couturiers, stylists and poster designers. Industry began making massive use of the work of the new artists for their advertising campaigns, in posters, brochures and articles in the illustrated press. Photography, now seen as an element in photomontages, photograms, or documentary shots, became a part of industrial business and some of the photographers who experimented in the field of new forms of expression came to discover its effectiveness for purposes of publicity. Among them were Max Burchartz, El Lissitzky, Albert Renger-Pätzch and A. Rodchenko, all of them linked to Constructivism and New Objectivity. The prestige and profits to be gained through photography for advertising were so attractive that few professionals were able to resist the temptation. Even Edward Steichen, one of the most emblematic proponents of the American Photo-Secession movement, began working for fashion magazines such as *Vogue* and *Vanity Fair* in 1923.[103] His example was followed by

CATALÁ PIC. Publicity photograph. 1935. (Catalá Roca Collection.)

some of the more talented young photographers, who succeeded in integrating avant-garde formal elements into the advertising idiom required by their new clients. Worth mentioning among them were Margaret Bourke-White, Ralph Steiner, Man Ray, Cecil Beaton, Adolf de Meyer, Martin Munkacsi and Peter Rose-Pulham.

This type of photography had little impact in Spain, one of the many reasons being the economic weakness of a country with such profound cultural and industrial deficiencies, and it is no coincidence that its strongest presence was in Catalonia during the opening years of the Republic. In this respect, Catalá Pic, an experienced and self-taught portraitist who was always on the lookout for professional innovations, played a decisive role. Catalá Pic was not only the person who contributed most to the development of informative photography in Spain, but he was also the creator of some of the best advertising photographs of the time. Josep Sala, linked to the magazine *D'Ací i D'Allá*, also worked in the general milieu of advertising, a field replete with creative potential, as Catalá Pic himself had observed. Emili Vilá, a poster artist and painter, successfully used photography in his designs for use in advertising and created some admirable images. Emili Godes made numerous professional incursions into industrial and advertising photography, using such techniques as photomontage, photograms and overprinting. An altogether different case was that of Ramón Batlles and Josep Masana, whose excellent professional work in the fields of fashion and advertising bears no resemblance to their pretentious and outmoded pictorialist creations. Other artists, such as Campañá and Goicoechea occasionally made formal experiments that are of little importance in the context of their work as a whole, and the same may be said of the Aragonese reporter Aurelio Grasa.

Two individuals with close ties to the world of painting merit special mention: Nicolás de Lekuona and Josep Renau. Lekuona's work, unmistakably influenced by Dada, Futurism and Constructivism, showed the clearest intent of any Spanish photographer of his time to break with the past and experiment. His expressive curiosity led him paint, write and photograph, using such techniques as photomontage and collage, as well as other formal innovations, in a body of work that, in spite of its lack of maturity, intimates the potential of its creator, who died at a young age in the strife-torn days of the Civil War.[104] Josep Renau

J. RENAU. The Commissary - Backbone of Our Popular Army. Photocollage, 1936. (Instituto Valenciano de Arte Moderno.)

had already made a name for himself in the avant-garde movements born in the flush of Republican enthusiasm and was one of the most prolific theorists of poster design and photomontage, through articles and books such as *Función social del cartel publicitario* (1937). His interest in the expressive potential of photography dated back to his student days, and his first photomontage, *El hombre ártico* (1929), was contemporaneous with his first and only exhibition as a painter. From then on, he worked constantly at developing the technique of collage, in a blend of the most extreme and revolutionary postulates of Dada and Mexican and Soviet poster art. Collage became his most effective means of expression, both during the Civil War and in his later work, such as the famous *American Way of Life* (1967).[105]

The cultural authorities of the Republic had little time to plan a substantial change in the means of promoting and exhibiting art, as demanded by artists' associations, which continually expressed their disappointment with the frustrating persistence of the officialist line in Spanish art. Some progress was made in photography with the formation of associations, particularly in Catalonia, where photographic associations and athenaeums linked to left-wing parties and trade unions proliferated. However, the predominance of the old officialist circles, such as the Agrupación Fotográfica de Cataluña, the Real Sociedad Fotográfica de Madrid and the Sociedad Fotográfica de Zaragoza, and the absence of mechanisms for publication and exhibition kept the so-called "artistic photography" mired in its fusty and obsolete aesthetic attitudes, giving rise to a profound division between the new creative trends and pictorialist fundamentalism. This explains the degree of formal eclecticism found in the work of photographers such as Campañá and Porqueras, and even a clear creative dissociation in the work of others, such as Masana, Batlles and even Pla Janini.[106]

On the other hand, the Spanish photography that could be seen as related to the avant-garde movements of the period between the wars, particularly with the European and American New Objectivity, clearly opted for a decidedly documentarist approach, as in the case of Joaquín Gomis. Linked to more progressive pictorialist circles, having founded and directed the group *Amics de l'Art Nou* (ADLAN) in 1930, Gomis was one of the leading figures of the artistic world in Barcelona during the Republic. He began taking photographs around 1920 and the brief flourishing of Spanish photography during the 1930s instilled in him an intense interest in forms, objects and details that had a profound effect on his clear, calm and technically impeccable images. Like Gomis, other photographers achieved similar results through purely intuitive means, assimilating without hesitation the dignity of the medium in which they worked. Some of them, including José Suárez, Aurelio Grasa, *Alfonso* and Agustín Centelles, were especially active in photojournalism, one of the fields that benefited most from the new cultural environment fostered by the Republic. Times were exciting once again for graphic reporting, marked by the splendid maturity of a second generation of excellent professionals, who had inherited the spirit of the pioneers and who benefited from the technical advances of the period and from the vigour of the illustrated press. Outstanding among these professionals were the photographers already mentioned and Díaz Casariego, Lluís Torrents, Joaquín Brangulí, Albero and Segovia, Santos Yubero, the *Mayo* brothers, Juan José Serrano and Luis Vidal Corella, prime examples of a whole generation of reporters who had to deal with the historical drama of the Civil War.

J. GOMIS. Fisherman. Sitges, 1936. (Gomis Collection.)

The Disasters of War

The victory of the parties grouped in the Popular Front in the February 1936 elections was insufficient to consolidate the Republican regime. It soon became clear that the overextended reformism of the Second Republic could not be maintained as an alternative to the old oligarchic system of the monarchy, which was supported by middle-class, religious and military fundamentalism. The conspiracies by these sectors, set in motion on the very day of the Popular Front's victory, culminated in a military uprising, in keeping with the deeply rooted 19th century tradition, that met with political failure in most of the country and plunged its inhabitants into the most brutal armed conflict of the modern age. Once again the old Spain of fixers, ruffians and bullies rose up against the Spain of rage and ideals, opening a breach filled with knives that led directly to the historical drama of the Civil War.

At a historic moment characterised by the irresistible rise of Nazism, the Spanish Civil War held the attention of the whole world, which saw here the opening battle between democracy and fascism. Leonardo Sciascia wrote "If it were not for the Spanish resistance, we would not have become aware of fascism." This exemplary, emblematic and premonitory nature of the Civil War attracted to Spain hundreds of correspondents from around the world, with the knowledge that their reports on the progress of the war would make a profound impression on their readers. Most of these reporters opted unequivocally for the legitimacy of the Republic, as did intellectuals and scientists, including André Malraux, Ernest Hemingway, Ilya Ehrenburg, Louis Aragon, John Dos Passos, George Orwell, Leon Blum, Arthur Koestler, M. Koltzov, Joris Ivens, and many others, whose work in Spain was as militant as it was professional. For them, the Spanish Civil War was the "last Romantic war" between popular democratic forces and an army in revolt defending the interests of a reactionary wealth-based oligarchy. This same sentiment inspired the work the most outstanding foreign photographers, who, in the words of Cornell Capa, constituted a veritable "international centre-left brigade armed with cameras".

For their part, Spanish photographers, much more closely involved in the events, very soon realised that their work, aside from its immediate usefulness, constituted an arm in the hands of the legitimate authorities who were fighting

ALFONSO SÁNCHEZ PORTELA. *Attack on the Montaña Barracks. Madrid, 20 July 1936.*
(Private Collection.)

the army in revolt. Also aligned for the most part in defence of the Republic, some of them, including Centelles, Torrents and *Gonzanhi*, in Barcelona, and *Alfonso*, Vidal, Benítez Casaus and Albero and Segovia, in Madrid, set to work on the same day that the uprising broke out, knowing that that they were in the process of laying the foundations of a photographic aesthetic based firmly on the ethical motives of the conflict. This identification with the Republican cause is especially evident in the work of *Alfonso*, Albero and Segovia, Díaz Casariego, the Vidal brothers, Gaspar, Torrents and particularly in that of Centelles and the *Mayo* brothers.[107] Others, including Casas, Catalá Pic, Sala, Renau and Centelles himself, approached their work as an unequivocal instrument of propaganda at the service of the constitutional government. According to Renau, in the extreme circumstances of war artists lost their personal and subjective character and became something collective, generous and "objective". He wrote in 1937 "The poster artist is subject in his social function to a purpose that is different from the purely emotional motivation of the free artist. The poster artist is the artist of disciplined freedom, of freedom conditioned by objective requirements, requirements that take precedence over his individual will." The artist – the photographer – serves the common cause, the collective task of defeating the enemy, as a necessary first step towards achieving the social justice and freedom that is being pursued.[108]

As Furio Colombo has pointed out, the Spanish Civil War gave rise to a new style of visual communication of events, marked by the photographer's commitment and the new potential offered by photographic techniques. Photographs of previous conflicts were only tangentially illustrative and lacked the artist's hallmark that they took on in Spain. This was not only because of the mechanical limitations that photographers had to overcome but also because they lacked the sense of solidarity, identification and passion – and compassion as well – that began to make itself so decisively felt during the Civil War. The former coldly and aesthetically professional perception was replaced by a new ethical, participatory and generous vision that prefigured the birth of a new era in photographic communication, marked by emotion, exaltation and militancy on the part of the photographer. A good example is that of Faustino Mayo, who left his job at *El Heraldo de Madrid* to join Enrique Líster's 5th Regiment as photographer. For their part, Centelles, Casas and Catalá Pic worked directly for the propaganda services of the Catalan Autonomous Government, Francisco *Mayo* and Benítez Casaus formed part of the so-called *Altavoz del Frente* (Loudspeaker of the Front); Díaz Casariego collaborated with the Republican air force and Josep Renau served in the Valencia Army Commissariat. This militant view of the photographer's work and the country's social, political and cultural circumstances left a profound impression on photographs taken in Spain in the period 1936-1939. The population – the people who fought and suffered in the war – became the central figure in these images. A figure that no longer acted but simply was, one that did not interpret a script determined by the photographer but instead lived, suffered and died in front of the cameras.

The interest stirred by the Civil War led the majority of the world's leading illustrated publications and graphic agencies to send their photographers to cover the conflict. With a few notorious exceptions, such as Cartier-Bresson, A. Kértesz

R. CAPA. Militiaman shot down at Cerro Muriano. ca. 1937. (Ministry of Culture Collection.)

and Felix Man, the leading reporters of the time travelled to Spain, including Robert Capa (*Vu, Regard, Life*), Gerda Taro (*Vu, Life*), George Reisner and Hans Namuth (*Vu*), Roman Karmen and B. Makaseev (*Smena*), L. Deschamps (*L'Illustration*), David *Chim* Seymour (*Life*), H. Mitchell (*The Illustrated London News*), Hollmann (*Illustrierte Zeitung*) and Walter Reuter (*Regard*), and some of them will always be remembered for their Spanish reports, such as Gerda Taro, consecrated by his tragic death on the front, Hans Namuth, Robert Capa and Walter Reuter, who ended up abandoning his camera to take up arms in the Andalusian militia. Worthy of special mention is Andrei Friedmann (Capa), who began publishing his first reports on the war in August 1936 in the magazine *Vu*, then edited by Lucien Vogel. After Vogel's resignation and the consequent change in the magazine's ideological direction, in the autumn of 1936, Friedmann – now definitively Robert Capa – continued working from Spain for *Regard* and *Ce Soir*. In 1938, *Life* began publishing his reports. Except for the brief intervals of his visits to China, Paris and New York in 1938 and 1939, Capa could be considered the graphic reporter who dedicated the most time to the Civil War, from the first days of the military coup to the withdrawal of the Republican troops and their confinement in the French concentration camps. Capa's photographs are more than a mere conventional narrative of the events of the war; they form understanding and compassionate chronicles of the life and death of the thousands of people who suffered the disasters of a war that they did not want and were forced into situations of extreme tension and violence. Their aesthetic is not only one of commitment, but also one of proximity: he was there beside the militiaman shot down on Cerro Muriano, he witnessed the moving farewell to the International Brigades, he observed the grievous collection of bodies on the desolate fields of Teruel, and shared in the distress of the people fleeing from death on the roads of Córdoba. For this reason, quite aside from its quality, his work has become the most important and emblematic photography from the Spanish Civil War.[109]

Hans Namuth and George Reisner had visited Spain before the outbreak of the Civil War. After leaving Nazi Germany they temporarily set up a studio in Pollensa and began working from there for *Alliance Photo*. They happened to be in Barcelona on 18 July 1936 to cover the Popular Olympics, which were never held. Their reports on the first day of the war were published with resounding success in the magazine *Vu*. This success and their own personal commitment led them to stay in Spain until March 1937. For over nine months, they travelled the country, producing excellent reports on Guadalajara, Barcelona, Madrid, Extremadura and Andalusia.[110] Walter Reuter, a w ll-known reporter for the magazine *AIZ* (*Arbeiter Ilustrierte Zeitung*), arrived in Spain in 1933. Having settled in Málaga, he travelled to Madrid on 18 July 1936 to take part in the defence of that city – he was a member of the Juventudes Socialistas Unificadas – and to work as a photographer for the Republican government's press departments. David *Chim* Seymour visited several fronts, taking extraordinary photographs of bombardments in Extremadura. Kati Horna also spent time in Spain and published unassuming photographs of daily life away from the fronts in the magazines *Tierra y Libertad* and *Mujeres Libres*. On the other hand, the foreign photographers who worked on the rebel side never came to identify with the motives of the conflict as did those who worked on the Republican side. A prime example is found in L. Deschamps, a reporter for *L'Illustration de Paris* who took hundreds of high-quality but thoroughly cold and distant images.

BRANGULÍ. Rally held by the UGT and PSUC trade unions at the Teatro Olimpia. Barcelona, August 1936. (Catalonia Historical Archives.)

As a rule, Spanish reporters lacked a background comparable to that of their foreign counterparts. Furthermore, Spain's illustrated press, in spite of the progress made under the Republic, had no clearly defined editorial policy, and this circumstance worsened during the early part of the war. Editorial levels were severely affected, as were photographers' working conditions. Film and photographic paper became alarmingly scarce during the first few months of the conflict. The almost total unavailability of standard negatives forced many photographers to go back to using their plate cameras and in some cases supplies of even glass negatives were exhausted. These difficulties affected almost exclusively the Republican side, since the Nationalist side had better access to supplies, thanks to assistance from the German authorities.[111]

The difficulty of procuring materials and of covering graphic information led photographers to form impromptu companies, for the purpose of meeting the growing demand from daily newspapers, magazines and propaganda offices. In Madrid, Santos Yubero and the Benítez Casaus brothers set up an agency that sent photograph to all Spanish publications. The *Mayo* brothers created the *España* agency, which distributed images to a wide range of Spanish and European publications, including *Smena* and *L'Humanité*. However, the largest and most pivotal group was the famous pool formed by Joaquín Brangulí, Carlos Pérez de Rozas, Josep María Sagarra, Lluís Torrents, Josep Badosa, Merletti, Joan A. Puig Farrán, Antoni Campañá and Ramón Claret. Their work as a co-operative allowed the members of the pool access to images of all current events but led to the inevitable confusion as to who had taken those photographs, a problem that was aggravated by the prudent omission of signatures and the dispersal of the photographers' own archives.[112] On a different level, the press underwent a radical transformation from the very outbreak of hostilities. Illustrated publications changed their content substantially and concentrated their reports on the events of the war. Most of them became partisan organs, while difficulties in obtaining supplies of paper caused the number of pages to dwindle and the quality of print to suffer as the conflict wore on. Nevertheless, the photographers continued working, although they were heavily conditioned by these technical problems and by the restrictions imposed by censorship. Outstanding among them were Alfonso Sánchez Portela, Albero and Segovia, Luis Vidal, Joaquín Brangulí, Sagarra, Torrents, Díaz Casariego, Pérez de Rozas and, above all, Agustín Centelles.

Centelles has become the best known Spanish reporter of the period, precisely because of his photographs of the Civil War. His were the best images, the most intense and dramatic, of the bloody events of 19 July 1936 in Barcelona. From then on, he worked incessantly, from the battles on the Aragon front to the Republican offensive against Belchite and Teruel. On 17 September 1937 he was assigned to the Photographic Services Unit of the Eastern Army and at the beginning of 1938 he was placed in charge of organisation of the photographic archives of the Catalonia Army, where he worked closely with the Catalan Autonomous Government's Propaganda Commissary, Jaume Miravitlles, and with Pere Catalá Pic, who was in charge of propaganda publication. As with Capa, Centelles's aesthetic is also one of commitment and proximity, of emotion and identification with the people he portrayed. This identification is particularly evident in his magnificent photographs of 19 July in Barcelona, his reports from the Aragon and Belchite front, the bombardments of Lérida and his images of daily life away from the fronts.

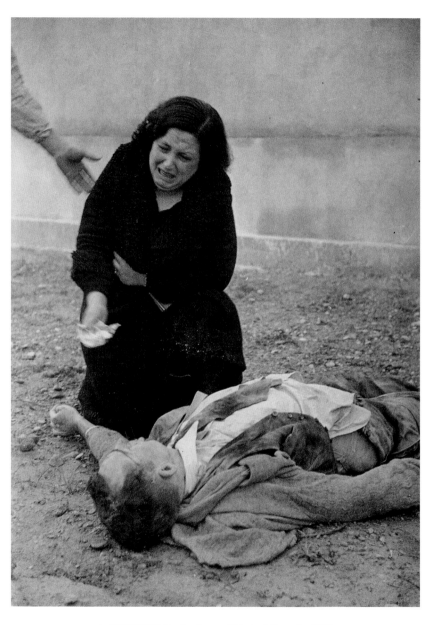

A. CENTELLES. Bombardment of Lérida. 2 November 1937.
(Centelles Archives.)

V. GOMBÁU. Colonel Millán Astray with two Falangist commanders. Salamanca, 1938.
(Filmoteca de Castilla-León.)

A. MERLETTI. Meeting at the CNT trade union offices. Barcelona, 1937.
(Institut d'Estudis Fotogràfics de Catalunya.)

His work, now recovered after having remained hidden for almost thirty years in a French town, is one of the most touching and emblematic bodies of work from the Civil War.[113]

Alfonso Sánchez Portela's war photographs are very different from Centelles's, even though they show the same curiosity and a similar interest in moving in close to the scenes of conflict. This curiosity led him to travel to the front on many occasions – Teruel, Andalusia, Guadarrama, Guadalajara – although he never approached his work with the commitment or proximity of the Valencian photographer. His images of Madrid during the first few months of the conflict show the same city as always, but ravaged now by the inclement gales of war. Memorable among his images are those of the attack on the Montaña Barracks and his depictions of daily life in the capital in which we sense the photographer's surprise and stupefaction at the ruin of the scenes that have undergone dramatic changes. The chronicle of the war itself is much more clearly present in the work of Albero and Segovia, who distinguished themselves during the opening days of the war as the most active photographers in Madrid. They were the leading figures of those days, although their work has been incomprehensibly ignored until now, like so many others that were dispersed, hidden or destroyed in the wake of the Republic's military defeat. This is true of Sagarra, *Gonzanhi*, whose photographs were often published bearing Centelles's signature, Badosa and Torrents, in Barcelona, Marina, Videa, *Piortiz*, Pepe Aguayo, Santos Yubero, Díaz Casariego and the *Mayo* brothers, in Madrid, Gil de Espinar and Espiga, in Bilbao, Marín Chivite, in Zaragoza, and Luis Vidal Corella, in Valencia.

As a rule, the photographers who worked on the rebel side lacked the quality, emotion and commitment of those on the Republican side. With few exceptions, the great reporters remained and worked in the cities that were loyal to the legitimate government, such as Madrid, Valencia and Barcelona. This fact, along with the absence of an ample editorial background, would explain the apparently poor quality of the work done by photographers on the so-called Nationalist side. Nevertheless, worthy of mention is the work of photographers such as Serrano, who followed Queipo de Llano's troops in Andalusia, documenting their entry into "liberated" towns, the advance on Madrid, and daily life away from the front. The Chilean journalist Boby Deglané produced a number of admirable reports for the weekly *Fotos*. However, the most outstanding photographic office was the one organised by General Aranda, head of the Galician Army, and including José Lombardia, Jaime Pacheco, José Longueira, Faustino Rodríguez, Ángel Llanos and Mario Blanco. This office's task was to take photographs of the enemy camp, photograph soldiers in the column and document its entry into occupied towns and cities. Also worth mentioning is the work done away from the front by Julián Loyola, Pablo Rodríguez, Luis Escobar, Sánchez del Pando and particularly Pascual Marín, Pepe Gracia and Jalón Ángel, the author of a number of the official portraits used by Nationalist propaganda services. The war brought activity in portrait studios effectively to a halt, although some professionals such as Jalón Ángel, Pascual Marín, Pacheco, Gracia, Gombáu, Amador, Rodríguez and *Alfonso* continued taking portraits of soldiers, militiamen and civilians. Lastly, the course of military events hastened the end of the major illustrated magazines, whose quality had declined steadily since the early months of 1937. Many of them did not survive until the end of the war. *Mundo Gráfico* published its last issue in December 1938. *Ahora* reduced its number of pages considerably after March 1938 and closed for

ALBERO AND SEGOVIA. Arrest of rebel soldier at the Montaña Barracks. Madrid, 20 July 1936. (Private Collection.)

good in February 1939. *Estampa* did the same in August 1938 and *Crónica* in September of that year. The end of the war brought final closure of all of these major illustrated magazines and the exile in Spain or abroad of the leading reporters of the time, who were forced to flee the country or suffer the widespread purges of the profession. The long, black night of the Franco regime forced Spanish photography back into the professional constraint of studios in irremediable decline and late pictorialist officialism that had been definitively superseded under the Republic. After a fierce struggle between the old and the new, the future, once again, was the past.

PART THREE

L. VIDAL CORELLA. Entry of Nationalist troops into Valencia. 29 March 1939. (Monasor Collection.)

The Autarchic Regime in Spain

On 1 April 1939, the rebel troops led by General Franco took their final military objectives, marking the beginning of a regime that was midway between austere fascism and the military and ecclesiastical dictatorship foretold by Azaña. In the wake of the military victory, Spain was subjected to a political system that was "nationalist, authoritarian, unified, ethical, missionary and imperial", to quote the rhetorical excesses of the time. The reality of the Spain governed by the groups of financiers, politicians and clergy who had supported the "Crusade", was described eloquently by the Falangist intellectual Dionisio Ridruejo. He wrote "The 1940s were, for the largest part of the population, years of distress, hunger, humiliation and fear of a regime of safe-conduct passes to travel and ration books to obtain miserable food rations. They were years of frivolous and offensive euphoria on the part of the small and profoundly vulgar class of self-important mandarins and rich speculators." They were also years of repression, punishment and terror. In the summer of 1939 there were 29 prisons in Madrid holding over one hundred thousand prisoners in squalor. Every morning, five extremely summary courts martial were held in the Salesian tribunals, judging and condemning between three hundred and four hundred defendants. This process was repeated in every city throughout Spain, where up to one hundred and fifty concentration camps were hastily set up. Count Ciano, who visited Spain around this time, noted in his diary "There are still a great many executions. In Madrid alone there are between 200 and 250 every day, and 150 in Barcelona and 80 in Seville." Even the Ministry of Justice officially admitted the existence of 271,000 political prisoners in December 1939 and 164,642 "violent deaths" by 1951. García de Cortázar and González Vesga write "The end of the armed conflict did not bring peace for the people of Spain; it merely brought social order. Hundreds of individuals were forced to change their behaviour and lives drastically to conform to the political and social demands of the new State. Thousands more fell before the firing squads. Those members of the defeated political organisations who remained in the country were subjected to unrelenting social exclusion."[114]

In his resolve to keep alive the fratricidal spirit that had made the Civil War possible, General Franco did not abolish the state of war until 1948 and the military tribunals continued to fulfil their repressive mission for almost forty years. Under these circumstances, the peseta was devalued by half of its 1936 value. In 1940, Spain's national income had dropped to the level of 1914, while per capita income had fallen to the equivalent of figures for the 19th century. By 1948, with 48.8 per cent of its population occupied in farm work, Spain was still a mainly agricultural and pre-industrial country. The working population had dropped by over one half million, while new jobs were reserved for "veterans" from the winning side and the army had over five hundred thousand officers and soldiers on its payroll. Until 1951, Spaniards' lives were marked by autarchy, economic stagnation and inflation. Repudiated by democratic countries, Franco's Spain closed in upon itself and condemned its people to a long and impoverishing period of international isolation.

In the area of culture, the situation was comparable to that of a barren expanse, since the authorities in charge of promoting and stimulating culture showed

ANONYMOUS. *Political prisoners in the old prison at Puerto de Santa María. June 1948. (Agencia Efe.)*

at best an unequivocal indifference towards it. Millán Astray's famous remark "Down with intelligence!" is no more than a local version of Goebbels' statement "When I hear the word culture I draw my pistol". With the military victory, Spanish cultural life was brutally truncated; most of the country's writers, artists, musicians and scientists went into exile, while others were imprisoned or purged or were forced into a semi-clandestine or underground life. In any case, their persecuted and banned works – the Franco regime compiled a list of over three thousand prohibited books – were not permitted to circulate until the very end of the dictatorship.

For obvious reasons, Spain's social reality during the period is not to be found reflected in the art, literature and certainly not the photography that, openly aligned with the neo-classical currents of the 1940s, reeked of the formol of a purist and jingoistic sentimentality. This Great and United – but by no means Free – Spain found it necessary to fall back on photographic academicism in the face of the prostration and indigence that even the regime's most accomplished propagandists were incapable of concealing. Pictorialism was the photographic style that best meshed with the triumphalist and mythicising spirit of the new authorities and with the dictatorship's moral and artistic abjection. Cultural nationalism took up the aesthetic ideology that had underpinned that movement, based on folklorism, picturesqueness, racial exaltation, tradition and the now imperial past, a movement that would characterise the work of the best known photographers of the postwar period. This circumstance was to remain unchanged until the last few years of the autarchic regime.

Photography for an Empire

In the atmosphere of patriotic exaltation fostered by the military victory of 1939, art was seen as a merely ceremonial accessory at the service of the State and the Empire, an accessory that should at once be pompous, reverential and conservative. The Franco regime's aesthetic, defined by such individuals as Giménez Caballero, José María Pemán, Eugenio Montes, García Valdecasas and Laín Entralgo, was a muddled jumble of rhetoric that owed much to pre-war pictorialism's repertoire of values: the greatness and unity of the Homeland, racial exaltation, tradition, and a baroque and rusty catholicity. According to the Falangist magazine *Jerarquía*, "Art requires a metaphysic to live and if instead of a metaphysic it is given a theology it will be that much stronger." It is not surprising that the Franco regime's cultural doctrine should appropriate the aesthetic of pictorialism, whose extended survival can only be explained by the determined support that it received from the upper echelons of the new regime.

José Ortiz Echagüe – the last of the pictorialists, as he has been called by Daniel Masclet – was unquestionably the leading proponent of this photographic style. He consistently placed his undeniable talent as a photographer at the service of an interpretative style of photography laden with unchanging values, the same values that were being stressed by the regime's press and propaganda offices. For this reason, and probably to his chagrin, Echagüe was recognised as the most representative photographer of the new Spain, where, according to Giménez Caballero, an artist also had to be a great soldier and a great Spaniard. This profound identification of Ortiz Echagüe's work with the national spirit of the Franco regime

J. ORTIZ ECHAGÜE. Burial at the Miraflores monastery.
1945. (Private Collection.)

was pointed out insistently by some of the most exemplary members of the new intellectual élite. Fray Justo Pérez de Urbel wrote in 1948 "Marching through his work we see the man of all provinces and times, the man who forged this colossal history that surpasses even the wildest flights of epic poetry. Here we see the hero of Numantia and the conquistador, the anonymous settler of the Reconquest, Don Quijote and Hernán Cortés..." As late as 1962, Miguel Tubáu was still brandishing similar arguments: "And therein lies the master's secret, beating in rhythm to a patriotic sentiment placed at the service of the art of photography, unswervingly, all the while making no concessions to imported liberalism."[115] In the midst of this rhetorical apotheosis, Echagüe was to finish his monumental tetralogy, begun with *España, tipos y trajes* (1933) and *España, pueblos y paisajes* (1938). *España mística* was published in 1943, and *Castillos y alcázares* in 1956.

Ortiz Echagüe remained active until 1973 and his unshakeable and schematic work showed no essential variation over the years, although towards the end it became more synthetic and "photographic". The magnitude of his "lordly and

E. SUSANNA. The Beggar's Prayer. *Bromoil, 1940s (published in* Sombras*).*

leading" figure was such that he overshadowed all of the other late pictorialists of his time, who, although less imbued with ideology, continued working in the old picturesque folkloric style and producing pretentious and affected compositions. Among them were a number who had already made a name for themselves in earlier years, such as José Tinoco, Pla Janini, Eduardo Susanna, Antonio Arissa, Casals Ariet, Mora Carbonell, Miguel Goicoechea, Antoni Campañá, who soon found a new direction in sports photography, the Marquis of Santa María del Villar, Carlos Gutiérrez and Joaquín Gil Marraco. Most of these photographers were entrenched firmly in the decorative preciosity that was so appropriate to the purposes of a regime that sought to conceal the country's dramatic situation by means of an art – and photography was thoroughly convinced that its artistic pretensions were justified – that was assigned a ceremonial and dissembling role. In this respect, late pictorialism was the country's photographic contribution to the autarchic regime to the same extent that it was a product of that regime.

J. TINOCO. Arenas de San Pedro. Bromide, 1946. (Real Sociedad Fotográfica.)

Special mention must be made of Joaquín Pla Janini, who, along with Ortiz Echagüe, had the greatest influence on Spanish photographers of the time. He was the most vocal advocate of pigmentarism, the one who put up the most tenacious resistance against new trends in photography and the one who most strongly defended a return to the true "artistic" photography, which, in his opinion, was pigmentary photography.[116] If he ever felt any desire for innovation in his working habits, for experimentation with new forms or with pure visual play, he soon returned to the old ways imposed by an exhausted, formally academicist and conceptually conservative aesthetic. In his later years he was unable to resist the temptation to take a documentary approach, as seen in such works as *Bajo los puentes* (1946) or in occasional bromides, in which he demonstrated a certain capacity for reporting.

The influence of Pla Janini, Ortiz Echagüe, Tinoco, Andrada and Susanna was decisive in the survival of pigmentation techniques among Spanish photographers of the 1940s and 1950s. These techniques were used by Smith de las Heras, Sigfrido Koch Bengoechea, Josep and Manuel Closa, Casals Ariet, Pau Barceló, Pere Sender, José A. Lassala and many of the leading members of the photographic associations of the time, whose work was exploited by the new cultural authorities, through the Plastic Arts Department of the Directorate-General of Press and Propaganda. Besides censoring works of art, this Department was responsible for organising the National Photography Salons through the photographic section directed by Augusto Vallmitjana, who was linked to the Agrupación Fotográfica de Cataluña. These salons, along with the associations and specialist magazines, had a decisive influence on the new generation of pictorialists, which was indebted to an informal folklorism that stressed the values of a "virile" Spain in contrast to an "industrial and liberal" Europe. Consequently, in their works, the epigones of late pictorialism exalted the peace, happiness, honour and "harmony without distress" of rural and agrarian life. This situation was maintained for several lustra by the leading lights of the movement, including José Loygorry, J. Domingo Bisbal, Manuel Cuadrada, Miguel Tubáu, Diego Gálvez, Rafael Gómez Teruel, Josep Massó, Pere Sender, José Veiga Roel and José Núñez Larraz. Some of them – Pere Sender, Veiga Roel and Núñez Larraz – served as a link to the realism practised by the following generation. The creative dissociation experienced by these photographers was clearly expressed by Veiga Roel in 1961 after the opening of the Oscar Steiner exhibition in Vigo: "I do not feel that I am ready to give an opinion on one approach or the other (classical or "modern"), especially since I am convinced that the old and outdated style urgently requires a drastic revolution, but what we are being presented with as new has yet to convince me that it is a sincere and spontaneous manifestation of art."[117] Veiga Roel gave an honest description of the conflict felt by many amateurs who were still mired in the dominant academicism but who had enough creative vigour to assimilate the airs of renewal that were then beginning to make themselves felt in Spain. Several of Veiga Roel's later works foreshadow this new documentary realism, whose origins can be seen in some of the images produced by Manuel Goicoechea, José Tinoco, Pla Janini and even Ortiz Echagüe, who always denied, with "ingenuous vehemence" that he was a pictorialist photographer.

The task of concealing, idealising and poeticising reality carried out by "artistic" photography in the postwar years was complemented by the work of the civil servants in charge of enforcing the censorship imposed by the authorities in order to watch over the purity of customs and safeguard the National Movement's moral values. Under Serrano Súñer's Press Act of 1938, all publications, shows and works of art were subject to censorship. Responsibility for censoring photography lay with Directorate-General of the Press and Propaganda. At a time when National Catholic orthodoxy insisted obsessively on morality, censorship concentrated on relentlessly suppressing even the most timid transgression in this respect, in addition to prohibiting absolutely any publication that infringed upon the regime's basic principles. Censorship was so stifling that nudes were banned from salons and competitions until well into the 1960s. As a result, photographers did not attempt to work in this genre until the eve of the transition to democracy, with the exception of the occasional admirable work by Otho Lloyd or Nicolás Muller, both of whom received their training in photography outside Spain. It is not until 1958 that we find the nudes by Ramón Bargués published in that edition of the *Afal* yearbook, after a determined struggle with government officials.[118]

However, it was not risqué subjects that most concerned those zealous guardians of the regime's moral and political orthodoxy; they were much more interested in concealing and disguising the miserable reality of Spain under autarchy, with its rationing and its black market. To this task, the officially sanctioned photography practised by Spain's leading late pictorialists and their legion of epigones and imitators made a significant contribution.

Industry and Autarchy

The political and economic circumstances of a country subjected fully to autarchy was immediately reflected in the commercial structures of photography, which, in the opening years of the postwar period, underwent a severe crisis. Photographers could not obtain paper, negatives, cameras or developers, driving many of them to the extremes of using glass negatives or waste material from the country's precarious film industry. The regime's political isolation made the situation even worse, since products could only be acquired from countries with sympathetic governments, such as Hitler's Germany. These products entered the country through official importers, who, under the restrictions imposed by the system of quotas, were able to supply the few specialist shops existing at the time. As with medicines and other staple goods, photography became the object of contraband traded on the black market.[119]

The Spanish camera industry had to overcome almost insuperable difficulties. In a sense, the autarchic regime fostered the development of a large number of modest domestic companies, which had to bring all their ingenuity to bear in order to fill the gap created by the lack of imported goods. Most of them manufactured cameras using foreign designs and patents, although they were hard pressed to obtain adequate optical materials. The first company to produce Bakelite cameras was Univex, which flooded the market with a wide range of inexpensive and simple models, including the famous *Supra*, *Marivez* and *Unica*, with rudimentary optical mechanisms. Between 1942 and 1954, Matutano, S.A. produced its popular *Perfecta* and *Capta-Baby* models. However, it was not until the 1960s that the Cerlex factory at Vic (Barcelona province) succeeded in improving on the quality of those basic products with its celebrated *Werlisa* line, whose plastic model achieved truly astonishing success on the market.[120] The manufacture of photosensitive material, paper and negatives, was practically monopolised by the companies Valca and Negra, although there were other small producers, such as Infonal, Mafe (Manufacturas Fotográficas Españolas) and Supremus.

Valca, whose full name was Sociedad Española de Productos Fotográficos Valca, started out producing plates for the graphic arts before moving to the manufacture of papers, films and chemicals. Its creation aroused a great deal of expectation and was greeted with profuse rhetoric in the specialist press of the 1940s. Negra i Tort recommenced in 1939 the manufacture of papers that it had begun in 1916. By 1952, this company was offering a wide range of the popular *Negtor* papers and had become one of the most competitive businesses in its line in Europe. Along with these emblematic companies, the Spanish photographic industry also included smaller businesses, such as Mafe, which was eventually absorbed by Agfa, and Infonal (Industria Fotoquímica Nacional), which began manufacturing very low quality papers in 1942.

However, the precarious Spanish photographic industry, which was increasingly invaded by German, American and Japanese products, never attained any sizeable volume nor produced enough to satisfy the modest needs of domestic consumption. In 1980, over forty years after the end of the Civil War, production

Although the Spanish photographic industry was never an important one,
brands such as Negtor and Univex were very popular.
(Miquel Galmes Collection.)

amounted to under 6,000 million pesetas. At that time, there were three companies dedicated to the manufacture of different varieties of specialised material:
Mafe, 40 per cent German-owned and with a yearly turnover of 3,373 million pesetas, Negra Industrial, 100 per cent Spanish-owned and with a yearly turnover of
2,061 million pesetas, and Valca, 100 per cent British-owned and with a yearly
turnover of 1,796 million pesetas. All together, these three companies had one
thousand three hundred employees and their yearly investments amounted to
4,000 million pesetas. Exports were few, amounting to under 1,490 million pesetas yearly, while imports in 1979 reached the substantial figure of 6,510 million pesetas.[121] The tax policy adopted under the 1959 Stability Plan and increasing
foreign competition eventually overcame the Spanish industry's weak resistance,
and the most emblematic brands, Negra and Valca, disappeared at the beginning of
the 1990s.

Nor were statistics on consumption encouraging. According to figures published by the magazine *Foto Profesional*, the average number of photographs taken
per person per year in Spain in 1986 was 8. This was equivalent to 0.4 rolls of film,

in comparison with 2.8 for Americans, 2.2 for the Swiss, 1.9 for the Japanese, 1.4 for the French, and 1.1 for the British. After forty years of official neglect and strict legal and union control, Spanish photography was in dire circumstances. In view of the practical non-existence of specialised schools and centres, manufacturers went so far as to petition the government for photography to be included in the curriculum of public schools. However, it was clear that the State was only interested in photography as a source of tax revenue. The Ministry of Finance's zeal in respect of tax collection led it to introduce the so-called *Responsible Business Credential*, controlled directly by the bureaucracy of the vertical unions. This credential was indispensable for anyone wishing to carry out any professional activity, and regulations for the training of professionals were set out in an order published by the Ministry of Science and Education on 11 February 1986. Nevertheless, in spite of these belated official guidelines, Spanish photographers continued to be effectively self-taught, as in the times of the old master *Káulak*.[122]

Officialist Photography

The Civil War had caused a severe breakdown in Spanish photography and in the activity of what had been until then its most influential circles, such as the Real Sociedad Fotográfica de Madrid, the Agrupación Fotográfica de Cataluña, the Photo-Club de Valencia and the Sociedad Fotográfica de Zaragoza. These historical associations accomplished little of note during the early years of the 1940s after reconstituting their executives and after their members, most of them from the wealthier classes and victors in the "Crusade", began working again. The work of these members, including Ortiz Echagüe, Pla Janini, Eduardo Susanna, Vicente Peydró, Gil Marraco, Claudio Carbonell and other old masters of Spanish late pictorialism from before the war, came to define a new photographic officialism, which had a decisive influence on the enthusiasts of the time. In addition, the formation of new societies was anything but easy, in view of the administrative obstacles interposed by the dictatorship. Associations were obliged to state clearly in their by-laws that their purpose was limited strictly to photography and to warrant that their members would not produce any works of a "realistic or immoral" nature that might inconvenience the all-powerful civil governors.[123] As a result, few associations were formed during this period. One of the best known ones was the Agrupación Fotográfica Gallega (AFG), created in Vigo in 1946 by amateurs, including José Veiga Roel, Inocencio Smith de las Heras and Raniero Fernández. The Agrupación Fotográfica Valenciana was founded in 1947 under the auspices of the Trade Union Education and Leisure Organisation and promoted by José Furió, José Asensi and Manuel Hernández. The influential Agrupación Fotográfica de Guipúzcoa was formed that same year in San Sebastián at the initiative of a small group of enthusiasts, headed by the Marquis of Rocaverde.

Administrative obstacles diminished gradually over the years while the timid economic recovery made for democratisation of the practice of photography, which, during the 1940s, could only be afforded by the more prosperous classes. In addition, the Trade Union Education and Leisure Organisation, which fully supported the regime, was an important presence and sponsored the creation of dozens of associations that became the "extended family" of enthusiasts and the centre through which they developed what J.D. Bisbal called "photographic camaraderie and friendship". The 1950s were the golden age of the association movement. In August 1950, the Agrupación Fotográfica Almeriense (Afal) was founded, followed two years later by the club centred on the Café Español in La Coruña that would subsequently evolve into that city's Sociedad Fotográfica (SOFOCO), under the auspices of the Education and Leisure Organisation and headed by Smith de las Heras. In 1955, the Agrupación Fotográfica y Cinematográfica de Navarra (AFCN) was founded in Pamplona by Pedro María Irurzun, Nicolás Ardanaz, Félix Elbusto and Fernando Galle. In 1956, and also under the auspices of the Education and Leisure Organisation, the Agrupación Fotográfica de Guadalajara and the Sociedad Fotográfica Alto Duero were formed at the initiative of Santiago Bernal and Manuel Lafuente Caloto.

In spite of their pompous names, their pretentious convocations for salons and the ceremonious discourse of their executives, these associations were charmingly modest and in most cases met in tiny, rented premises. Nevertheless, they were the only institutions that kept the flame of amateur photography burning through those years of darkness. Their humble headquarters became impromptu schools where the neglected enthusiasts of the time could acquire basic notions on technique, meet one another and show their work. The courses, seminars and shows that they organised provided enthusiasts with what meagre theoretical background they had at a time when there were no specialist centres and, owing to the regime's political isolation, no news whatsoever of international photographic activity reached the country. However, the very weight of their systematic functioning, the boredom of routine and their executives' resistance to change soon marred the atmosphere in these associations and turned them into mere clubs or recreation centres, in spite of the fact that officialist sectors succeeded in having them recognised in 1972 as "Collaborating Artistic Organisations". This recognition turned out to be almost totally ineffective, owing, on the one hand, to the seriousness of the problem that it was meant to solve, and, on the other hand, to the unsteadiness of a political regime that was on its last legs. The creation of official schools and courses and the publication of new specialist magazines and fascicles plunged these societies into an even deeper crisis, although in the 1980s new associations were founded in Castile-León, Andalusia and Extremadura. Worth mentioning among these is the Agrupación Fotográfica de Córdoba (AFOCO), founded in 1981 at the initiative of José Gálvez, Alicia Reguera and Juan Vacas. At present, these associations are in decline, the victims of their endogamy and their lack of any attractive offering for their members. Some of them, however, have redirected their activities and are looking back to their origins. Institutions such as the RSF in Madrid, AFOCO in Córdoba and the SFZ have recently undertaken programmes of cataloguing, restoring and exhibiting their collections, an activity led by the example of the work begun in 1975 by Josep María Ribas Prous at the Agrupación Fotográfica de Reus.

Over its half-century of existence, the association movement generated an aesthetic that perpetuated itself through the institution of salons and whose pervasive influence encumbered the work of several generations of enthusiasts. This hierarchy of merit gave rise to a photographic aristocracy formed by the most outstanding practitioners of the technicist and academicist preciosity propounded by the associations themselves. However, among their members, certain photographers produced work that aroused considerable interest. Worth mentioning in the Agrupación Fotográfica Gallega were Luis Zamora, Raniero Fernández, Luis Rueda, Manuel García Ferrer and Veiga Roel himself. Within the Photo-Club de Valencia, outstanding work was produced by members of the group known as *El Forat*, formed in 1962 by José Segura Gavilá, Francisco Sanchís, José Miguel de Miguel and Francisco Soler Montalar. José Luis García Ferrada, linked to the Agru-

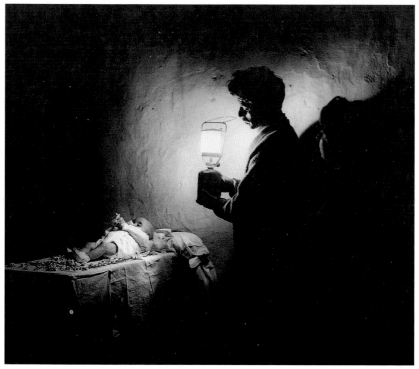

EL CANTERO. El Herradero. 1959. (Centro Nacional de Arte Reina Sofía.)

J. OLIVÉ. The Dead Baby. Alforja, 1965.
(Societat Fotogràfica de Reus. Obra Cultural Caixa de Tarragona.)

VEIGA ROEL. Fulfilling
the Vow. *1960s. (José Veiga
Collection.)*

pación San Juan Bosco de Burriana since 1962, took photographs that succeeded
in reflecting the simplicity of everyday life. Of even greater interest is the work of
Manuel Cruzado Cazador, a pioneer in photography with anthropological themes.
In connection with the Agrupación Fotográfica y Cinematográfica de Navarra, the
work done by Pedro María Irurzun, Nicolás Ardanaz and Félix Aliaga, a true clas-
sic in competition photography, is worthy of note. Outstanding work was produced in Andalusia by Emigdio Mariani and Juan Vacas, from Córdoba. The
Agrupación Fotográfica del Casino de Comercio de Tarrasa produced work by Jor-
di Vilaseca Parramón and other members of the *El Mussol* group, including José
María Albero, A. Montcaujussá and Ignacio Marroyo. Worthy of note in the Real
Sociedad Fotográfica de Madrid were Leonardo Cantero, Rafael Romero, Gregorio
Merino, Sifgrido de Guzmán, Juan Antonio Sáenz, Nieto Canedo and the leading
members of the so-called *Madrid School*. In the Agrupación Fotográfica de
Cataluña, noteworthy work was done by Jaume Jorba Aulés, Ramón Vilalta Sensa-
da, Pedro Martínez Carrión – an excellent reporter and an outstanding representa-

J.M. RIBAS PROUS. Calatañazor,
1969. (Author's Collection.)

tive of the so-called "grainy" generation – and Pere Sender, who developed his style from the use of pigmentation techniques to a documentarism replete with spontaneity and charm. Particularly outstanding in the Sociedad Fotográfica de Zaragoza were Carmelo Tartón Vinuesa, Pascual Martín Triep and José Antonio Duce. Worth mentioning in Castile were Santiago Bernal, the president of the Agrupación Fotográfica de Guadalajara, and José Núñez Larraz, who, from the Agrupación Fotográfica de Salamanca, went on to join the Grupo Libre de Fotografía, which rejected representation and leaned towards a brand of abstraction. Also approaching photographic abstraction were Ángel Úbeda, from La Mancha, and Ton Sirera, a member of the Agrupación Fotográfica de Lérida. Outstanding members of the Agrupación Fotográfica de Reus were Josep Massó, Salvador Terré and, especially, Josep María Ribas Prous, a pioneer in nudes and an excellent reporter. Jordi Olivé, the founder of the Agrupación Fotográfica de La Alforja, merits special mention. Far from any hint of artistic puerility, he succeeded in penetrating the daily reality of the village and expressed it through his simple, considered and touching images.

With a precise and effective technique, Olivé connected with the humility and intuition of the great popular masters and produced one of the most accurate and profound depictions of a small, rural Spanish community. Ángel Quintas, a highly creative photographer and the author of a very admirable body of documentary work, resists classification.

The photographic societies were also the driving force behind specialist magazines, many of which were created from within those societies, such as *Sombras* or the newsletter *Afal*, or served as their unofficial publications, such as *Arte Fotográfico*. *Sombras* appeared in June 1944 as the organ of the Real Sociedad Fotográfica de Madrid. Founded by Domingo de Luis, this magazine constituted a veritable platform for the late pictorialist aesthetic cultivated by its most assiduous contributors, such as Ortiz Echagüe, José Tinoco, Francisco Andrada, the Count of La Ventosa, Pla Janini, Mora Carbonell, Vicente Peydró and the Marquis of Santa María del Villar. Following months of editorial indecision, *Sombras* ceased publishing in 1952 after trying unsuccessfully to transform itself into the organ of the association movement. This objective was to be attained by Ignacio Barceló, who began publishing the influential *Arte Fotográfico* that same year.

From its launch in 1952, *Arte Fotográfico* served as the unofficial organ of the photographic associations, which shared a sense of orphanhood at the lack of any specialised publications. The chief merit of *Arte Fotográfico* was precisely that it was able to attract the enthusiastic collaboration of the associations to such an extent that it became the great "national magazine at the service of photography" that J. Domingo Bisbal had advocated in 1951 from the pages of the humble newsletter of the Agrupación Fotográfica de Igualada. Its status as the unofficial newsletter of the associations and the mirror and spokesman for their interests and activities, as well as those of the Spanish photographic industry, determined the editorial policy of *Arte Fotográfico*, which, at its peak, attained print runs of around twenty-five thousand copies. Born as an offshoot of *Sombras*, *Arte Fotográfico* inherited that magazine's spirit and its stable of contributors, to which were gradually added the most outstanding epigones of late pictorialist officialism, including José Loygorry, Diego Gálvez, J. Domingo Bisbal, José María Marca, José de la Higuera, *Arcilaga*, and Ignacio Barceló himself. For over thirty years, the pages of this magazine became the unavoidable pulpit from which illustrious mediocrities exercised a decisive influence and were held up to the credulous amateurs of the provinces as examples of the desiderata of photographic art. In this respect, *Arte Fotográfico* was a decidedly officialist, mothballed and reactionary magazine. However, like the associations themselves, it was also a useful – and almost unique – source of technical information for the photographers of the time, who lacked even a minimum infrastructure for instruction, promotion, exhibition and publication of their work. The magazine also presented the work of the most lucid proponents of photographic reformism of the time, including Gerardo Vielba, Gabriel Cualladó and Josep María Casademont, as well as the work of important foreign photographers, such as Daniel Masclet, Roger Doloy and Emmanuel Sougez.

Under the title of *Revista Bimestral de Fotografía y Cine*, the newsletter of the Asociación Fotográfica Almeriense (*Afal*) was founded in 1956 by José María Artero and Carlos Pérez Siquier, who shortly afterwards created an Editorial Board including Oriol Maspons, Xavier Miserachs, Gonzalo Juanes, Ricard Terré and Gabriel Cualladó, among others. This magazine was published in one of the provinces that were hardest hit by poverty and emigration and its existence was erratic and plagued with difficulties. In spite of its modest editorial ambitions, *Afal* soon became a sort of standard-bearer for the new documentary realism of the 1950s and 1960s, which J.M. Casademont came to label as the second Spanish photographic avant-garde. An avant-garde that, like its predecessor during the Republic, still had as its rallying point the vociferous criticism of pictorialism. The magazine, however, did not limit itself to being a platform for young Spanish photography, but also opened its pages to the more innovative international trends, through contributions from Gonzalo Juanes, Roger Doloy, A. Thevenez and J.A. Chnoll.[124] From 1958 – when it published its first and excellent yearbook – onwards, the newsletter managed to survive upsets and silences until 1963, when, as a result of insuperable financial difficulties, it ceased publishing.

The magazine *Imagen y Sonido* took up where *Afal* left off. It appeared in 1963 and under the editorship of J.M. Casademont, and became the platform for a photographic documentarism that had run wild and been assimilated by the new realist orthodoxy. *Imagen y Sonido* retained close ties to the association movement but opposed the latter's stiff academicism with a certain reformism tinged with ambitions of integration and eclecticism. In 1969, Casademont was replaced by G. Pasías Lomelino, although he maintained his presence through articles signed with the pseudonym *Aquiles Pujol*. The magazine tried to survive its own demise in the form of *Eikonos* (1975), which, under the editorship of Casademont, had a brief existence. With a clear delay and going very much against current trends, if we bear in mind that *Nueva Lente* appeared in 1971, the first issue of *Cuadernos de Fotografía* was published in 1972, created and edited by Fernando Gordillo, with Cualladó, Paco Gómez, Leonardo Cantero, Gerardo Vielba, Pedro Pascual and Fernando de Giles on its editorial board. Its elegantly printed pages presented almost exclusively the work of photographers linked to the editorial staff, including some contributions from members of the conservatives sectors of the literature and journalism of the time. Aside from these publications – *Nueva Lente* will be discussed elsewhere – little else was available to amateurs in the postwar period, except for the modest newsletters of the different associations. The best and most interesting of these was published by the Agrupación Fotográfica de Cataluña, with contributions from Lluch Oliveres and Rosario Martínez Rochina. The newsletter published by the Real Sociedad Fotográfica de Madrid was even more modest, until it greatly improved its quality from 1960 onwards with the incorporation of contributors such as Cualladó, Vielba, Jorge Rueda, Elías Dolcet, Miguel Oriola and Cristina García Rodero.

Competitions were another of the pillars sustaining officialist photography during the postwar years. In the depressed cultural environment of the time they offered amateurs their only opportunity for recognition of their work's merits. According to Ignacio Barceló's rhetoric, they were also an ineluctable means of attaining popularity and "a technical, moral and human training ground". At the height of the academicist apotheosis, the quality of the works submitted to the competitions was judged on the basis of its conformity to the standards imposed by juries that were entrenched in the pictorialist and technicist aesthetic. The inevitable results were preciosity, mediocrity and cliché.[125] Against this aesthetic dictatorship of salons and competitions there gradually arose a sort of insurgent movement, whose paradigm may be found in the lucid criticism of Oriol Maspons, who, in 1957, coined the term "salonism" to define the endemic of competitions of the time. By salonism, Maspons meant the phenomenon that institutionalised a type of photography – "that remains pictorialist" – whose only purpose was to win prizes by conforming to the demands of embalmed jurors selected from the executives of the associations and elevated to the status of zealous guardians of the most unbending orthodoxy.[126]

During the 1950s there were a few attempts at renewal in connection with the competitions, as initiatives from within the ranks of the associations themselves in reaction to their progressive and alarming loss of credibility. The most important of these was promoted by Luis Navarro – the pseudonym of Luis Conde Vélez – with the organisation in 1954 of the Avant-garde Photography Salon, which was eventually sponsored by the Agrupación Fotográfica de Cataluña after the untimely death of its promoter. In 1955, the Agrupación Fotográfica del Casino de Comercio de Tarrasa convoked competition for the Egara trophy, and five years later the Real Sociedad Fotográfica de Madrid instituted the Contemporary Photography Salon, promoted by Gerardo Vielba and Gabriel Cualladó. The repercussions of this timid *aggiornamento* of the salons were felt even by the Negtor Prize, created in 1953 by Higinio Negra and considered the true "prize of prizes".[127] However, renovation was not possible, since the rusty edifice of Spanish photography was unable to undertake the measures needed in order for the mummified structures of the competitions to be overcome. The lack of any channels for promotion, marketing and publishing still conditioned the impoverished situation of photography in Spain, and so the competitions continued for years to be, and to a certain extent still are, almost the only opportunity for photographers to show and promote their work, and, as Campañá put it in 1961, the "necessary stimulus for development of artistic sensibility among enthusiasts".

On the Eve of Reality

In the cultural wasteland of the postwar years it was not easy for photographers to approach the *modern* photography that some young people were beginning to demand, be it expressionist, abstract, impressionist or realist. José María Artero asked in 1956 "What are we to offer in opposition to the modern concept of photography? Why, simply, pictorial photography. These are the elements in diametrical opposition. (...) A life that is borrowed, parasitic, imprisoned by a mimicry without horizons, or a life that is free, splendorous and infinite." However, in the midst of the retro-pictorialist apotheosis, this free and splendorous life sought by the young protagonists of the future renewal of Spanish photography was only ever reflected – with rare exceptions – by the popular photographers whose lack

M. FERROL. Emigrants' farewell. La Coruña, 1956.
(Author's Collection.)

H. PATO. Beggar outside the Restaurant Llardy.
Madrid, 1940. (Agencia Efe.)

of pretension delivered them from artistic excesses of the time. In contrast with the artificiality, the mimicry and the so-called stylistic vocation of the artists of the camera, the work of these popular photographers, in spite of its technical limitations, is alone in offering us a glimpse of the lives led by the Spaniards of the time and the reality of their daily surroundings. Alejandro Cirici wrote in 1958 "Within photography itself, photographs taken with no regard for correct technique so often have an extraordinary vitality and help to us to know the world and even ourselves, while, on the other hand, these competition photographs, taken impeccably with faultless technique, are so often totally lacking any importance."[128]

The popular photographers kept alive the spirit of the old itinerant photographers of the prewar period and responded still to the growing demand from the local people, who, by means of their portraits, and the portraits of those close to them, were trying to rebuild the emotional geography of their family circles, now doubly devastated, not only by illness and distance, but also by imprisonment, exile and so many deaths on desolate and unknown fronts. In the economic precariousness of those years of penury, only the work of these itinerant portraitists and reporters in the provinces allowed the survival of a trade that, in turn, guaranteed the persistence of those simple and ingenuous images that we still find in family albums and in our grandparents' trunks and chests of drawers. Antonio Muñoz Molina writes "Fortunately, photography has, for the greatest part of its history, remained a trade, and photographers are still people who try to make an honest living with their work. A great painting or a great sculpture can only be viewed in places that are specially created to show them, while a masterful photograph can move us in a museum or under the spotlights of a gallery, but also by chance as we leaf through a newspaper or glance at a shop window, or even as we look through our parents' photograph albums."[129]

Along with this naive type of photography, practised by those anonymous and unsung professionals, also current was a sort of popular reportage whose ability to surprise and astonish was based squarely on its creator's simplicity and lack of pretentiousness. In spite of their limited means, precariousness and improvisation, the images produced by the occasional reporters of the time provide us today with a touching record of a repressed Spain, a Spain that was still licking its wounds from the war. In contrast with official reporters, these unsophisticated professionals had no interest whatsoever in concealing the humiliations of reality and, to the

P. MENCHÓN. Social Assistance canteen. Lorca, 1945.
(Lorca Municipal Archives.)

extent that circumstances allowed, they went about creating a sort of reverse image of the one disseminated by the regime's Press and Propaganda offices. If not a photograph of silence, fear or impotence, the forgotten and semi-decayed images produced by these reporters constitute a mirror that reflects for us the desolate territory of defeat and the sombre world of exclusion and suffering. Even the very photographs used at the time to offer a hyperbolical image of the Homeland, now, a mere half-century later, become an implacable accusation against their protagonists, a veritable negation of victory that bears witness precisely to the opposite of what they were attempting to preach from the heights of official rhetoric.

Among these provincial photographers, worth mentioning are several who had already begun working earlier, such as Luis Escobar, Antonio Avilés, Fernández Trujillo, Pedro Menchón, Jaume Calafell, Federico Vélez, and others who were only then starting out in the trade, such as José Castellanos, Rufino and Pedro Reales. A singular case is that of Manuel Ferrol, a studio portraitist and all-terrain reporter, who produced a splendid report on emigration in 1956, with the sole resources of his intuition and talent. Ferrol used a concise, direct language to communicate a message charged with profound pathos: out-of-focus faces, hetero-dox composition, blurred figures, saturated light, a whole catalogue of "errors" and technical flaws that not only did not diminish the narrative effectiveness of his photographs but in fact heightened their drama. In the same geographical area, worth mentioning is the work of Virgilio Vieitez, a modest professional from the town of Soutelo de Montes in the province of Pontevedra who created a monu-mental and moving chronicle of rural Galicia over the course of twenty years. Taken with a simple and effective technique, Vieitez's portraits not only fill the memory with satisfaction but also constitute an astonishing visual record of a time and place that are gone forever.

Outside the bounds of officialism, photographers such as Joaquim Gomis, José Suárez, Otho Lloyd and Francesc Català Roca produced worthy and ad-mirable work. Gomis was linked to Catalan artistic circles of the time. His prox-imity to Joan Miró made him the visual chronicler of the artist's life and personal universe. Otho Lloyd worked in a number of different genres, although it is in his urban scenes that his exquisite sense of light and composition is most evident. Suárez was forced into exile in Argentina, where he continued to work as a press photographer. He returned to Spain in 1960, bringing to the depressed panorama of photography his mastery of vision and composition. However, Català Roca was the most important photographer of his time and served as a link between pre-war avant-garde and the new documentary avant-garde of the 1940s and 1950s. He re-ceived his professional training from his prestigious father, Pere Català Pic, and in-herited from him his technical dexterity and the formal daring of some of his earliest works, including *The Pianist* (1936) and the view of the monument to Columbus (1951). His photographs, published in books such as *Tauromaquia* (1953), *Barcelona* (1954), and *Cuenca* (1956), show us a mature professional who has successfully combined a thorough familiarity with technique and a con-siderable creative capacity in a body of work that appears to give priority to pure vi-sual instinct and accurate perception of reality over any concern with or attempt at style. Over the years, Català Roca turned his steady gaze on the crucial details of things, with the intent of communicating his own vision of the world in a direct and effective manner. Planted firmly on the steps of certainty, he was always con-vinced of the validity of his own perceptions and this is doubtlessly the essential characteristic of his best photography, a photography that marked the demise of

VIRGILIO VIEITEZ. Soutelo de Montes, ca. 1960. (Vieitez Archives.)

pictorialist puerility and exercised a decisive influence on the work of the generation of realists of the 1950s and 1960s.

On a different level, only a very few episodic minority experimental movements succeeded in breaking the routine imposed by associations and salons.
One of these was the postist skirmish, involving Gregorio Prieto, Eduardo
Chicharro and Carlos Edmundo de Ory in the 1940s, a mere theatrical pirouette
that had little if any impact on the cultural scene of the time. In the area of photography, this inoffensive second-hand surrealism produced nothing more than
one or two mundane and mostly forgettable collages by Gregorio Prieto. However, aside from these innocuous efforts and the production of photographers who
laid the groundwork for documentary realism, the accurate diagnosis made by
Juan Antonio Bardem of Spanish cinema in 1956 could also be applied to Spanish photography of the time: it was politically ineffective, socially false, intellectu-

F. CATALÁ ROCA. Advertisement. *Barcelona, 1957.*
(Catalá Roca Family Collection.)

ally feeble and industrially rickety. And it would remain so until the years of the transition to democracy.

Under these circumstances, the image of Spanish life must also be sought in the work of a number of leading foreign reporters who had much in common with the documentary and humanistic aesthetic best exemplified in the *Family of Man* exhibition organised by E. Steichen in 1955. Among these, the most widely known work was by Eugene Smith, who produced the celebrated report *Spanish Village* in 1950 in the Extremaduran village of Deleitosa. This was the first time that the Franco regime allowed a foreign photographer any degree of freedom to travel and work in Spain. Aside from its importance in the history of photography, Smith's photo-essay is one of the most penetrating graphic records of the rural Spain of his time and a sort of homage to the pride and moral fortitude of a group of people forced to survive under extremely difficult conditions.[130] At a great remove from Smith's vision is that of Jean Dieuzaide, who travelled through Spain between 1949 and 1951 gathering material to illustrate the book *Southern Spain*. Dieuzaide was not looking for clichés or picturesque scenes, but rather the unusual. With their extraordinary technical quality, his photographs are among of the most spontaneous and personal of the time. Cartier-Bresson, who visited Spain in 1953 to work on his book *Europeans* (1955), has a colder vision. Also similar to the great French photographer's view is that of Inge Morath, who took hundreds of photographs between 1953 and 1957 brimming with sincerity, understanding and tenderness.

Other excellent reporters worked incidentally in Spain, including William Klein (1956), Edouard Boubat (1957) and Marc Riboud, who depicted the contrast between the real and the official Spain, on the occasion of the inauguration of the Valle de los Caídos monument (1959). In the 1960s, the country was visited by reporters of the stature of Gianni Berengo (1966), Ferdinando Scianna (1969), Lucien Clergue (1965), Irving Penn (1965), and Jean Mohr (1965 and 1971). Along different lines, other photographers, including Brassaï and Fulvio Roiter, produced excellent illustrated guides, of the type that was so popular in Europe at the time. More ambitious was the report by the Swiss photographer Michael Wolgensinger, compiled in the magnificent and surprising book *Spanien* (1956).

The case of the Hungarian Nicolás Muller, forced to flee his country in 1938 by the onslaught of Nazism, is exceptional. After brief sojourns in France,

Portugal and Morocco, he finally settled in Madrid in 1947. In this culturally deprived environment, marked by the obsolescence of an aesthetically exhausted photography, Muller constituted one of the few windows opening onto modernity. A member of a brilliant generation of Hungarian photographers in exile, he was one of the photographers who best succeeded in depicting postwar Spain, through hundreds of photographs published in books such as *España clara* (1966) and in a half-dozen illustrated regional guides (1967-1968). In spite of editorial impositions, Muller's work was always pervaded with dignity and avoided the picturesque clichés that were so heavily exploited by Spanish photographers, who were determined to exhibit an idealised Spain that did not exist outside the totally misjudged official rhetoric.

The Last Portraitists

The subject of professional photography in Spain in 1939 still includes portrait photography. The cultural anaemia of the dictatorship confined professionals to the redoubts of studios that were on their last legs. In 1949, ninety percent of Spanish professional photographers were portraitists and the precarious portrait industry provided a living for those professionals who had survived the disasters of the war and the postwar period. Circumstances obliged some of the most highly respected reporters of the prewar period to survive as itinerant portraitists in towns and villages. A prime example is that of Alfonso Sánchez Portela, who, like other members of his generation, found it necessary to join the legion of photographers that travelled, in wooden trains or the quaint coaches of time, from town to town during those dark years, known popularly as "the time of hunger".[131]

The middle class supporters of the Franco regime and the new élites that had grown up in the shadow of hasty business deals soon went about recovering the habits of the prewar bourgeoisie and residual aristocracy. The demand for portraits by these political and economic classes provided impetus for the established studios and facilitated the definitive consolidation of professionals who, like Jalón Ángel, Pascual Marín and Gyenes, succeeded in placing themselves nearest the circles of power. This growing demand for portraits opened a new golden age for the studios, which once again proliferated in Spanish cities. Figures published in the

JALÓN ÁNGEL. *Celia Gámez. 1934.*
(Private Collection.)

AMER-VENTOSA. *Admiral Carrero Blanco.*
ca. 1955. (Muller Collection.)

Bailly-Baillière yearbooks indicate that there were 79 portrait studios in Madrid in 1949, 120 in 1950, 198 in 1958 and 231 in 1968. There were 15 on Calle Montera alone, and another 10 on the Gran Vía. In Barcelona, studios were concentrated on streets such as Calle Pelayo, where there were up to 10 portraitists working in 1950.

As in the golden age of studio portraiture, the professional photographer's goal was to satisfy the customer rather than to produce good portraits. To this end, portraitists adopted the decadent aesthetic of the masters of the previous era, with abuse of the *flou* effects and soft focus characteristic of large format cameras, and continued along these lines until well into the 1960s. The old 18 × 24 *Globus* was replaced around 1950 by the 9 × 12 *Linhof*, the *Anaca*, and others such as the *Plaubel "Peko"* and the *Técnica Jordan*, also 9 × 12. Studios were equipped with pretentious stage settings, using the real furniture and decoration so popular with the European middle classes of the 1930s. In his studio on Madrid's Gran Vía, Alfonso Sánchez Portela installed a neo-classical staircase with backcloths covered in silver- and gold-dust. To this range of accessories, portraitists added all types of religious and secular scenery, decorated with pianos, real or false fireplaces, copies of classic works of art, and anything else that might create the illusion of bourgeois and aristocratic surroundings and stress their subjects' social standing. The studios began using colour around 1950 and Jalón Ángel was one its most active proponents.

Some of the more prestigious studios of the postwar period had already established a solid reputation in the 1920s and 1930s and more than a few portraitists had collaborated actively with the new authorities during the military uprising. This was the case of the Aragonese Jalón Ángel, who produced a series of flattering portraits of the inspirers and protagonists of the Rebellion, compiled in an album entitled, significantly, *Forjadores del Imperio* (Builders of the Empire). With their style reminiscent of the pompousness of the photographic academicism of the time, these portraits were essential to the creation of the new regime's iconography. Jalón Ángel succeeded in positioning himself, if not as General Franco's official court portraitist – the dictator also had portraits taken by the younger *Campúa*, Gyenes and Marín – at least as one of his favourites, and he took official portraits from the days of the Civil War until 1956. Jalón Ángel's professional success was rivalled only by that of the historical partnership Amer-Ventosa. Amer had been a well known portraitist during the Republic and had operated up to four different studios at once in Madrid. In 1944 he destroyed his archives and transferred the business to his assistant Francisco Ventosa; together they set up a new studio that became the busiest in Madrid. Another of the favourite portraitists of high society under the Franco regime was Juan Gyenes. Hungarian by birth, he arrived in Madrid in 1940 and, after working for several years with the younger *Campúa*, set up his own studio in 1948, which soon attracted a prosperous clientele. Outside the studio, commissioned by the cultural authorities, Gyenes worked for over thirty years as graphic chronicler of the Madrid theatre scene. The case of Alfonso Sánchez Portela was somewhat different. Purged after the Civil War, he had to overcome the initial hostility of certain social and media circles in order to regain the professional prestige lost in the course of so many years of uncivilised irrationality.[132] Nevertheless, and in spite of taking a number of excellent portraits, he never recovered the vigour and moral freshness of his best known works from before the war.

N. MULLER. Pío Baroja strolling in el Retiro. Madrid, 1950. (Muller Archives.)

Established in Madrid in 1947, Nicolás Muller demonstrated a rare capacity to delve into his subjects' personalities and an extraordinary technical quality, with the result that he soon became one of the most widely known portraitists of his time. Like the old studios of the beginning of the century, Muller's was a sort of backroom and meeting place for liberal artists and intellectuals linked to the magazine *Revista de Occidente*. However, Muller did not limit himself to the meagre space of his studio and was known on occasion to go outdoors to take some of his more memorable portraits, such as those of Azorín (1947) and Pío Baroja (1950). Other notable portraitists included *Manuel*, Ventura and Cartagena, whose studios were visited by the members of Madrid's smart set in the 1940s and 1950s. In 1951, a very young Vicente Ibáñez, the last in a family of professional photographers dating back to the times of the *carte de visite*, opened his studio on the Gran Vía. Ibáñez had an enviable command of technique and his portraits had little in common with the standard variety, using delicate compositions and unusual lighting in search of impeccable backgrounds and certain effects of shading on the subject's face. He soon became one of the more fashionable portraitists and the favourite of Madrid's singers, artists and bullfighters.

The 1940s and 1950s were also years of prosperity for the portrait industry in Barcelona, although, in those times of exacerbated centralism, that city's studios did not attain the same level of popularity as the capital's. Worth mentioning among them were those of *Napoleón*, Meyer, Boiada and Navarro, some of them with a long professional history behind them. Other outstanding portraitists in Barcelona were Guirau, Lucas, Ramón Batlles, Josep Compte, and M. Duart, the successor to the historical Suñé. A different type of work was produced by Pau Barceló, who had been purged by the authorities of the Franco regime and who eventually combined his work portraying actors and show-business people with contributions to the press of the period.

Portrait fever was not limited to the largest cities. In Valencia, the most active studios were those of Plá, Derrey and Sanchís, all three of them with a professional history dating back to the 19th century. In Murcia, studios were operated by Mateo, Almagro and Manuel Herrero, who produced the *Fotos-Jerárquicas* series of portraits of the provincial leading lights of the time. In San Sebastián, Pascual Marín and Sigfrido Koch Bengoechea were particularly active; in Vitoria, Schommer Koch; in Pontevedra, Joaquín Pintos; in Pamplona, Pedro María Irurzun and José Galle; in

A. SCHOMMER. *The dancer* Antonio. *From the* Retratos Psicológicos *series*
(1969-1973). (Author's Collection.)

J. DOLCET. The painter Manolo Millares. 1960. (Dolcet Family Collection.)

L. POMÉS. *Portrait of Elsa. 1962. (Author's Collection.)*

Zaragoza, Manuel Coyne; in Salamanca, Cándido Ansede; in Bilbao, Vicente Garay; in León, Pepe Gracia; in La Coruña, Ángel Blanco; in Santiago de Compostela, Luis Ksado; in Seville, Luis Arenas, Antonio Cubiles and Francisco Crespo del Castillo; and in Vigo, Pacheco. Perhaps the most interesting among them was Pedro María Irurzun. His portraits stand out mostly because of his use of lighting and composition, particularly after he abandoned the pretentiousness of his earliest work.

The traditional studio portrait entered on an irreversible crisis towards the end of the 1960s, one that was manifest not only in the number of customers visiting the studios, but also, and most particularly, in the nature of demand by popular figures. This crisis had a number of different causes, including the spectacular increase in amateur activity, changes in consumer tastes and the growth in sales of cameras, although the professionals' corporatist complex blamed it on unfair competition and the entry of unqualified people into the profession.[133] The new audio-visual culture and recommendations by managers', publicists and publishing consultants all marked the work done by the young people entering the profession with no studios of their own who brought with them a renewed aesthetic that was closer to the demands of European fashion and advertising studios. One of the pioneers in this new brand of portrait was Juan Dolcet, who worked frequently with figures involved in the plastic arts and brought to bear a certain formal audacity, an impeccable technique and a considerable capacity for introspection.

However, the most popular representative of this new breed of portraitists was Alberto Schommer. With a background in painting and advertising, in 1969 he began his famous *Retratos Psicológicos* (Psychological Portraits) series for the press (1969-1973), in which he distanced himself from the austerity of photographers such as Irving Penn, Richard Avedon, Diane Arbus and Gisèle Freund, and instead constructed bombastic settings based on an accumulation or articles supposedly defining his subject. Schommer used a baroque symbolism that established his own presence in his portraits, as he designed the staging, directed the subject's pose and gestures and prepared the ambience of the image, for the purpose of presenting a theatrical and supposedly interpretative vision of the subject. Such an approach obviously involves a risk, if the photographer is mistaken in their perception of the subject.[134] Without denying the worth of this risk, Schommer's greatest merit is having succeeded in taking this approach with well-known figures from the worlds of politics, culture and finance, who, probably allowing themselves to be flattered by the possibility of being contemplated by the camera's selective eye, entertain the secret hope that this gaze will favour them, when, and it must be pointed out, that gaze is not necessarily respectful or flattering.

Among the most significant practitioners of this new type of portrait were Leopoldo Pomés, who produced portraits brimming with intuition and with touches of irony and complicity with the subject, with a surprising formal refinement and a rare sense of composition. Also filled with irony, self-assurance and a certain critical distance – not lacking in self-criticism – are the portraits taken by Oriol Maspons, author of the surprising book *Animales de compañía* (1995). *Colita* also took admirable photographs of personalities of cultural life in Catalonia, compiled in the exhibition *La gauche qui rit* (1972). María Espeus also established a solid reputation as a portraitist after setting up in Barcelona in the 1970s. In her work, compiled in the exhibition *Hola Barcelona*, her subjects, most of them from the world of show business, seem to emerge from the image as reincarnations of themselves. Also working in the same cultural milieu, Toni Vidal made an excellent series of portraits towards the end of the 1960s. Miguel Galmes, linked to the world of the stage, produced a series of portraits of actors between 1962 and 1964, which he later gathered in the exhibition *Retratos del teatro* (1967). Nearer to a symbolism with hints of surrealism and expressionism are the portraits of Luis Buñuel by Antonio Gálvez, also known for his series of portraits of the exiled Spanish and Latin American intelligentsia in Paris.

Little by little, the crisis of the portrait studios came to affect their traditional clientele, with the massive invasion of photo booths that began appearing in Spanish cities from 1963 onwards. The end of photographic studios foretold by the old masters was consummated. *Káulak* wrote in 1910 "The day will come when the skilful and conscientious work of studio portraitists will no longer be necessary, threatened as they are by the uncontrolled advance of new techniques and the intrusion of a legion of unqualified practitioners." Sixty years later, the old studios began to disappear and nowadays they are sadly languishing, reduced to secondary professional work.

The Law of Silence

The impoverishment of Spanish cultural life after the Civil War was particularly evident in the press. While the Republican period saw the publication of up to two thousand newspapers and magazines, there were only eighty-seven in 1945 and over half of those belonged to the Movement's publishing group. The number of readers was extremely low and distribution networks barely covered the area of the major cities. On another level, the press had to operate within the narrow margins of freedom imposed by the 1938 Press Act, which remained in force until promulgation of the so-called "Fraga Law" in 1966. The Press Act had been drafted during a period of exception marked by the Civil War and was based on the fundamental principle that the press ought to serve the creation of the new State as a soldier would.[135] For this purpose, strict censorship was imposed and a School of Journalism was founded in 1941 with the objective of converting new journalists into true "apostles of the thought and faith of the Nation saved to fulfil its destiny". At the same time, access to the profession was controlled through the Official Registry of Journalists, restricted to graduates of that School, although access could be granted discretionally to anyone whom the authorities considered worthy of the title on the basis of their "patriotic merits". For the same reason, access was denied to anyone not considered to be a supporter of the new regime. Lastly, the State had competence to "determine the number and dimensions of periodical publications", appoint editors, censor information and order the obligatory publication of political directives, editorial comments, articles and photographs.

In this context of repression and media intervention, Spanish journalists were subjected to sweeping purges that were carried out under the Political Responsibility Act of 1939 or by special courts, such as the Tribunal for Repression of Freemasonry and Communism (1940). In fact, the purges had begun in 1939 at the hands of the Cultural and Educational Purity Commission, presided by José María Pemán, whose mission was to further the "jubilant dawning of a new Golden Age of Christianity, civilisation and Spain". In line with these criteria, universities, schools and editorial staffs were decimated. The purges were especially intensive in Madrid, Barcelona and Valencia, where the leading graphic reporters had worked, and many of these were forced into exile in France or Latin America.[136] In this way, a new aristocracy in the trade was gradually formed, based not on professional merit, but rather on the intensity or purity of unswerving or circum-

SANTOS YUBERO. Departure of the Blue Division.
Madrid, June 1941. (Comunidad Autónoma de Madrid.)

A. MERLETTI. Authorities giving the Fascist salute at an official act. Barcelona, 1945. (Institut d'Estudis Fotogràfics de Catalunya.)

stantial loyalty to the Franco regime. This drive for control reached such ludicrous extremes that, during the first few triumphal years, the Movement's Directorate-General of the Press made graphic reporters wear uniforms, in fulfilment of a long-standing dream of the ineffable Juan Aparicio, the Director-General of the Press and Propaganda.

Among the more active reporters during this blue period of the Spanish press were Pérez de Rozas, the Brangulís, Joaquín María Domínguez, the Merlettis and Josep Comte, in Barcelona, Santos Yubero, Contreras, Pastor, Hermes Pato, Olegario Pérez de Castro and the younger *Campúa*, in Madrid, Juan José Serrano, in Seville, José Cabrelles Sigüenza, in Valencia, Hermenegildo Vallvé, in Tarragona, Ángel Blanco, in La Coruña, Pascual Marín, in San Sebastián, Federico Vélez, in Burgos, and Jaume Calafell, in Lérida. These more or less official reporters were soon joined by a heterogeneous group of professionals who covered graphic information during the early years of the postwar period. Worth mentioning in Barcelona were Antonio Sáenz Guerrero, who contributed to *Destino*, *Diario de*

H. VALLVÉ. Prisoner's wife trying to hand a letter to General Franco. Tarragona, 1949. (Foto-cine Vallvé.)

Barcelona and *Mundo Deportivo*, Josep Postius, who, after his internment in a concentration camp at Miranda de Ebro, began working for *Diario de Barcelona* in 1942; Josep Valls Gili, Merletti's assistant, who worked from 1945 to 1970 with his son, Josep Valls Sorolla, and Pérez Molinos, who, after several years in prison, worked for the Provincial Propaganda Authority. In Madrid, there were Contreras and Luis Alonso Martín, who worked for *ABC* and Agencia Efe; Hermes Pato, who formed Efe's graphic service, Rogelio Leal, who joined *La Actualidad Española* in 1953, and José Pastor, who joined the staff of *Arriba* in 1940. In Valencia, Luis Vidal Corella, José Penalva and Manuel Sanchís *Finezas*, signed their photographs jointly. In Seville, there were Ángel Gómez Gelán and Serafín Sánchez Rengel; in Córdoba, Ricardo Rodríguez, Francisco Rodríguez *Frama* and Ladislao Rodríguez; in La Coruña, Alberto Martí Villardefrancos; in Zaragoza, Luis Mompel and Miguel Marín Chivite; in Vitoria, S. Arina and *Arque* (Federico Arocena and Gregorio Querejazu); and in Pamplona, José Fernando Galle and Zubieta and Retegui.[137] In general, these reporters' work holds little of interest, as it was encumbered by censorship and the officialist routine of the dictatorship, although some of the images by Pato, Arque, Vallvé, Pérez de Rozas, Vélez, Martí Villardefrancos, Calafell and Luis Vidal Corella are truly memorable.

In this context, reports on bullfighting attained a considerable level of quality, thanks to the rapid incorporation of the leading figures from before the war. They were joined by the great reporters who came to the fore during Manolete's career, such as Paco Mari, Arjona, Hermes Pato, Paco Cano, Cuevas, Fernando Galle and the Botan father and son team, who worked profound changes in the speciality, comparable to the changes in bullfighting itself. Sports reporting also reached a notable level of quality, thanks to the work of veteran reporters such as Ramón Claret, Joan Bert, Álvaro, Luis Vidal and Luis Sánchez Portela, and the decisive incorporation of Antoni Campañá, Agustín Vega Peña, Ramón Dimas, Jacinto Maíllo and Paco Alguersuary. Towards the end of the 1960s a new generation of reporters joined their ranks, including Manu Cecilio, Horacio Seguí, Avelino Pí, Raúl Cancio and the brothers Josep María and Jaume Alguersuary, who worked a sweeping transformation in the speciality.

The State also controlled information through Agencia Efe, which monopolised not only political information but also graphic information, through an extensive network of correspondents directed by Manuel Cortés and Hermes Pato. In 1963, the agency installed its first permanent telephotography line, thereby strengthening its monopoly on information, which it maintained until the eve of the transition to democracy. Political control of information was supplemented through Pyresa (Agencia de Prensa y Radio Española), created in 1945 by the Movement's Press and Propaganda Office. The agency Europa Press, linked to the Opus Dei, was created in 1957. This agency was more modern and competitive than Efe and created an excellent graphic service, with contributions from reporters of the status of Paco Ontañón, Antonio Alcoba and César Lucas.

Graphic information was also characterised by the absence of the major illustrated publications from before the war, such as *Estampa*, *Crónica*, *Blanco y Negro* and *Mundo Gráfico*, which were replaced by *Fotos*, *Revista* and *Destino*. This last magazine appeared in 1947 and was linked to Falangist circles, with contributions from photographers including Catalá Roca, Ramón Dimas, Ernest Vila and Montserrat Manent. Under the editorship of José María Verges, *Destino* became a veritable professional platform for young Catalan reporters, such as Xavier Miserachs, Jaume

CÉSAR LUCAS. Luis Miguel Dominguín and El Cordobés *at a shooting party. 1968. (Author's Collection.)*

Buesa, Eugenio Forcano, *Colita* and Toni Catany. *Revista* was created in 1952 in direct competition with *Destino*, and had Catalá Roca as a permanent contributor. However, the leading graphic publication under the regime was *Fotos*. With the subtitle "National Syndicalist Graphic Weekly", it was founded in 1937 by Manuel Fernández Cuesta in San Sebastián. It was printed in excellent photogravure and initially had contributions from Pascual Marín, the younger *Campúa*, Compte, Carlos Pérez de Rozas, Santos Yubero, Badosa, Videa and Contreras. Its editorial offices were moved to Madrid in 1940 and Cecilio, Zarco, Gyenes and Claret were added to its list of contributors. After years of slow decline, it ceased publishing in 1963. The most notable newspapers were *La Vanguardia*, in Barcelona, and the Falangist daily *Arriba*. Various generations of Catalan photographers worked for *La Vanguardia*, from Pérez de Rozas, Vallvé and Buesa, to the younger photographers Josep María Alguersuary and Toni Catany, who was a contributor from 1967 to 1969. *Arriba* dedicated eight pages of photogravures to graphic content, with contributions from Pastor, Contreras, Cano and Zarco, among others.

The large graphic weeklies, such was *Gaceta Ilustrada* and *La Actualidad Española*, commenced publishing in the 1950s. *Gaceta Ilustrada* first appeared in 1955, with work by such prestigious photographers as Catalá Roca, Luis Hernández Calderón, Oriol Maspons, Ramón Masats, Xavier Miserachs, Julio Ubiña and a young Manuel López Rodríguez. With links to the Opus Dei, *La Actualidad Española* was created in 1952 and published work by Paco Ontañón, César Lucas, Rogelio Leal and Antonio Navas. However, these were not propitious times for large illustrated magazines. The graphic publishing formulas applied by magazines such as *Vu*, *Life*, *Picture Post*, *Paris-Match* and *Stern* seemed to have been exhausted and they disappeared in the period between 1957 and 1970. In Spain, competition from television eventually led to the closure of the best illustrated weeklies between 1977 (*La Actualidad*) and 1984 (*Gaceta Ilustrada*). Reporters such as Masats, Ontañón, Miserachs, Forcano, Ubiña, Maspons and César Lucas found it necessary to revamp their approach to work, at a time when new perspectives were opening for professional photography, thanks to the economic impetus provided by the successive Development Plans. Some moved to the daily press or television itself, while others began working for the emerging daily newspaper Sunday supplements, or sought new horizons in the fields of fashion, advertising or book illustration.[138]

In addition, as in the early years of Spanish photojournalism, photographers' work was still looked down upon by publishers. Even after the advent of democracy, Spanish photojournalists lacked the proper cultural and technical background and few of them had any training for work in the field of graphic publishing.[139] However, in spite of so many limitations and deficiencies, a new generation of graphic reporters was to be the protagonist of the most sweeping renovation of Spanish photojournalism since the days of the Republic. After almost forty years of censorship, directives and repression of information, these new reporters revived the old spirit of vindication of the pioneers in the field, in full awareness of their responsibility to society in the common struggle for democratic liberties. Here was a new brand of journalism, one that was deeply committed to its times, accompanied by a renewed and militant photographic language. This new journalism began appearing in the sectors that were most active in the democratic opposition to the Franco regime. The young photojournalists' work bore witness to the reality of a country committed to a long and unflagging opposition to the dictatorship. Many of the events that they were to portray involved clear risks. In addition, given their status as freelancers and the extreme instability of their employment conditions, they had to deal with a situation of total defencelessness against employers and political and government authorities. The new generation of photojournalists found themselves, almost certainly unintentionally, involved in a threefold campaign of demands: with their commitment to the struggle for democratic liberties, their determination to foster in Spain a new and modern approach to their work, and their demands for better working conditions. Owing to the persistence of strict censorship towards the end of the Franco regime, the images captured by these young reporters – images of urban insurgence, police brutality, and the trade union and student struggles – had to be published outside Spain or in underground newsletters. In order to distribute these images and provide them to the foreign press the so-called *Grup de Producció* was formed in Barcelona in 1973 with the participation of photographers linked to the clandestine political party PSUC. This core later gave rise to the CIS agency, whose contributors included Paco Elvira, *Colita*, Josep Armengol, Manel Armengol and Pilar Aymerich. For his part, Jordi Socias had already created the *Agencia Informativa Popular* (API) in 1972. Similar initiatives were taken in Madrid by Juan Santiso, Guillermo Armengol, the brothers Antonio and Gustavo Catalán, Germán Gallego, López Rodríguez and J.L. de Pablos. These reporters, along with Pepe Encinas, Carlos Bosch, Sigfrid Casals, Quim Llenas, Lluis Salom, the father and son team Jordi Soteras and Jordi Soteras, José Miguel Gómez, Eduardo Rodríguez, Pérez Barriopedro, Manuel Hernández de León, César Rus, Fernando García Herranz, Francesc Simó, Jordi Morera, Francesc Llovet, Marisa Flórez, Bernardo Pérez, Carlos Corcho, Elio Bugallo, Antonio Tiedras, Xurxo Lobato and, on an occasional basis, Enrique Sáenz de San Pedro, *Shaba* (Aurora Fierro), *Pizzi Press* (Jorge Rueda), the *Yetis* (particularly Félix Lorrio) and Paco Jarque, formed the nucleus of reporters who were the central figures in the renewal of Spanish journalism on the eve of the transition to democracy. Some of them formed a group associated with Jordi Socias and Aurora Fierro, who, in 1981, created *Cover*, the most emblematic Spanish graphic agency of the transitional period.[140]

Nevertheless, and in spite of the admirable quality of the many of these photographers, the Spanish press still underestimated the value of graphic information, with only a very few exceptions, such as *Primera Plana*, *Cambio-16*, *La Calle* and

M. ARMENGOL. *Police repression of a pro-amnesty demonstration. Barcelona, 1976. (Author's Collection.)*

M. PÉREZ BARRIOPEDRO. *The coup leader Tejero in parliament. 23 February 1981. (Agencia Efe.)*

JORDI SOCIAS. Demonstration for the Catalan Statute of Autonomy.
Barcelona, 1976. (Author's Collection.)

Cuadernos para el Diálogo, which had excellent graphic editors in the persons of Carlos Bosch, Victor Steinberg, Jordi Socias, Eduardo Rodríguez and Manuel López Rodríguez. However, even though there were obvious improvements in graphic publication, many of the problems of press photography persisted long after democracy was fully established. In 1981, at the First Catalonia Seminar on Photography, the Catalan Association of Press and Media Photographers, founded in 1977, deplored the poor handling of graphic elements by the press and the instability suffered by graphic reporters in their employment situation. These problems were further complicated by others stemming from the gradual imposition of the new routine that followed upon the creative enthusiasm of that brief reawakening of Spanish photojournalism, which lasted basically from 1972 to 1980.

The Thaw

During the 1950s, the Franco regime entered a period of greater political flexibility, with the aim of leaving behind its nationalist burden and moving the country closer to a neo-liberal capitalist model. Spain joined the UN and then the OECD and the International Monetary Fund, in line with the new economic direction mapped out by the Opus Dei technocrats who were beginning to take control of the government, edging out the fundamentalist relics of the Movement. The need to adapt to the demands of the new economic orthodoxy led the government to promulgate the 1959 Stabilisation Plan, which called for a substantial devaluation of the peseta, strict wage controls and an economic adjustment to allow Spain's integration into the emerging Common Market. As a result, the industrial population grew at the expense of the rural and agrarian population, with the accompanying intensive and traumatic migratory movements. It is estimated that between 1961 and 1965 approximately nine hundred thousand people left the country's most backward regions to move to the conurbations of Madrid, Barcelona and Valencia. In addition, the number of workers forced to seek employment on the more prosperous European labour markets neared two million. According to the Ministry of Labour, subsidised external emigration amounted to 1,742,428 persons between 1959 and 1970, although experts such as Salustiano del Campo believe that this uncontainable exodus was actually much greater than indicated by official figures.[141]

Spain was opening up: emigrants were pouring out and tourists were pouring in. The number of arrivals of foreigners in Spain went from 1,263 in 1951 to over twenty-four million in 1970, while foreign currency remittances by emigrants soared during the same period. Foreign investments also grew steadily from 1962 onwards, turning many of Spain's leading companies into mere branch offices of the major multinationals. The entry of American capital increased substantially after the bilateral accords of 1953 and reached astronomical figures during the 1960s. This economic penetration constituted a veritable Trojan Horse for a cultural colonisation without parallel in the modern history of Spain, one that was further intensified with the arrival of television in the country's towns and villages – now mere numbers in the computers of the global village – and the consequent entry of the empire's neo-liberal philosophy into Spanish homes. The ubiquitous English-speaking cultural presence, the massive migrations and the influence of tourism led to the immediate loss of moral and cultural models and references and the irreversible decline of the traditional Spanish way of life. However, these profound structural changes in the country's economy had barely any effect on the political situation, given the nature of a regime supported by police repression and the total strangulation of democratic liberties.

In the area of artistic creation, the 1950s were a crucial period. The *Salon de Octubre* was created in 1948 and that same year saw the birth of the *Dau al Set* group, formed by Antoni Tapies, Joan Ponç, Modest Cuixart, Joan Brossa and Juan E. Cirlot. Two emblematic groups in contemporary Spanish art were formed in 1957: *El Paso* and *Equipo 57*, promoted by artists such as Rafael Canogar, Manolo Millares, Antonio Saura, Luis Feito, Martín Chirino, Manuel Rivera, Pablo Serrano and Agustín Ibarrola. At the same time, painters such as Zamorano and José Ortega advocated a type of art centred on denunciation and deeply committed to reality, while similar stances were adopted by musicians, filmmakers, playwrights, novelists and poets, who, in the words of Juan Goytisolo, turned their work into a "mirror of the obscure, humble and daily struggle by the Spanish people to regain their lost freedom".[142]

Photography, still at a distance from artistic and cultural circles, and still looked down upon and ignored by the most representative figures in those circles, remained immune to that creative tension, a circumstance that, while preserving it from the dialectic excesses of some of the members of that generation,

P. SENDER. *Neighbourhood cinema. Barcelona, 1955. (Private Collection.)*

also cut it off from its invigorating passion and its renewing, iconoclastic and protean power. The political transition, which had had a certain impact on other areas of creativity, was barely felt by photography, which was dramatically cloistered in the endogamous world and the puerile aesthetic affectedness of the associations and salons. However, the end of autarchy brought with it the exhaustion of the regionalist and nationalist tradition and, consequently, of the ideological basis for the largest part of the artistic premises of late pictorialism. The wave of economic development in the 1960s also brought with it new factors of cultural penetration and new ways of approaching the concept of photography, marked by the international avant-garde movements linked to humanist realism, embodied most emblematically in the monumental *Family of Man* exhibition (1955). Although clearly late, Spanish photographers began questioning the late pictorialist academicism whose morbid influence was still firmly predominant in the officialist circles of the time. As pointed out by José María Artero in 1956, the "radically opposed" con-

CATALÁ ROCA. Young women strolling on the Gran Vía. Madrid, 1953. (Catalá Roca Family Collection.)

cepts were those of *pictorial* photography and *modern* photography, the photography that was still a "poor imitation of painting" and the photography "of our times". It was – still – a question of returning to the aesthetic propositions at the base of the photographic revolution of the period between the wars, expressed repeatedly in the work of such photographers as Man Ray, Paul Strand, Brassaï and Catalá Pic himself, and stressed once again by Artero, over thirty years later: "We did not want our works to look like paintings, but to be, simply and straightforwardly, photographs."[143]

The struggle for renewal of photography involved a parallel struggle against the officialist circles the old pictorialist academicism remained firmly entrenched. This conflict was not limited to Spain, since it was also being fought in other countries by such important photographers as Bill Brandt, Helmut Gersheim and Cecil Beaton in England, Fulvio Roiter, Mario Giacomelli and Silvio Pelegrini in Italy, and Jean-Claude Gautrand, Jean Dieuzaide and Roger Doloy in France, through such influential groups as *La Bussola* (1947), *Friulano per una Nuova Fotografia* (1955), *30x40* and the *Cercle des XII*. In Germany, the *Fotoform* group was created in 1949 by Peter Keetman, Wolfgang Reisewitz and Otto Steiner, the theorist of the so-called *subjective photography*, which advocated the photographer's creative freedom to take creative photographs, but "always using the possibilities inherent in the technique". In the United States, this renewal was centred on photographers such as Paul Strand, Edward Weston and Minor White, with whom creative photography was to shed the last remains of its servitude to painting. These developments had a decisive influence on young Spanish photographers, as did the publication of books such as W. Klein's *New York* (1956), Robert Frank's *The Americans* (1958), and the *Family of Man* exhibition (1955), which sent veritable shock waves through the sleepy backwaters of Spanish photography of the time.[144]

However, in contrast with other countries, the renewal of photography in Spain began from within the associations, whose most advanced members understood the old reformist adage that something must change in order for everything to remain essentially the same. To this end they situated themselves at the head of the renewal movement in order to lead the inevitable change, control its scope and reap its artistic benefits. One of the apostles of this renewal was Luis Navarro (the pseudonym of Luis Conde Vélez), a member of the Agrupación Fotográfica de Cataluña, whose article *El momento fotográfico español* (1952) was a veritable wake-up call for the photographic circles of the time. He wrote "Our photographic artists are old and have been unable to renew themselves. (...) It is a tragedy for a person to live in a time later than their own, but it is even more of a tragedy to live in a time earlier than one's own." And he returned to the subject a year later: "New sentiments are of no value if they are expressed in old modes, and new modes of expression are of no value unless they are accompanied by new sentiments. (...) We are advancing towards the doors opened to us by a generation of photographic artists, of young people who see with fresh eyes and who are now hesitating before the distress represented by a past era and the hope of a new and unknown time for their flights."[145]

The new generations were seeking a photography removed from the reigning technicist preciosity. As already observed by Maspons, in 1951, technique was no longer the main quality required for a photograph to be considered "artistic". Gonzalo Juanes wrote in 1957 "We do not wish to denigrate technique. In the Spanish salons, everything is secondary to technique, so much so that it stifles the idea, if there is in fact an idea. The result is an artificial, monotonous, cliché-ridden photography." It became a matter of avoiding photographic artifice, rhetoric and symbolism and seeking instead a simple photography, one that was "deliberately understated, in comparison with the photographic ostentation predominating in Spain".[146] However, the road to renewal was by no means clear of obstacles, and it soon encountered the frontal opposition of the more orthodox and conservative sectors. Artero remembered in 1991 "Although the particular language of photography was understood in the rest of Europe, in Spain we still lived in the 19th century and photo-reportage, the capture of the instant and the reflection of everyday reality were considered by some to be works lacking in any 'pictorial' worth, by others as an easy option for those with no skill in the *art of the camera obscura*, and by still others, these being the most dangerous, as evidence of a latent threat to the preservation of social order." A social order that the censors and zealous guardians of the national virtues saw under threat when creators – as denounced by Carmen Conde in 1946 – chose the "putrid, reeking, repugnant or subhuman" as the theme of their works, rather than the "creative, luminous and beautiful".

Although photographers were still a long way from the creative approaches taken by novelists, filmmakers, painters and playwrights, and from their profound social and moral commitment, this incipient and timid move in the direction of reality was opposed tenaciously by the mandarins responsible for watching over the racial purity of Spanish photography. However, in spite of the determined resistance of the officialist sectors and the influence still wielded by the old masters – it is important to remember that Ortiz Echagüe published his book *Castillos y alcázares* in 1956 – the groundwork for photographic insurgence was already laid and was firmly supported by the more talented young photographers who were then setting out on their careers.

Documentary Renewal in the 1960s

Although the wave of renewal originated from within the associations, the genuine photographic renewal soon transcended the cramped environment of their salons. Photographers such as Masats, Maspons, Miserachs, Pomés, Colom, Terré

F. ONTAÑÓN. Wedding in Salamanca, 1960. (Author's Collection.)

and Ubiña made an attempt in Barcelona to break away from the antiquated Agrupación Fotográfica de Cataluña, which was incapable of assimilating the new trends, going beyond the *new photography* propounded by Luis Navarro.[147] Between 1955 and 1959, at a time when the country was beginning to shake off a little of the dust of autarchy, this group of photographers began showing their work in the few galleries existing in the city, such as Galerías Layetana and the Sala Aixelá. These activities and the informative efforts of the Lumen publishing house, which began publication of its excellent collection "Palabra e Imagen" (Words and Images) in 1961, provided an excellent platform for these young photographers, whose work tended towards a documentary realism influenced by the documentarism of Català Roca, French poetic realism and touches of Italian neo-realism. With the magic of Maspons, the intuition of Colom, the creative daring of Masats, the subtlety of Pomés and the analytical capacity of Miserachs, this group, with the clearly inappropriate name of the Barcelona School, took a decisive step on the one-way road towards the future of Spanish photography.[148]

R. MASATS. From the report Los Sanfermines. *Pamplona, 1960. (Author's Collection.)*

J. COLOM. Barcelona, 1959 (From Izas rabizas y colipoterras*). (Author's Collection.)*

C. PÉREZ SIQUIER. La Chanca (Almería), 1962. (Author's Collection.)

Ramón Masats was the first to practise pure reportage in his excellent monographic works *Neutral Corner* (1962) and *Los Sanfermines* (1963), in which he distanced himself definitively from the traditional photographic language, showing a surprising audacity to break with the conventionalisms of the time and a superb intuition and creative capacity. After publishing *Viejas Historias de Castilla la Vieja* (1964), he alternated his work as a photographer with growing involvement in the cinema and television. Oriol Maspons brought a corrosive critical and demythologising approach to his work in a full range of genres. In his images, which often contain a glimpse of his talent and taste for provocation, there is always a wink of complicity to the beholder and a covert tenderness. Julio Ubiña began working with Maspons in 1957, and together they produced a magnificent book, *Toreo de salon* (1962). Ironic and mocking, he practised a brand of documentarism free of conceptual complexity, with a direct language and great narrative efficacy.

From his very first works, Xavier Miserachs transcended the world of appearances to offer an analytical vision of reality, one that is full of wisdom. Some of these photographs were compiled in the emblematic book *Barcelona en blanc i negre* (1964), an exciting exercise in visual contemplation of the life of the city from a purely documentary, but also critical and interpretative, standpoint. This analytical style pervaded with connotations and nuances was maintained in *Costa Brava Show* (1966) and other later works by Miserachs, who also published admirable material of an informative and theoretical nature. Leopoldo Pomés, a creator of photographs full of suggestive and delicate subtleties, was linked to the *Dau al Set* group at the beginning of his career. His photographs blur the distinction between fact and fiction and invite the beholder to dream in a way that has as little of gratuitous escapism about it as it does of simple evocation of the immediate. Pomés gradually abandoned photography to dedicate himself almost exclusively to creative filmmaking and advertising.

There are certain similarities to Pomés's subjective perception in the work of Ricardo Terré. More than a mere attempt to reflect reality, here we find a determination to transcend it. With his limited repertoire of themes – death, ritual, childhood – Terré has a tendency to timelessness. Obsessed with the semantic proximity of death, he used the most appropriate technique to emphasise his own sensations in the face of the inscrutable language of ritual. His images therefore become metaphors for his own inner world. Paco Ontañón used a simple language, free of any experimentalist pretensions, but tremendously direct and effective. Although he worked in Madrid, he always maintained certain links with the Barcelona group and had his book *Los días iluminados* (1964), a penetrating look at Easter week, published by Lumen. With her parallels to the aesthetic approach of the Barcelona School, *Colita* may be considered its most characteristic epigone. She began working with Miserachs and Maspons, and is another all-terrain photographer, as at home with portraits as with reportage and advertising. Her book *Luces y sombras del flamenco* (1975) was the final entry in the "Palabra e Imagen" series and shows an admirable ductility and command of reportage.

Other Catalan photographers, such as Colom, Forcano and Martínez Carrión worked more fully within the Agrupación Fotográfica de Cataluña. Colom was always at home in the marginalised world of the poorer neighbourhoods. His memorable depiction of the underbelly of social life in Barcelona constitutes one of the

X. MISERACHS. Flirtatious compliment on the Vía Layetana. Barcelona, 1962. (Author's Collection.)

most daring, moving and fascinating photographic works of his generation. With his simple and highly intuitive language, he took dozens of excellent photographs, a selection of which were printed by Lumen in the book *Izas, rabizas y colipoterras* (1964). Situated at a point equidistant from pure reportage and the technicist preciosity promoted by the Agrupación Fotográfica de Cataluña we find the work of Eugenio Forcano, whose talent as a photographer prevented him from succumbing either to officialist excess or the risks of his own inspiration. A contradictory and "self-absorbed" photographer, with an undeniable creative and protean capacity, Forcano was an island in the renovation of Catalan photography.

In contrast to Barcelona, photographic renewal in Madrid commenced within the bounds of the Real Sociedad Fotográfica, whose most alert and informed members were profoundly influenced by the work of Ramón Masats, who had moved to Madrid in 1957. Masats himself, along with Gabriel Cualladó, Gerardo Vielba, Leonardo Cantero, Paco Gómez and the Asturian painter Joaquín Rubio Camín,

R. SANZ LOBATO. *Miranda del Castañar, 1971. (Author's Collection.)*

formed the short-lived group *La Palangana* (1957), which was soon joined by Joan Dolcet, Rafael Romero, Paco Ontañón and Gonzalo Juanes. Just a few months later, Rubio Camín, Masats, Ontañón and Juanes stopped attending the group's informal meetings, to be replaced by Fernando Gordillo and several members of the future *La Colmena* group, including Carlos Hernández Corcho, Rafael Sanz Lobato, Sigfrido de Guzmán and Felipe Hernández Tarabillo. Between the reformist aspirations of the original core members and the more argumentative and rebellious attitude of the members of *La Colmena*, a formal and conceptual synthesis arose that was to evolve into the doubtful – and at times suspicious – rural poetics that characterised a substantial part of the work of what came to be known as the Madrid School.

While Catalan photographers were permanently in close contact with the most advanced cultural circles in Barcelona, their colleagues in Madrid – the majority of them members of the social classes most closely identified with the Franco regime – remained cloistered in the endogamous world of the Real Sociedad Fotográfica. Isolated from their city's cultural milieu, the members of the Madrid School were anchored firmly in a mellifluous lyricism that only rarely transcended a cloying

G. CUALLADÓ. Secretary to the Town Council of Alarcón (Cuenca). 1968. (Author's Collection.)

"praise of village life" or the reflection of a reality idealised by the photographer's supposedly poetic inspiration. However, it is only fair to point that the ones who, given their background and training as artists, would naturally have seemed destined to maintain the officialist essence of the Real Sociedad Fotográfica, ended up being the key figures of a renewal movement that, in spite of its limitations, was an honest attempt to break with the puerile academicism of the time. Among the most notable members of the group were Cualladó, Paco Gómez, Gerardo Vielba, Fernando Gordillo, Juan Dolcet, Carlos H. Corcho and Sanz Lobato.

   Although Cualladó's work contains decidedly documentary elements, what is in fact documented is the photographer's own personality. In spite of his express admiration for Smith, none the great American reporter's ethical commitment is to be found in Cualladó; in its stead there is the vision of a man who always aspired to simplicity. However, we should not be misled by the apparent simplicity of his photographs, since that simplicity is in fact the confirmation of their technical complexity and their overwhelming perfection. Cualladó succeeded in creating a world of nostalgia pervaded with mystery and defining a characteristic and instantly

F. GÓMEZ. Wall and tree. 1962. (Author's Collection.)

recognisable photographic language. The world of Paco Gómez is another intimate one. With the awareness that honesty is the foundation for any truly creative work, Gómez retreated to a limited and personal world to build an austere and deeply original language that he could use to attain the natural poetry of things of which Brassaï had spoken. It is this simplicity charged with evocativeness and nostalgia that embodies the magic of Paco Gómez, the most advanced member of the Madrid group, the subtlest and the most ironically tender and likeable.

Juan Dolcet provides a prime example of work well done, of pure, simple and penetrating photographic perception. An excellent reporter and accomplished portraitist, his works show the meticulousness of a jeweller and a profound sweetness. Gerardo Vielba was the group's leading theorist and his dedication to questions of doctrine encumbered his photographic efforts to a certain extent. However, Vielba was a gifted photographer and produced worthy images bordering on tenderness but without every falling into exaggeration. Between 1960 and 1970, Fernando Gordillo produced an admirable report on the village of Pedro Bernardo in the province of

Ávila, with a number of excellent images. Deliberately avoiding any evocation of wretchedness or squalor, his express purpose was to present an idyllic and attractive image of rural Spain. Hernández Corcho and Sanz Lobato are the two great forgotten figures of the Madrid School. Corcho had a caustic and biting vision, and was the first to break the mellifluous and technicist philosophy of the Real Sociedad Fotográfica and turn his gaze towards urban scenes, paving the way for other young photographers. Sanz Lobato began taking photographs in the early 1960s, concentrating on analytical documentation of the customs and ritual celebrations of Castilian towns and villages. In this sense, he was, along with Corcho, Dolcet and Cruzado Cazador, one of the pioneers of anthropologically-based photography.

However, the most radical movement in Spanish photography in the 1950s was the one formed around the *Afal* group, promoted from Almería by José María Artero and Carlos Pérez Siquier. The movement was constituted informally in 1956 and its theoretical basis was a pugnacious opposition to late pictorialist academicism and a determined commitment to the social reality of the time. Gonzalo Juanes wrote in 1956 "A photographer can never distance himself from the vital concerns of his contemporaries." Nevertheless, as Juanes himself admitted, *Afal* never attained the degree of commitment found in other European groups, such as *Friulano per la Nuova Fotografia*, which advocated a brand of photographic militancy as a denunciation of an aggressive and unjust situation. Nor could *Afal* take its insurgency much farther, in view of the rigid control to which it was subjected by censors and government authorities. The group's influence soon spread beyond the geographical boundaries of Almería. From the outset it had the decisive participation of Juanes, from Gijón, and Maspons, from Barcelona. They formed the doctrinal core of the movement along with the two founding members and occasional contributions from Miserachs, Gabriel Querol, Cirici Pellicer, Roger Doloy and André Thevenez.[149] Its impact was so extensive that all of the renewal movements that arose in Spain – *El Mussol*, in Tarrasa, *El Forat*, in Valencia, and even *La Palangana*, in Madrid – claimed, with greater or lesser justification, to be members of *Afal*. In this sense, it is safe to say that it was the most influential and effective of the movements for photographic renewal that arose on the depressed Spanish cultural scene in the period following the war. It was through *Afal* that the most outstanding proponents of the documentary avant-garde in Spain, such as Masats, Maspons, Miserachs, Ontañón, Terré, Colom, Gómez, Cualladó, Pomés, Schommer and Pérez Siquier, became known.

O. MASPONS. *Bullfight with young bulls in town in La Mancha. 1961. (Author's Collection.)*

Carlos Pérez Siquier was one of the group's founders. From the social documentarism of his earliest photographs, he evolved towards a sort of magic realism, midway between analytical documentary and pure formalist rigour. He later went on to refine this aesthetic of the magical, adding certain surrealist and tenebrist nuances as seen in his final works. Gonzalo Juanes is one of the more neglected members of *Afal* and one of those who made the greatest contribution in the area of doctrine and theory. His relentless consistency led him to abandon photography in 1963 and destroy his negatives. Alberto Schommer contributed work replete with freshness, avoiding any sort of artificiality, rhetoric or symbolism, an approach that he did not keep to consistently in later years. An extraordinarily versatile photographer, Schommer worked in a wide range of genres and maintained an enviable creative vitality, as seen in his later works, such as *El Viaje* (1994) and *La Vida (La Habana)* (1994).

In that time of cultural and political prostration, *Afal* played a decisive part in breaking Spanish photography's persistent international isolation through its contacts with such important groups as *La Bussola*, in Milan, *30 × 40*, in Paris, and

Fotoform, in Germany and through its participation in the leading international biennial exhibitions and competitions. This activity took on such importance that Spanish photography came to be identified with this group's work, as observed by Emmanuel Sougez in 1959. Over the years, its rebellious and galvanising spirit lost its edge, owing to the lack of a sincere desire to break with the past on the part of a good many of its later members, many of them linked to more conservative photographic circles. Maspons writes "The form was renewed, but not the content." What followed was a sort of documentary mannerism, already deplored by Pérez Siquier in 1957. This new brand of officialism was soon integrated into the routine of the associations, which were concerned solely with adapting to change in order integrate that change into their antiquated and rusty philosophies.[150]

On the other hand, many of the most representative members of *Afal* left the group to work as professional photographers. Maspons, Masats, Miserachs, Ontañón, Pomés and Ubiña eventually went into the field of advertising photography, a speciality that they alternated with graphic reporting and book illustration.

Other younger photographers, including Gianni Ruggiero, the brothers Antón and Ramón Eguiguren, Toni Riera, Antonio Molina, José María Ferrater, J.M. Oriola and César Malet, worked almost exclusively in fashion and advertising photography, returning to a speciality commenced in the 1930s by photographers such as Catalá Pic, Sala and Masana and that had barely had any opportunity to develop an aesthetic of its own in Spain under the autarchic regime. This absence of a tradition and the lack of proper training were behind the mediocrity of Spanish advertising and fashion photography, although recognition must be given to the quality of the work done by Maspons, Toni Riera, José María Ferrater, Antonio Molina and, later, in the 1980s, by Javier Vallhonrat, Spain's most brilliant and highly respected advertising photographer.

There were also other areas of photographic creation where not much progress had been made. With the timid attempts at reforms and breaking away exhausted and tamed, Spanish photography became mired in the officialism of the new documentary orthodoxy and there were few voices raised to break the monotony of that mediocre, limited and debilitating panorama.

The Dawning of the Future

In the lee of the prosperity of the international economy, Spain had implemented three Development Plans between 1963 and 1975 that, by the final years of the dictatorship, had positioned it as the world's tenth industrial power. The foreign currency revenues generated by the tourist industry and the mass migrations of the 1960s helped to maintain a healthy balance of payments, at the cost of the sacrifice of a condemned and despised rural Spain. Over four million people were obliged to leave their hometowns during that period, while industry became increasingly dependent on large multinationals that were coddled by a political regime that needed them.

Economic change did not bring with it any corresponding political or cultural change. The dictatorship remained firm in its systematic prohibition of civic liberties, with the support of the more conservative sectors of the army, the church and finance. Any expression of demands was strangled by means of police repression, as in the days of Serrano Súñer's Press Act. However, strike movements grew during the final years of the Franco regime and, beginning in 1969, were met with successive states of emergency. Labour unrest became increasing organised around the underground Comisiones Obreras trade union, which eventually rendered the regime's union organisation meaningless. In addition, nationalist movements resurfaced in the Basque Country and Catalonia, while members of the democratic opposition met in Munich in 1962 to find political alternatives to the Franco regime. The government's response to this growing defiance was an indiscriminate intensification of repression. Leading figures of the cultural and academic worlds were arrested and deported, while the police broke up such demonstrations as the act of homage to Antonio Machado in Úbeda (1966), the *Caputxinada* in Sarrià (1966) and the sit-in by intellectuals at the Montserrat monastery (1970).

The assassination of Admiral Carrero Blanco (1973) precipitated the crisis of the Franco regime. Beginning in the summer of 1974, the political opposition entered a phase of intense activity, centred on the Junta Democrática and the Plataforma de Convergencia Democrática, which grouped all of the parties, unions and citizens' movements. In October, the two organisations banded together to demand the democratic rights and liberties prevailing in western countries. This marked the end of the regime that, like its creator, was at death's door, in a climate of intense repression marked by trials by the so-called public order tribunals and the execution by firing squad of ETA and FRAP activists. In this context, Spanish art experienced in an especially intense manner the conflict sparked on the international stage by the creative tensions arising from the crisis of informalism, the rise of a heavily politicised pop art, and the new figuration. The special circumstances that defined cultural reality under the late Franco regime – the persistence of censorship, the non-existence of an art market worthy of the name, and the social commitment of the country's leading intellectuals and artists – had a profound effect on the art produced during those years. Valeriano Bozal writes "It is undeniable that the relationship between art and politics was a close one, although the most important aspect here is that, as in the transition from the 1950s to the 1960s, this did not degrade the quality of art; on the contrary, it acted as an incentive, feeding a dynamism that was not only ideological but also stylistic."[151]

The photographers of the time – with the exception of a few young photojournalists – remained oblivious to these dialectic tensions, cloistered in the limbo of the new documentary orthodoxy, or barricaded behind the suspicious

P. PÉREZ MÍNGUEZ. *Cover of the magazine*
Nueva Lente. *October 1971.*

J. RUEDA. *Cover of the magazine*
Nueva Lente. *April 1976.*

"subversion of the essential" preached by the *newest* sectors with links to the magazine *Nueva Lente* (1971). These sectors were in close contact with some of the most representative practitioners of new Spanish art who, in the face of the ethical commitment of the preceding generation – for whom they felt a genuine "generational phobia" – advocated an art that was "artistic" and apolitical in the turbulent and bloody closing years of the dictatorship. These artists, including Carlos Alcolea, Guillermo Pérez Villalta, Carlos Franco, Rafael Pérez Mínguez and Juan Antonio Aguirre, united through the Amadís gallery and the *Nueva Generación* movement, strongly influenced the new photography propounded on the pages of that magazine. Enric Mira writes "*Nueva Generación* was unquestionably the strongest influence on the incipient new Spanish photography. (...) The photographic image of the first phase of *Nueva Lente*, created according to a "*poetics of the absurd*", was a clear exponent of this playful-irrational bent and its iconographic embodiment, a photographic alternative based on the aesthetic category of ambiguity as its fundamental value."[152]

Considered by many to be the source of all contemporary photographic avant-garde movements in Spain, the magazine was an appendix of this playful-ir-

M. FALCES. Untitled. 1975 (original in colour). (Author's Collection.)

F. LORRIO. Fried Spain. 1976 (original in colour). (Author's Collection.)

rational spirit taken up by the new artistic currents and a home-grown version of certain aesthetic movements in the English-speaking world that took in all styles, from conceptualism and pop art to the underground aesthetic found in posters, pamphlets and fanzines, which would be devoured by an iconoclastic generation that saw itself as representing the very essence of modernity and progress. Among its defining traits were its determined ambiguity, a certain eclecticism rooted in postmodernism and a militant disregard for politics. Another of its identifying marks was its radical negation of the photography practised by the preceding generation of documentarists and a vital drive to break with the immediate past. Beginning with the very first issue, the editors of *Nueva Lente* wanted to draw a clear dividing line between the past and the future that was being born with their magazine, with the supposed revolution that they would be working through its pages. In Mira's words "An ingenuously mistaken concept, based on ignorance of the historical past of Spanish photography. This fact points up the intellectual poverty of the arid cultural panorama of the early years of the decade [of the 1970s] and its inability to stimulate research and therefore to know that historical past."[153]

During its first phase (1971-1975), *Nueva Lente* was characterised by a puerilely provocative attitude that proclaimed that reality had been exhausted as subject matter for photography. The leading proponent of this doctrine was Pablo Pérez Mínguez, a representative of what Joan Fontcuberta has defined as the "funny revolution". This initial phase was essentially experimental and, in the shadow of Christian Vogt, Duane Michals, Paul de Noijer and Bernard Plossu, it produced images that were pretentious, self-indulgent, ingenuously oneiric and technically facile and immature. Among its most frequent contributors were Pablo and Luis Pérez Mínguez, Elías Dolcet, Juan Ramón Yuste, Paco Roux, Jorge Rueda and the sisters Cristina and Marigrá García Rodero. In 1975, the magazine entered a new phase, under the editorship of Jorge Rueda, who turned in the direction of a type of photography tending more towards the fantastic, one that had little respect for reality and was indebted to the aesthetic of Topor, Delvaux and Magritte. The photomontage became the technique used most commonly by the young photographers of this period, who were heavily influenced by the photomontage fever then sweeping Europe, embodied in the monumental Ingolstadt exhibition (1969) and the satirical publications born in the wake of May 1968 in France, such as *Charlie Hebdo* and *Hara-kiri*.

J. RUEDA. My Sister's Fiancées.
Photomontage, 1971.
(Author's Collection.)

Rueda himself, Joan Fontcuberta, Pere Formiguera, J.M. Oriola, Rafael Navarro, Antonio Gálvez, Eduardo Momeñe, Manuel Falces, the brothers Antón and Ramón Eguiguren and the *Yetis* were the most frequent contributors during the magazine's second phase.

Of the dozens of photographers who made their début on the pages of *Nueva Lente*, few have survived as photographers, most of them having been "obscured and consigned to oblivion by their brilliant mediocrity", as Carlos Serrano and Pablo Pérez Mínguez had accurately foretold. Those who managed to remain on the scene would take years to mature and find their own personal means of expression. The sole exceptions would be Pablo Pérez Mínguez and Jorge Rueda. The former used irony and parody as essential elements of a sort of photography that deliberately avoided reality to cloister itself in its creator's world, in an exercise in narcissism that also marked the work of Luis Pérez Mínguez. The photography practised by Jorge Rueda sprang from his innate rebelliousness, an intense honesty and an astonishing imagination. His work – both in the area of photomontage and reportage, one of his most neglected and admirable facets –

R. NAVARRO. Diptych-8.
1978. (Author's Collection.)

constitutes a profound subversion of the routine, photographic conformism and system of values of Spanish society during the final years of the Franco regime.

The 1970s also saw other crucial events that defined a pivotal decade for the future development of Spanish photography. A dozen new galleries and exhibition rooms opened, new magazines were published, new schools and academies were founded, and the groundwork was laid for the development of an incipient photographic market, thanks to the efforts of such key figures as Albert Guspi, the founder of Barcelona's Spectrum gallery (1973) and the Grup Taller d'art Fotogràfic (1975).[154] The Redor gallery opened in Madrid in 1970 and the first *Spafoto* yearbook as published in 1972, followed in 1973 by the *Coteflash* and *Everfoto* yearbooks. The first issue of the magazine *Flash-Foto* appeared in 1974, and the multi-role Photocentro, directed by Aurora Fierro, opened in Madrid that same year. The Centros de Enseñanza de la Imagen (CEI) were founded in 1976, join-

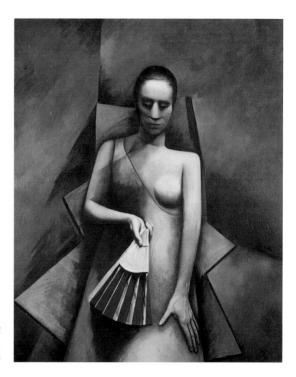

J. VALLHONRAT. From the Homages series. 1983. (Author's Collection.)

ing the already important Institut d'Estudis Fotogràfics de Catalunya (1972), directed by Miguel Galmes. In 1976, Photocentro began publishing the Spanish version of the magazine *Zoom*, and two years later Spanish photography began figuring among the participants in the International Meetings at Arles. These developments were complemented by a wide range of activities organised by the photographic associations themselves, such as the Photomostra show in Lérida and the Photography Week in Guadalajara.

On another front, Spanish photojournalism was experiencing its finest moment since the years of the Republic and the Civil War. In the convulsive times of the final years of the Franco regime, the work of the country's young reporters attained admirable levels of quality and contributed a renewed style to publications that had atrophied after so many years of censorship, self-censorship and legal restrictions imposed by a political regime that had relentlessly persecuted civic liberties and particularly the freedom of expression.

T. CATANY. From To Dream of Gods. *1984. (Author's Collection.)*

Latest Trends: Between Reality and Fiction

Franco's death and the laborious process of the transition to democracy had a number of immediate effects on the area of culture. With the dictator's demise, the last barriers to Spain's political normalisation disappeared. The anti-Franco commitment was to give way to a new, more "artistic", decorative and indulgent art, coinciding with the integration into the structures of political and cultural power of the members of the anti-establishment youth who had inherited the spirit of the French May 1968 and who, with the enthusiasm of converts, were anxious to offer a new image of Spain, as a country no longer mired in its reactionary and chauvinistic past, one that was more liberal, progressive and definitively aligned with the international currents of modernity.[155] On a different level, the collective and militant spirit that had reigned among photographers during the 1960s was gradually replaced by a marked individualism, appropriate to the intense competition imposed by the mandarins of the new international order and their local deputies. The new photography began moving along trails blazed by a creative bent with a conceptual foundation, in contrast to the documentary vanguards of the postwar period. With the exhaustion of reality as subject matter for photography capriciously declared, photographers felt the need to create or conceive images that, in the words of Duane Michals, would now project their own "inner landscapes". With this rejection of documentary photography – Jean-François Chevrier and François Hers had solemnly stated that "reportage photography is dead because there is nothing left to photograph" – making photography into a mere medium for aesthetic experimentation, a substantial part of the new photographic academicism was born, along the lines of a number of interdisciplinary artists such as Cindy Sherman, Anna and Bernard Johannes, Thomas Ruff and particularly Jurgen Klauke, a leading proponent of the Concept Art of the 1980s, for whom the camera was merely accessory in the creation of his works.

These developments had a decisive influence on the new Spanish photography that had been evolving since the early days of Nueva Lente. It was a photography marked by the euphoria of breaking away and a reverent attitude to any manifestation of foreign culture, in confirmation of Spanish photographers' international bent, seduced as they were, in the words of Eduardo Subirats, by the "rhetoric of a tamed and politically neutralised avant-gardism and by the absolutely servile mimicry of models bearing the seal of approval of international criticism".[156] These playful, ambiguous and "uncommitted" currents eventually established their primacy and edged out any sort of moral responsibility to society on the part of the photographer. The new avant-gardes linked to postmodernity are more pragmatic and less idealist than those related to modernity in the period between the wars and humanist and documentarist currents of the 1950s and 1960s. Rather than destroying the past, as the surrealists and dadaists had intended, the only objective now was to ransack it. Umberto Eco writes "The postmodern response to modernism consists of admitting that, since the past cannot be destroyed, as this would lead only to silence, what must be done is to revisit it, with irony and without naïvety."[157] This explains the eclecticism of postmodern art in general and postmodern photography in particular, its tendency to look to the past and its willingness to plagiarise, which, added to the increased blending of techniques and styles, has so profoundly marked the production of a substantial number of the members of the latest generations. The solemn regard of these photographers for themselves, similar to that observed by Barthes in the classic pictorialists, has led them gradually away from photography, to assume the procedures and techniques of other disciplines, such as sculpture, installations and painting.

The new avant-garde orthodoxy, defined by a legion of impromptu critics, curators, experts and dealers, propounded a sort of neo-pictorialism, one that was more sophisticated and baroque than its predecessor but just as indebted to the old Victorian defence of photographs as art objects, or, as pointed out by Walter Benjamin, more properly as "objects of commerce", to the same inferiority complex in respect of painting, and to the same lack of humility on the part of its creators. A neo-pictorialism born of postmodernist mystification and the dehumanisation of post-industrial society that led to the disappearance of all strains of resistance to and rebellion against power, to the end of idealist ethics, to the destitution of the old values of solidarity, with the alibi of an economic development that would drive the market for a sumptuary and indulgent art that would, finally, include photography.

As in the golden age of pictorialism, the photographer feels the need to be and see himself as an artist, as the only means of reaching this desired photographic market. Vicenç Altaió writes "Photographers, other than those who make a living from advertising or journalism, want to be artists." Pere Formiguera stated in

J. FONTCUBERTA.
La Nascita de Venus
(Double Body *series*).
1992 (original in colour).
(Courtesy of IVAM.)

1980 "I refuse to define or categorise my work once it is finished. It might be photography, painting or collage. I consider myself an artist who manipulates his photographs, and when that manipulation is taken to its utmost limits, it might become painting."[158] In order to attain this status, photographers have not hesitated to abandon their condition as such, distancing themselves hygienically from any suspicion of depicting reality and accepting with resignation the deconstruction of the fundamentals of its language as dictated by fashion and an art market plunged into uncertainty and paralysis. This would be a new attempt to subjugate photography and would dangerously narrow its margins of creative freedom as an autonomous language. Just as the old pictorialists used the so-called noble emul-

P. FORMIGUERA. From the series Nosología. *1989. (Private Collection.)*

sions, young photographers use a wide range of techniques to manipulate media, including collage, clastotypes, cascographies, photo-sculptures, photo-installations, photograms and overprinting, the modern descendants of the bromoils, carbons and gum bichromates with which – as observed by Brassaï in 1932 – the "artistic" photographers tried to remove all trace of photography from their works. Nor can it be said that photography has been particularly original in this respect. In recent years, with the absolute denigration of craftsmanship, artists seem to be condemned to accept the prior destruction of the techniques pertaining to their language, be it painting, literature, or photography. These techniques appear to be of no interest to anyone, and least of all to artists themselves or aspiring artists, who thus find themselves freed from the long and painstaking process of learning their art. However, in spite of photography's increasing subjection to the standards dictated by gallery owners and dealers, collectors continue to ignore them.[159]

Fontcuberta was one of the earliest voices raised in Spain in defence of the photographers status as creator, advocating the revision of prevailing ideas

OUKA LELE. The Mystery
of Life. *Tinted photograph,
1989-1990. (Private Collection.)*

on photographic representation and veracity, through series that were less and less photographic, such as *Herbarium* (1984), *Fauna* (in conjunction with Pere Formiguera), and later ones, such as *Frottogramas* (1989) and *Sputnik* (1998), using collage and superimposition of negatives and objects on patterned papers, reproductions of famous paintings, representations of media pornography and three dimensional objects. On the basis of the principle that the camera "is no match for external reality" – as he stated in 1984 "It is a waste of time to go out with your camera over your shoulder and the intention of seeing the world in a different way. For photography, reality has been exhausted; we must create new realities." – it ceased to be an indispensable tool for creating his images, becoming instead a mere accident of work. Other photographers, such as Pere Formiguera, Pedro Avellaned, J.R. Yuste, Ciuco Gutiérrez, Jorge Rueda, the Yetis, Antonio Gálvez, Elías Dolcet, Manuel Falces, Jordi Guillumet, América Sánchez, Jorge Ribalta and Manuel Vilariño, work with a range of different manipulation procedures and invent or manufacture images. *Ouka Lele* started off with certain influences from this

R. ZABALZA. Mocejón. 1984. (Author's Collection.)

K. CHAMORRO. San Fermines series. Pamplona, 1977. (Authror's Collection.)

C. GARCÍA RODERO. Confession. *Saavedra, 1978. (Author's Collection.)*

group and from the so-called Madrid scene, and her artistic pretensions have led her not only to paint on photographs – as a number of painters, such as Darío Villalba, have been doing since the 1960s – but also to create scenes that are often highly reminiscent of the allegorical world of early pictorialism. In his series centred on homage to painting (1983), *Autogramas* (1991), *Cajas* (1996) and *Lugares intermedios* (1998), Javier Vallhonrat questions the language of photography, including its most basic aspects, producing images whose photographic nature is all but imperceptible.

In other areas of photographic creation, the 1980s witnessed the consolidation of a vigorous documentary current, embodied in the works of Koldo Chamorro, Cristina García Rodero, Cristóbal Hara, Fernando Herráez, Benito Román, Enrique Sáenz de San Pedro and Ramón Zabalza, who were unwilling to renounce reality and who accepted without reservation the dignity of their medium. In contrast with the "creative" photographers who preferred to produce their images within the confines of their studios, these photographers saw the world as their studio and kept alive the old passion for observing, discovering and being moved by the never-ending show of reality, and adopted Moholy-Nagy's statement to the effect that photography should be judged as much for the human and social intensity of its representation as for its aesthetic values. Seeing photography as an act of appreciation and humility, the new documentary photographers, heirs to the best of the realist and humanist tradition of the postwar years, became honest witnesses to the changing reality of Spain during a period marked by the apotheosis of neo-liberalism responsible for the decline of rural life and traditional cultural and moral points of reference. Faced with a Spain that was disappearing, they wished to leave a record of its celebrations, rituals, popular customs and ways of life and death, by means of a photography that was pure and free of any type of manipulation. Although the work of this group of photographers commenced in the mid-1970s, it matured and became known in the following decade, reaching a wide audience in domestic and international cultural circles. A decisive factor in this recognition was the publication in 1989 of Cristina García Otero's splendid work *España Oculta*, an astonishing reflection of traditional celebrations in rural Spain, captured in surprising, captivating and extraordinarily plastic images and showing, with great emotion and wisdom, the religious and profane reality of the ancient Iberian rites. The image of this disappearing Spain is also found in such ex-

C. CÁNOVAS. Cardedeu, Vallés Oriental, 1990. (Author's Collection.)

traordinary works as *4 cosas de España* (1990), *Lances de aldea* (1992) and *Vanitas* (1998), by Cristóbal Hara, *Vestigios* (1990, by Fernando Herráez, the *España mági-ca*, *Los Sanfermines* and *El nacimiento de una nación* series, by Koldo Chamorro, exhibited in 1989 and compiled in the monograph *Koldo Chamorro* (1998), *Imágenes gitanas* (1995), by Ramón Zabalza, and *España, fiestas y ritos* (1992), also by Cristina García Rodero.

A new type of photography started appearing in the 1980s, with intimist roots, using diverse themes, blending magic, dream and mystery, seen in the work of Manolo Laguillo, Marta Povo, Ferrán Freixa, Carlos Cánovas, Humberto Rivas, Manel Úbeda, Eduard Olivella and Manel Esclusa, whose images cross the traditional boundaries of photographic genres and have been categorised, with evident inaccuracy, in the field of the so-called intimate documentarism. It constitutes a return to pure photography, showing the melancholy and degradation of urban and industrial scenes and characterised by technical perfection and formal quality and by its distance from the subject matter: old shops, decadent spas, decaying

A. GARCÍA ALIX. *Three Females. April 1989. (Author's Collection.)*

buildings and landscapes, poor urban neighbourhoods, and objects deteriorated by abandonment. Along similar lines to this brand of photography are the splendid works *La meva mediterrània* (1990) and *Obscura memòria* (1994) by Toni Catany, the author of an unforgettable series of still lifes of great subtlety and chromatic quality (1987). His accentuated pragmatism and protean capacity have led him to experiment with techniques as diverse as calotypes and Polaroids transferred to watercolour paper or raw silk, obtaining still lifes, nudes and portraits of extraordinary beauty, compiled in books such as *Somniar Deus* (1994) and *Fotografies* (1997).

The 1980s also saw the failure the specialist galleries, coinciding with the opening of exhibition galleries administered by government organisations, such as the Instituto Valenciano de Arte Moderno (IVAM), the Sala Parpalló, in Valencia,

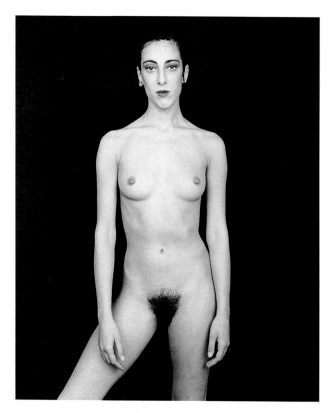

H. RIVAS. Magda. 1986. (Author's Collection.)

the Canal de Isabel II and the Círculo de Bellas Artes, in Madrid, the Palau de la Virreina and the Centro de Arte Santa Mónica, in Barcelona, the Kiosko Alfonso, in La Coruña, and the Palacio Sástago in Zaragoza. Particularly outstanding in this connection are the initiatives taken by private institutions, such as the Fundación Caixa de Cataluña and Fundación "la Caixa", in Barcelona, the Obra Social de Caja Madrid, in Madrid, and the Fundación El Monte, in Andalusia, all of which have carried out important work in the area of exhibitions and publishing, complementing the efforts of publishers such as Gustavo Gili, La Fábrica y TF, Omega, Mestizo, Blume, and especially Lunwerg Editores, which has just celebrated its twentieth anniversary and whose prolific work has been decisive in making Spanish photography known in international circles. In this area, worth mentioning is the appearance of magazines such as *Foto Profesional* (1983), *La Fotografía* (1986),

C. MADOZ. Untitled.
1987. (Private Collection.)

J.M. CASTRO PRIETO. ▶
Muñopepe, 1986.
(Author's Collection.)

FV (1989) and, on a more theoretical level, *PhotoVision* (1983), which, in sense, has taken up where *Nueva Lente* left off. *Archivos de la Fotografía*, published by the Zarautz Museum of Photography, appeared in 1995 and specialises in the study of photohistory. Also of prime importance was the creation of biennial exhibitions and meetings patterned on the Arles International Meetings, which brought many Spanish and foreign photographers to the attention of the public at large. Worth mentioning among these are the Primavera Fotográfica, in Catalonia (1982), the Fotobienal, in Vigo (1982), the Jornadas Fotográficas, in Valencia (1984), Foco, in Madrid (1985), Fotoplín, in Málaga (1985), the Bienal Internacional de Fotografía Isla de Tenerife (1991), Imagina, in Almería (1990), Tarazona Foto (1987), and Huesca Imagen (1995), only a few of which are still held.[160] At the same time, the short-lived Photography departments at the old Spanish Museum of Contemporary

Art (1984) and the Fundación Miró (1985) were created, along with the Fundación Española de la Fotografía (1981), which, under the direction of Eduardo Momeñe and Manuel López Rodríguez, constituted an admirable effort to bring photography closer to the government. More recently, and also with government sponsorship, important institutions have been created, including the Centro Andaluz de Fotografía (Almería, 1992), with the objective of setting up a centre for research, compilation and diffusion of photography as a cultural manifestation. The CAF has presented important exhibitions and photographic meetings, organises workshops and conferences, and sponsors the work of recovering the historical photography of Andalusia. La Fábrica (Madrid, 1998) is in a different category, as a private undertaking with the objective of becoming a cultural centre with the capacity to develop projects closely linked to the world of photography. In the short

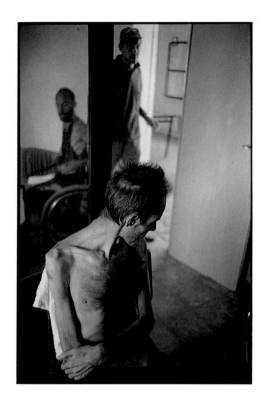

C. BERNAD. AIDS Patients
(from Woe is Us). Chinchón,
1995. (Author's Collection.)

span of its existence to date, La Fábrica has held two editions of the ambitious festival PhotoEspaña, started up the PhotoGalería, and, with the sponsorship of the Obra Social de la Caja Madrid, begun publishing a series of pocketbook monographs on Spanish photographers.

The 1980s were also decisive in the area of training. Cinema, Photography and Video departments were created in 1981 in the Fine Arts faculties in Madrid and Barcelona and subsequently at all other Spanish universities. At the same time, important private training centres were created, such as the Escuela de Fotografía Grisart (1985), the Escuela de Altos Estudios de la Imagen y el Diseño (1982), in Barcelona, the Visor Centre Fotogràfic, in Valencia (1982), and the Taller Fotográfico Spectrum (1977), in Zaragoza, which were successors to the Institut d'Estudis Fotogràfics de Barcelona (1972) and the former PhotoEscuela de Madrid (1974). Under the direction of Miquel Galmes, the Institut carries out an extraordinary

RAFAEL TROBAT. Solentiname, 1990. (Author's Collection.)

range of educational activities, as well as programming exhibitions and conferences and creating a magnificent photographic archive. Similarly, the EFTI school in Madrid (1988) does not restrict its activities to teaching, but has also set up one of the few permanent photography exhibition galleries in the city. Admirable work is also done in this area by a number of centres, including the Railowsky bookshop in Valencia and the Kowasa bookshop in Barcelona, which have created a new commercial formula in the tradition of historical galleries such as Tartessos, which have a regular programme of exhibitions and are making a considerable contribution to the development of an incipient trend to photograph collection. Lastly, important work in the area of recovery and study of Spain's photographic past was begun in the 1980s by pioneering authors such as Lee Fontanella, Marie-Loup Sougez, Joan Fontcuberta and Miguel Ángel Yáñez Polo, re-creating the history of Spanish photography, unknown until then. They were later joined by Bernardo

Riego, in Cantabria, Francisco Grabifosse, in Asturias, María Teresa Zubizarreta and Matilde Muro, in Extremadura, Fernández Rivero, in Málaga, María José Mulet, in the Balearic Islands, Jesús Rocandio, in La Rioja, Carlos Teixidor and Carmelo Vega, in the Canary Islands, Ana Gutiérrez, in Madrid, Enrique Acuña, Manuel Sendón, X. Luis Suárez and José Luis Cabo, in Galicia, Carlos Cánovas, in Pamplona, José Huguet, José Aleixandre and José Ramón Cáncer, in Valencia, and Ricardo González, in Valladolid.[161] Their work has been decisive in making various government organisations aware of the value of early photography as a true public heritage, including the collections of negatives in the archives of museums and cultural centres. Also worthy of note in this connection are the efforts at conservation and diffusion carried out by several regional centres, including the Filmoteca de Castilla y León, and by municipal archives, such as those of Gerona, Sevilla and Vitoria.

Towards the end of the 1980s, several of the currents that appeared in preceding years were consolidated, although a renewed eclecticism and the effects of the new experimental officialism have fostered a trend towards the mixing of techniques and styles, in line with the direction being taken by most contemporary art. Photography has gradually become more dependent on the circumstances of art and the conditions prevailing on the conventional market. The uncertainty seen in the new photography has much to do with the confusion and perplexity reigning on the market, which has given rise to a deliberate avoidance of any sort of dogma. Consequently, the diversification of styles in photography is now limitless, leading to an increasing fragmentation, as observed by experts in painting. Spanish photography of the present has therefore now embarked on multiple and undefinable meanders that make any effort at taxonomy pointless. However, in spite of this difficulty and the lack of sufficient critical distance, what we can say is that young Spanish photographers are following innumerable paths, from those who use photographic techniques and media only circumstantially, to those who accept the dignity of their medium and practise pure photography. The former continue to use every conceivable type of procedure for intervention and manipulation, from all varieties of photograms, to installations, painted photographs and photo-sculpture, by way of chemigrams, infograms, collage and other mixed techniques borrowed from painting, to the extent that they have made the camera a wholly unnecessary instrument. The artists working in this field include Tomi Ceballos,

CARLOS DE ANDRÉS. Squatters. From the Spanish Youth series. Madrid, 1988. (EFTI Collection.)

XURXO LOBATO. Cannibalistic Galicia. 1995 (original in colour). (Author's Collection.)

Mabel Palacín, Marc Viaplana, Antonio Bueno, Julio Álvarez Yagüe, Daniel Canogar, David Escudero, Paloma Navares, Jorge Galindo, Felicidad Moreno, Alberto García Sáenz, Eduardo Cortils, Pedro López-Cañas, Ceferino López, Iñigo Royo and Ramón David.

At a distance from this attitude of distrust for the very nature of the photographic language, there are a number of different currents, from the different types of reportage (Rick Dávila, Kim Manresa, Carlos de Andrés, Delmi Álvarez, Javier Bauluz, Gervasio Sánchez, José Antonio Carrera, Matías Costa, Txema Salvans Tino Soriano, Consuelo Bautista, Xabier Ribas), documentarism (Xurxo Lobato, Clemente Bernard, Manuel Sendón, Juan Manuel Díaz Burgos, Rafael Trobat, Marta Sentís, José Muñoz, Jorge Lens, Miguel Trillo), portraiture (Alberto García Alix, Rafael Vargas, Pablo Pérez Mínguez, Juan Ramón Yuste, Carles Fragas, Jorge Represa, Hernando Toro, David Nebreda, Sofía Moro), advertising and fashion photography (Oriola, Isabel Muñoz, Xavier Guardans, Javier Vallhonrat, Carlos Navarro, Eduardo Momeñe, Antoni Bernal, Joan Garrigós, J. Antonio Deorlegui, Fernando Manso), book illustration (Genín Andrada, Chema Conesa, Juan Manuel Navia), and a sort of magic and oneiric documentarism, derived from the current that arose in the 1980s (Juan Manuel Castro Prieto, Manuel Sonseca, Vari Caramés, Pilar Pequeño, Alejandro Sosa, Toni Gumella, Javier Campano, Baylón, Luis Asín). Worth mentioning in the area of conceptual photography is the work of Chema Madoz, who has created a personal world that is instantly recognisable from evocative visual inventions captured by the camera with no tricks or manipulations of any sort. For their part, some of the most emblematic members of the preceding generation continue to follow their own creative directions (Ferrán Freixa, Toni Catany, *Ouka Lele*, Cristina García Rodero), while others have adopted new techniques or themes (Manel Esclusa, Antonio Tabernero, Rafael Navarro, Fernando Herráez, Jorge Rueda) or recycle old craft techniques (Isabel Muñoz, Jordi Guillumet, Martí Llorens). One exceptional case is that of Alberto García Alix, who has been producing a fascinating chronicle of his times and himself via portraits of a segment of his generation, those who have been most ill-treated by fortune, weakness or neglect, individuals who are dignified by the wise, sincere and kind vision of this extraordinary photographer, whose work was shown in an memorable retrospective show at the Círculo de Bellas Artes in Madrid in 1998.

MIGUEL TRILLO. Leaving *El Gran Musical* at the *Consulado* discotheque.
Madrid, 1980. (EFTI Collection.)

RICK DAVILA. From the Slaves of Gran Sol series. 1995. (Author's Collection.)

VARI CARAMÉS. 'Un "cortao"'. *La Coruña, 1985.*

Lastly, the 1990s saw the first effects of the technological revolution beginning to make themselves felt, with the infinite potential for deconstruction and manipulation offered by the digital age, which seems to move photography even
farther away from the old ambition of its pioneers, who dreamed of using it to obtain a faithful record of reality. The newest, state-of-the-art computers have abrupt-
ly shattered all of the old technical conventions of visual representation. Some fear
and others hope that today's digital revolution might be more than mere technological change and become the serpent's egg of a new era in the history of art,
profoundly affecting the future of the analog audio-visual media, including the cinema, video, television and also photography. It is no coincidence that people are
now beginning to speak of the work of art in the era of digital representation, just
as Benjamín spoke in his time of the work of art in the era of technical reproducibility, and there is no shortage of prophets of an imminent cybernetic and decidedly post-photographic age. This has given rise to a certain techno-fetishism,
which has substituted the art-fetishism that so profoundly marked the work of a
great many young photographers after reality was declared to have been exhausted as a subject matter for photography on the eve of the 1970s. In effect, this

CIUCO GUTIÉRREZ. From the Interior Landscapes or the Colour of Memory *series. 1997 (original in colour).*

overwhelming development of technology is already playing a central role in the current debate on photography, now midway between reality and fiction. Digital procedures are already an important factor in the work of artists such as Juan Urríos, who manipulates images using a computer, superimposing close-ups of different faces to create new, non-existent ones. Photographers with long experience and recognised and respected creative capacity, such as Ciuco Gutiérrez, have begun using computers in their process of visual creation; Rosa Muñoz and Pablo Genovés are also working in this area, as a number of painters of the most recent generation have been doing for some years.

Spanish photography has recently been the subject of growing interest in other countries and many important exhibitions have been held (*Contemporary Spanish Photography*, University of New Mexico, 1987, *Photographic Creation in Spain*, Musée Cantini, Marseilles, 1988, *Four directions*, Centro de Arte Rein Sofía, 1991, *Spanish Vision*, Spanish Institute, New York, 1992, *Vanishing Spain*, International Photography Center, New York, 1991, *Open Spain*, Chicago-Madrid, 1993), showing, from different points of view, an ample panorama of contemporary trends in photography. At the same time, there is much interest in the study of photohistory and the work of the participants in the photographic renewal of the postwar years is being re-examined.[162] However, in spite of the undeniable vitality of Spanish photography and its growing national and international recognition, its commercial, editorial and exhibition structures remain unchanged. It is only thanks to efforts on the part of photographers themselves – many of whom have found it necessary to act simultaneously as critics, researchers and directors of exhibitions – along with the admirable dedication of publishers and a timid public and private sponsorship that photography has been able to begin, slowly, to establish itself as an element of the country's cultural habits.

NOTES

PART ONE

The Daguerreotype in Spain

1. *El Semanario Pintoresco Español, January 27 1839.*
   Marie-Loup Sougez and Lee Fontanella have made detailed studies of photography's beginnings in Spain in their works *Historia de la fotografía*, Madrid, Cátedra, 1981, and *La historia de la fotografía en España, desde sus orígenes hasta 1900*, Madrid, El Viso, 1981.

2. Published in *El Museo de las Familias*, vol. II, Barcelona, May-December 1839.
   Monláu himself proposed that the Academy acquire a daguerreotype camera brought by Ramón Alabern from Paris. The camera was acquired at a price of 1,946 silver reales.

3. The newspaper *El Constitucional* reported on November 11: "The Plaza de la Constitución was crowded with onlookers attracted by the novelty of the event and the elegant hats of the ladies who had been invited and the harmonious strains of the orchestra gave the rooftop surroundings a placid and picturesque air."

4. The article published in *El Corresponsal* the same day reads: "The subject chosen was a view of the Real Palacio. (...) Calculations were made most carefully and the plate was exposed for the space of 60 minutes. (...) In spite of all of the setbacks, the resulting picture is an amazing miniature with a delicate finish, reproducing every detail with the fidelity of which only nature itself is capable."

5. These events do not seem to have been imbued with same air of public entertainment as was the case in Barcelona on November 10, although Hysern claims that the Regent, Maria Cristina, was present. This seems highly unlikely, since there is no mention of her presence in the article published in *El Corresponsal*.

6. Recent research has uncovered the existence of other texts referring to the daguerreotype and dating from 1839, in the form of two appendices to Physics textbooks, published by Francisco Álvarez and Nicolas Arias.
   Kurtz, Gerardo, in *150 años de fotografía en la Biblioteca Nacional*, Madrid, El Viso, 1989.

7. The 28 March edition of the newspaper *El Diario Mercantil* reads: "We have had the pleasure of examining the results of these experiments and they reveal the impressive potential of this invention, which, although still in its infancy, is already capable of such enchantment, beauty and perfection."

8. Further information on the origins of photography in Valencia may be found in the essay by José Huguet in the joint work *Fotografía en la Comunidad Valenciana*, Barcelona, Lunwerg, 1992.

9. Reported by Miguel Ángel Yáñez Polo y Márquez de Castro in his paper presented to the 1st Congress on the History of Photography in Spain, held in Seville in May 1986.

The First Professionals

10. Juan Antonio Fernández traces the professional activities of Count Lippa and the Lorichon family in detail in his book *Historia de la fotografía en Malaga durante el siglo XIX*, Malaga, Miramar, 1994.

11. The papers presented at the Seville Congress mentioned above by Yañez Polo, Manuel Carrero, Alfredo Romero, Bernardo Riego, Ricardo González, Ignacio Pardo, Xosé Luis Cabo, María José Mulet Guillermo Merk and Joaquín Arazuri provide abundant details on

the activities of those groundbreaking daguerreotypists.

María Ribas's unpublished dissertation, *Los inicios de la fotografía en Barcelona (1839-1859)*, is particularly well documented and illustrative.

12. *El Fénix*, Valencia, November 3 1944. Quoted by José Huguet.

13. Newhall, Beaumont. *Historia de la fotografía. Desde sus orígenes hasta nuestros días*. Spanish edition by Gustavo Gili, 1983.

14. Between 1839 and 1841, the price of daguerreotype cameras dropped by one third. According to Gisèle Freund, two thousand cameras and five hundred thousand copper plates were sold in Paris in 1846. The daguerreotype's expansion in the United States was extremely rapid. In 1851, the two thousand daguerreotypists working in that country took three million photographs. Gisèle Freund. *La fotografía como documento social*, Gustavo Gili, Barcelona, 1976.

The Reproducible Image: Calotypes

15. In 1842, the Spanish press publicised the work *El Orbe Pintoresco y Daguerrotípico*, including 104 "very handsome plates engraved on steel", with accounts of voyages "by land and sea to the world's five continents" by Tissot and Chateaubriand.

16. *El Genio de la Libertad*. Palma de Mallorca, 26 April 1840. (Quoted by María José Mulet in her address to the 1st Spanish Photography Congress, Seville, 1986.)

17. Clifford, Charles, *A Photographic Scramble Through Spain*. Although undated, this pamphlet was most probably written in 1862.

18. Lacan, Ernest. *Esquisse Photographiques*, Paris, 1856.

19. Wheelhouse, C.G. Text accompanying the album *Photographic Sketches of the Mediterranean*.
R. Hershkowitz observes "How many photographers, beginning with Wheelhouse himself and finishing with Thomson, thirty years later, were taken for warlocks or spies by disconcerted and intransigent natives?" Robert Hershkowitz. *The British Photographers abroad. The First Thirty Years*, London, 1980.

20. Lacan, Ernest. Op. cit.

21. *Revue Photographique*, Paris, 5 July 1986.

22. Fontanella, Lee. "El calotipo en Sevilla", in *PhotoVisión*, no. 12, Madrid, 1985.

23. Huguet Chanzá, José. *Benito Montfort y Pascual Pérez Rodríguez, dos pioneros de la fotografía*, Valencia, 1990.

The Ascendancy of Photograpy

24. Mayer and Pierson. *La Photographie, histoire de son decouverte*, Paris, 1862.

25. Lacan, Ernest. Op cit.

26. Disdéri, André Adolphe. *Application de la Photographie à la reproduction des Oeuvres d'Art*, Paris, 1861.

27. Rouillé, André. *L'Empire de la Photographie, 1839-1870*, Le Sycomore, Paris, 1982.

28. Report by the Jury of the 1885 Universal Exposition in Paris. Quoted by André Rouillé. *La expansión de la fotografía (1851-1870)* in *Historia de la Fotografía* (ed. J.C. Lemagny and A. Rouillé), Spanish edition, Alcor, 1988.

29. Cánovas del Castillo, Antonio (*Káulak*). "El porvenir de la fotografía profesional", in *La fotografía moderna*, Madrid, 1912.

According to Rouillé, the business volume of Parisian photographers in 1868 was twenty times greater than in 1848. In 1868, Mayer and Pierson noted that "photography has now become a major industry". In 1863, Anthony and Co. were producing 3,600 celebrity portraits daily, prompting *Humphrey's Journal* to comment that "a revolution is taking place in the photographic business". André Rouillé, op. cit.

30. After opening his Surrey studio, Frith hired a large team of assistants. His company's photographs of Spain bear the stamp *Frith Series* or *Frith and Co.* used by Frith's successors after his death in 1898. However, this does not necessarily mean that they were taken after that date, since by then the company had accumulated an immense stock of images.

31. López Mondéjar, Publio. *Cien años de fotografía y ferrocarril*, Lunwerg Editores, 1988.

32. Especially noteworthy is the work of the Briton Charles Piazzi Smith and the Austrian Oscar Simony, who photographed the Canary Islands during the course of their visit there for the purpose of astronomical observation. Piazzi Smith published his book *Tenerife: An Astronomer's Experiment* in 1858, including 20 stereoscopic views of different parts of the island.

Two Foreigners in Isabella II's Court: Charles Clifford and J. Laurent

33. Herrero de Collantes writes "His artist's temperament and his rapport with any political force or effort in that arena stand out clearly in his photographs. Thus, Clifford was, if not the most efficient, at least the most truthful of those who were called upon to serve those ends of monarchic propaganda."
Herrero de Collantes, Ignacio. *Viajes oficiales por España de Isabel II*, Gráficas reunidas, Madrid, 1950.

While he was the most important, Clifford was not the only photographer who recorded Isabella II's royal visits. Others, such as the Asturian Alfredo Truán, also contributed to the graphic chronicle of those royal progresses. According to Collantes, Truán sold three collections of views of Asturias to the Palace for 2,650 silver reales.

34. Clifford, Charles. *A Photographic Scramble...* This work was sponsored by the King and Queen of Spain, the Emperor and Empress of France, the Emperor of Russia, the Queen of England and the Duke of Montpensier. These and other facts have led to speculation as to Clifford's status as royal photographer. Collantes, one of the most reliable sources on the photographer's relations with the Palace, writes "Within the bounds of his modest position in Spain, he was the first to rightly use the title "Photographer to Her Majesty." It is nevertheless significant that the photographer does not figure on any of the known lists of the Queen's entourage on her celebrated voyages, and is mentioned only once, in passing, in the chronicles of those voyages.

35. Andersen, Hans Christian. *Viaje por España*, Alianza Editorial, Madrid, 1988.

36. Further information on Clifford is found in the catalogue for the exhibition *Charles Clifford, fotógrafo de la España de Isabel II* (El Viso, Madrid, 1996), with texts by Lee Fontanella and Gerardo Kurtz. Kurtz gives a detailed account of the photographer's career, from his arrival in Madrid in 1850 until he began work on documenting Spain under Isabella II in photographs.
In addition, the Isabella II Canal published a magnificent edition of the album *Vistas de las obras del Canal de Isabel II, fotografiadas por Clifford*, with forewords by Juan Benet and Publio López Mondéjar (Madrid, 1988).

37. Dozens of photographers worked for Laurent's company and many of them subsequently went into business for themselves. Clifford was not the sole author of all of the photographs in his catalogue. Ricardo González mentions his arrival in Valladolid in 1854 accompanied by his partner Juan Pérez. González, Ricardo. *Luces de un siglo. Fotografías en Valladolid en el siglo XIX*, ed. Gonzalo Blanco, 1990.
On the subject of Laurent, in 1983 the Ministry of Culture published the catalogue *La documentación fotográfica de la Dirección General de Bellas Artes. J. Laurent-I*, with texts by Ana M.V. Gutiérrez and Carlos Teixidor.

Democratisation of the Portrait

38. Francastel, Galienne and Pierre. *El retrato*, Cátedra, Madrid, 1978.

39. In 1897, two Catalan engineers, Pedro Cabanach and Rafael Calvet, invented an automatic tintype machine. Such machines were installed in parks and other public places and produced portraits for 10 centimos, and for a further 10 centimos provided the corresponding brass frame.
La fotografía práctica, no. 44, Barcelona, February 1897.

40. Lacan, Ernest. Op. cit.

41. Flores, Antonio. *La sociedad de 1850*, Madrid, 1868 (from his book *Ayer y Hoy*).

42. Mesonero Romanos, Ramón de. *El antiguo Madrid*, Madrid, 1861.

43. Ramón y Cajal, Santiago. *Mi infancia y juventud*, Espasa-Calpe, Madrid, 1976 edition.

The Spread of Photography

44. Already in 1859, the Count of Benazuza made reference to the work of Reigón, Corro and other painters, who had "contributed on countless occasions to enhancing and increasing the value of photographic proofs with their beautiful miniatures".
Conde de Benazuza. "Noticias sobre la historia de la fotografía", in *La América*, 8 October 1859.

45. Ramón y Cajal, Santiago. Op. cit.

46. This may be deduced from notes made on the back of many images – Madrazo's hands photographed for a portrait of Benito Murillo, for example – or from examination of a portrait of Isabella II that is practically identical to drawings by Madrazo himself. Joaquín de la Puente writes "I would not be at all surprised if one day it were to be proved that [Madrazo] made use of the sizable body of photographic images available and even of photographs taken purposely and planned and composed by him for each particular subject to be portrayed."
De la Puente, Joaquín. *Federico de Madrazo por entre su estirpe y su tiempo*, in the catalogue *Los Madrazo, una familia de artistas*, Madrid, 1985.

The Proliferation of Studios

47. Cánovas del Castillo, Antonio (*Káulak*). "De cómo se aprendía a ser fotógrafo hasta hoy", in the magazine *La Fotografía*, 1904.

48. Figures given in the *Anuario Martí*, 1862, the *Bailly-Baillière* yearbook, 1898, and the collection of the magazine *La Fotografía*.

49. Cánovas del Castillo, Antonio (*Káulak*). "Estado presente de la profesión fotográfico". Article published in the magazine *La Fotografía* and reprinted in the book *La fotografía moderna*, Madrid, 1912.

Uses of Photography

50. For further reading on this subject, see Gerardo Kurtz's well-documented work "Sobre

el retrato fotográfico y el proyecto fotográfico-policial de Julián de Zagasti", in *Archivos de la Fotografía*, no. 1, summer 1995.

Amateur Photography

51. Notes from the Marquess of Valmar to Álvarez Sereix, transcribed by Marie-Loup Sougez in *Historia de la Fotografía* (2nd edition), Cátedra, Madrid, 1985.

52. Ramón y Cajal, op. cit. Texts such as these have led some to affirm that Ramón y Cajal was the inventor of photographic emulsions and even colour photography systems. The simple truth is that he was an attentive and well-informed amateur who was fascinated as a young man by the development of the exposed image upon treatment with pyrogallic acid.

Journalistic Photography

53. Lacan, Ernest, in *La Lumière*, no. 15, 21 July 1856.

54. Roman Gubern writes "We might say that photography tended to take on the traditional function of landscape painting, while, paradoxically, drawing generally made up for the infant photography's momentary inability in the area of action reporting."
Gubern, Roman. *Mensajes icónicos en la cultura de masas*, Lumen, Barcelona, 1974.

55. Heribert Mariezcurrena, Joan Serra, Miguel Joaritzi and Josep Thomas provided *La Ilustración* with the techniques used by that magazine to publish the Spanish press's first photocomposition in 1881. A year later, *La Ilustración* published the first lined photoengraving, by means of a technique different from the one used by Meisenbach that same year in Germany.
Fabre, Jaume, in the catalogue for the exhibition *Història del fotoperiodisme a Catalunya*, Barcelona, 1990.

56. An indispensable reference work on the history of photomechanical reproduction in Spain is Marie-Loup Sougez's documented essay "Imagen fotográfica en el medio impreso", included in the catalogue of the exhibition *150 años de fotografía en la Biblioteca Nacional*, Madrid, 1989.

PART TWO

Spain in 1900

57. Tuñón de Lara, Manuel. *La España del siglo xx* (Vol. 1), Laia, Barcelona, 1974.

58. Chamberlain, John. *El atraso de España*, Valencia, undated (quoted by Antonio Flores in *La España del siglo xx*, Ed. Cuadernos para el Diálogo, Madrid, 1972).

59. Between 1916 and 1921, 17,082 Spanish conscripts and 2,395 professional soldiers were killed in Morocco, and Spain spent the enormous sum of 82.5 million pesetas on the war in 1912 alone.
Bachoud, Andrée. *Los españoles ante las campañas de Marruecos*, Espasa-Universidad, Madrid, 1988.

Let Others Invent!

60. The exaggerated protectionist attitude on the part of professional photographers is particularly evident in several of the Assembly's conclusions, which went so far as to sanction a petition to the authorities for imposition of a fee for amateurs "for permission to take photographs out of doors". Conclusions of the National Assembly of Professional Photographers, Valencia, 1908.

61. *La Fotografía*, March 1902.

62. The Barcelona company Riba based its advertising on its status as importer of photographic lenses and devices "made by the leading

foreign companies" and as exclusive agent for Ilford, Goerz, Gaumont and Taylor and Taylor. Riba published a specialist newsletter, which it sent free of charge to its customers.

63. "A Success Story of Spanish Industry. Photographic Plate Factory in Madrid". Report published in the magazine *Mundo Gráfico*, 16 August 1922.

64. José Echegaray had dealt with the subject of colour photography two years before Ramón y Cajal, although in less detail, in his work *Vulgarizacion científica*, published by R. Gutiérrez Jiménez, Madrid, 1910.

Photographic Circles

65. "La Sociedad Fotográfica de Madrid", published in *La Fotografía*, January 1901.

66. As earlier as 1896, a proposal for the creation of a national photographic society had been published in the magazine *La Fotografía*. This longstanding ambition was finally realised in 1891, with offices in a building on Plaza Cataluña, but the only result of its ephemeral existence was a photographic competition advertised in the magazine *Las novedades fotográficas*, Bilbao, September 1891.

67. For further information on this subject see Horacio Fernández's work "Fotografía en revistas y revistas de fotografía" in the catalogue for the exhibition *Arte moderno y revistas españolas, 1898-1936*, Madrid, 1996.

Denial of Reality – Pictorialist Photography

68. A magazine of the time reports: "Models, costumes, carpets, furniture and decorations, everything that the painter transfers without expense from his imagination to the canvas, must be gathered physically by the photographer and arranged to produce the desired effect."

"La fotografía artística", unsigned article published in the magazine *Hojas selectas*, Madrid-Barcelona, 1907.

69. Melon, Marc. "Más allá de lo real: la fotografía artística", in *Historia de la Fotografía*, ed. Jean-Claude Lemagny and André Rouillé, Alcor, Barcelona, 1988.

70. Strand, Paul. "Artistic Motivation in Photography", published in *The British Journal Photography*, 1923. (Included in Joan Fontcuberta's book, *Estética Fotográfica, selección de textos*, Barcelona, 1984).
Miguel Huertas had expressed a similar opinion in 1922. "To find a way of making photography appear to be something else is to avoid and scorn it." *Criterium*, April 1922.

71. King, Carl, S. *The Photographic Impressionists in Spain*, The Edwin Mellen Press, 1989.
Coloma Martín writes "What was practised was neither pictorialism nor its older opposite, but rather the premises on which pictorialism was based. In other words there was a movement contrary to the use of fuzziness or blurring of the image, but no opposition to the theatrical and literal approach to the theme." Coloma Martín, Isidoro, *La forma fotográfica*, Universidad de Málaga, 1986.

72. Escobar, Luis, Marquis of Valdeiglesias. *Tres fiestas galantes* with photographs by Christian Franzen and Antonio Cánovas (*Káulak*). Limited edition with photogravures by Dujardin, Madrid, 1905.

73. Jaime Brihuega has analysed the subjects of the paintings shown at the National Painting Exhibitions between 1900 and 1936. "Anecdotal-*costumbrista*" scenes with a rural and arcadian slant, exotic and religious subjects with oriental and biblical settings and symbolic scenes with a "purely ornamentalist and decorative" approach were particularly abundant.

Brihuega, Jaime. *Las vanguardias artísticas en España, 1900-1936*, Istmo, Madrid, 1981.

Artists, Patriots and Other Excesses

74. Ortiz Echagüe always insisted on the documentary nature of his work and on his rejection of the techniques used to imitate paintings. "I deplore absolutely any type of process tending to imitate painting and I do not wish to be classified among those known in the English-speaking world as pictorialists."
Quoted in *José Ortíz Echagüe, sus fotografías*, Incafo, Madrid, 1978.

75. At the 7th Zaragoza Salon in 1931, 218 bromide prints were shown, in comparison with two gum bichromates, 7 *fressons*, 27 bromoils, 5 carbon transfers and 5 resinotypes. Figures published in *El Progreso Fotográfico* (quoted by C.S. King, op. cit.).

76. Bozal, Victoriano. *Historia del arte en España* (vol. II), Istmo, Madrid, 1975.

77. Gerardo Vielba writes "For example, for the images of the Castilian shepherd of Calatañazor, since a genuine article of the appropriate costume could not be found, he had to content himself with finding an original length of the material and the last living tailor who had cut and sewn such peculiar capes, and having him make one up expressly for the shoot."
Vielba, Gerardo. "Personalidad de un fotógrafo singular", included in the monograph *José Ortiz Echagüe, sus fotografías*, Incafo, Madrid, 1978.

78. Carlos Cánovas writes "In Goicoechea there is no *mise en scène*, none of the vulgar and at times horrendous stagings so common at the time. (...) In spite of Goicoechea's pictorialist manipulations, the underlying substance is always clearly documentary."

Cánovas, Carlos. *Fotógrafos históricos de Navarra*, Pamplona, July 1986.

79. Mir Escudé wrote on the subject of *Municipal Guard* "An aptly chosen model, a fine example of the classical type of our municipal guards, in whose visage we see the combination of goodness and roughness that are characteristic traits of the Catalan race."
Mir Escudé, Andreu. "L'Obra de Dr. Pla Janini", in *Art de la Llum*, October 1934.

The Decline of Portraiture

80. Cánovas del Castillo, Antonio (*Káulak*). *La fotografía moderna*, Madrid, 1912.

81. Figures published in the magazine *La Fotografía* (May 1900) and in various *Bailly-Baillière* yearbooks.

82. Barceló, Pau. "Mig segle enrera", included in the catalogue for the exhibition *Masana, Fotògraf*, compiled by Miguel Galmes, Barcelona, 1984.

83. Photographers' wives and daughters were invariably retouchers, tinters and clerks. This was the case with the wives of Luis Escobar and José Oliván, the wives and daughters of Alfonso Sánchez García, and the daughters of Francisco Perea and Francisco Garay. In some instances they took over the business themselves, as did the widows of Clifford, Oliván and Prospéri, who took charge of the family studios on the death of their husbands.

Popular Photography

84. Sontag, Susan. *Sobre la fotografía*, Edhasa, Barcelona (1981 edition).

85. Maside, Carlos. "En torno a la fotografía popular", in the magazine *Índice*, Madrid, 30 March 1954.

86. Weston, Edward. "Seeing Photographically", in *The Complete Photographer*, no. 49, 1943. (Included in the anthology Estética Fotográfica, ed. Joan Fontcuberta, Blume, 1984).

87. A comprehensive anthology of Luis Escobar's photographs was published in the book *Retratos de la Vida* (1980), along with those of other popular photographers such as Benito Pons, Justo Hortelano and Manuel Soler. The most recent edition of this book (Lunwerg, 1989) also includes photographs by Julián Collado.

88. There have been attempts in some areas to transform the affliction of death into an act of celebration. Margaret Hooks has analysed this subject lucidly in her essay "Memories of Innocence", published in the magazine *Luna Córnea*, no. 9, Mexico City, 1996.

89. In some cases, the moral pretext for the nude was sought in subjects of biblical or allegorical inspiration. Some photographers used clearly exotic and anachronistic themes (*The Sultan's Favourite*, by Antonio Prats, or *The Slave*, by Amador) that are highly reminiscent of similar compositions by second-rate painters such as Jiménez Aranda, Sáenz Martínez and Enrique Simonet.
The subject of pictorialism is dealt with in greater depth in *Las Fuentes de la Memoria (II)*, Lunwerg, Barcelona-Madrid, 1992.

Fascicles and Postcards

90. According to Káulak himself, he sold the considerable number of one hundred and eighty thousand collection in this series in under three years. From *¡Quién supiera escribir!*, a short philosophical poem by Ramón de Campoamor, illustrated with photographs by Antonio Cánovas. Paris, 1905.

91. A new edition of Hielscher's book was recently published, edited by Agustín Núñez, Edilux, Granada., 1991.

92. Langdon Coburn, Alvin. *An Autobiography*, ed. Helmut and Allison Gersheim, New York, 1978.

The Eyes of History

93. Jaume Fabre edited a catalogue on the subject of Catalan graphic journalism for the exhibition *Història del fotoperiodisme a Catalunya*, Barcelona, March-April 1990.
In addition, between 1989 and 1993 Josep Cruañas published a well-documented section in the magazine *Capçalera* on Catalan press photographers.

94. On the occasion of the king's wedding, in May 1906, the daily newspaper *ABC* offered the sum of 25 pesetas for each photograph of the event that it published. As a result, hundreds of aspiring reporters took to the streets to photograph the royal procession, thus affording the opportunity for the spectacular images of the assassination attempt taken by amateurs, including Mesonero Romanos, Pérez Pech and Caterina Lefevre. The impact produced by these photographs obliged the newspaper to print several editions of its June 1 issue with the famous image of the assassination attempt taken by Eugenio Mesonero Romanos.

95. Díaz Casariego commented "At the time of the Anwal massacre, the High Commissioner gave orders that journalists were not to witness operations from close up. In order to ensure that no trickster would be able to evade his prohibition, General Berenguer made all of the journalist board a ship and had it put out to sea."
Díaz Casariego, José. Interview published in *La Esfera*, Madrid, 10 April 1926.

96. Ayala, Francisco. *Recuerdos y Olvidos (Vol. 1)*, Alianza, Madrid, 1984.

97. J.M. Sánchez Vigil and M. Durán have published a well documented book on the his-

tory of photography of bullfighting, *Historia de la fotografía taurina* (Espasa Calpe, Madrid, 1991). The origin and development of sports photography is dealt with in my book *Visiones del deporte, 1860-1939* (Lunwerg, Madrid, 1991).

98. Pérez, Darío. "Cosas del oficio: el repórter fotógrafo", in *La Libertad*, Madrid, April 1907.

99. At the time, Germany was taking the lead in the field of graphic publishing. Publications such as *Arbeiter Illustrierte Zeitung* (AIZ), *Münchner Illustrierte Zeitung* (MIZ) and *Berliner Illustrierte Zeitung* (BIZ) all achieved press runs of over one million copies. It is no coincidence that the great reporters of the time were either German or worked for German magazines. Outstanding among them were Erich Salomon, André Kértesz, Robert Capa, Alfred Eisentstaedt, Felix H. Man, Martin Munkacsi, the Gidal brothers and László Moholy-Nagy. The rise of Nazism brought this vigorous photographic activity to a halt and caused most of these reporters to leave the country and go to work for the French and American press.

A Certain Avant-garde

100. Ehrenburg, Ilya. *España, república de trabajadores*, 1932, reprinted by Júcar, Madrid, 1976, and Crítica, Barcelona, 1976.

101. Catalá Pic, Pere. "La evolución fotográfica" in *Revista Ford*, Barcelona, June 1932. Catalá Pic was also the author of other theoretical and informative texts, such as "La revolución fotográfica moderna", in the magazine *Mirador*, 22 December 1932.

102. Dalí, Salvador. "La fotografía, pura creación del espíritu", in *L'Amic de les Arts*, Sitges, 30 September 1927.

103. An American magazine from 1920 reads "Art is the new weapon in domestic and international competition and America leads the world in the application of art to business." *Printer's Ink*, 28 April 1920, quoted by Christoper Phillips in "Los Estados Unidos: la sociedad americana", in *Historia de la fotografía*, ed. André Rouillé and Jean-Claude Lemagny, Spanish edition, 1988.

104. Lekuona's photographic work has been compiled, analysed and published by Adelina Moya in the catalogue for the exhibition *Nicolás de Lekuona. Obra fotográfica*, Bilbao, 1982.

105. Renau wrote "The objective and the ultimate purpose of Spanish art go beyond [these] concessions to a standard aesthetic. In the new Spain, the poster will win back its historical heritage and develop traditional values along the lines of the new realism, and will attain the status of indisputable artistic creation, with the dignity implied by the total fulfilment of a socially and historically necessary mission."
Renau, Josep. *Función social del cartel publicitario*, Valencia, 1937.

106. Joan Fontcuberta writes "Tradition and avant-garde, classicism and innovation appeared, as a rule, as attributes whose confrontation was not experienced as tension, but rather as natural manifestations in one and the same creative spirit."
Joan Fontcubera. "Spanish Photographers: memory and avant-garde", in the catalogue *Idas and Chaos*, Madrid, 1985.

The Disasters of War

107. Julio Mayo stated "Our political struggle was more powerful than our struggles with the camera. When the misnamed Spanish Civil War broke out on 18 July, the fighting took two forms: one with the camera, the other

with rifles, mortars and machine-guns." Statements made to John Mraz in the weekly supplement of *La Jornada*, Mexico City, 17 December 1989.

108. Renau, Josep. "Contestación a Ramón Gaya", in *Hora de España*, Valencia, February 1937.

109. Some of the photographs signed by Capa were taken by David Seymour or Gerda Taro, a circumstance that has made their correct attribution more difficult. In this connection, Carlos Serrano's revealing study is indispensable for its examination of the close personal and professional ties between the three photographers prior to Gerda Taro's tragic death on 26 July 1937.
Serrano, Carlos. Robert Capa. *Cuadernos de guerra en España (1936-1939)*, Diputación Provincial de Valencia, 1987.

110. A selection of Namuth and Reisner's photographs, along with Namuth's war diary, has been published in the book *Spanisches Tagebuch 1936*, Berlin, 1986.

111. Walter Reuter told me that from October 1936 onward he obtained photographic paper form Robert Capa, who brought it from Paris. (From a letter dated October 1991.) Julio Mayo recalled: "The material that we used during the war was Agfa paper at first, until it ran out. After that we used Soviet paper, which was of terrible quality, since the heat raised blisters on it and the emulsion separated from the backing." (From a letter dated 7 February 1990.)

112. The attribution of a number of photographs to Centelles is doubtful, since his archives may contain negatives by other photographers, such as Torrents and *Gonzanhi*. Some of these images were distributed and signed by those photographers in the press of the time. These and other facts make this subject a delicate one and make any research on the subject difficult, given the dispersal of archives and the fact that most of the people involved are no longer alive.

113. An excellent monograph has been published on Centelles, edited by Pere Formiguera, with texts by Albert Balcells, Cornell Capa, Joan Fontcuberta and Jerald Green. Catalogue of the exhibition *Agustí Centelles, fotoperiodista*, Fundació Caixa de Catalunya, Barcelona, 1998.

PART THREE

The Autarchic Regime in Spain

115. Tubáu, Miguel. In Arte Fotográfico, Madrid, May 1962.

116. Pla Janini wrote in 1940 "Pigmentation techniques are the only means for revealing the photographer's artistic taste and skill (...) Only [transfer] provides the ability to move the image onto the type of paper used by draftsmen and etchers that removes the unpleasant aspects of the photograph and give it the similitude of a good drawing or etching."
Pla Janini, Joaquín. *La intervención en fotografía de arte* (unpublished manuscript from 1939-1940), printed in PhotoVision, no. 9, October-December 1983.

117. Quoted by Manuel Sendón and X. Luis Suárez Canal in the catalogue of the exhibition *En Galiza nos 50. As agrupacions fotográficas*, Concello de Vigo, 1990.

118. The nude was persecuted so obstinately during the National Catholic apotheosis that Ribas Prous has stated recently that this genre became, for the members of his generation, a form of disobedience to the dictatorship's moral and cultural oppression. As

late as 1973, Juan Domingo Bisbal warned in the June issue of Arte Fotográfico "We must be careful with nudes in photography, and make sure that they always abide by the strictest moral tenets."

Industry and Autarchy

119. Gerardo Acereda states "Goods were frequently exchanged for the cameras brought in by ships' crew members. In Barcelona, the prostitutes who plied their trade with this type of customer would offer their services in exchange for cameras that they would later sell to dealers in the trade."
Acereda Valdés, Gerardo. From correspondence with the author, 29 January 1994.

120. According to Acereda Valdés, approximately twelve million of the popular *Werlisas* were manufactured in Certex's thirty-year existence.
Acereda Valdés, Gerardo. "Cámaras fotográficas españolas", in *FV*, no. 64, Madrid, 1993.
The Spanish photographic market was so unsteady in the postwar years that some craftsmen began producing their own cameras to satisfy the existing demand. One of these was Hipólito Gil, from Seville, who began marketing his *Ultra* camera in 1944, a simple model of which he sold 2,800 in Spain. And the enterprising manufacturer could have sold even more if rolls of the 127 film that his camera used had been more easily available.
Gil Chaparro, Francisco. *El privilegio de la creación. Hipólito Gil Rodríguez, mechanic, photographer and inventor*, Seville, 1999.

121. Figures published by the magazine *Cambio-16* in its 13 July 1981 issue.

122. Manuel López Rodríguez asked in 1985 "Where does one learn photography in Spain? Where does one register to study press photography, or industrial, fashion or advertising photography? To date, the only reply is silence on the part of the authorities."
López Rodríguez, Manuel. "La fotografía, una realidad desenfocada", in *Foto Profesional*, no. 34, Madrid, October 1985.

Officialist Photography

123. Carlos Cánovas writes "Any purpose not strictly limited to photography, and one might say any purpose not strictly limited to technical considerations, was prohibited. Photographs of nudes or social denunciation could cause problems for these entities."
Cánovas, Carlos. "Apuntes para una historia de la fotografía en Navarra", in *Panorama*, Pamplona, 1992.

124. *Afal* also promoted Spanish exhibitions of the work of E. Weston, Cartier-Bresson, the Paris *30 × 40* group, E. Steichen and Otto Steiner, to whom the newsletter dedicated a special issue in 1961, ten years after it had first presented his *subjective photography*, which had so greatly influenced the artistic photography of the time.

125. Miserachs wrote in 1965 "The lack of any market for so many years reduced to a state of absolute amateurism anyone who, being interested in photography as a source of personal aesthetic satisfaction, had competitions as the only forum for their experiments and the only reward for their successes. This led to the proliferation of a brand of photography whose highest aspiration was to be of "competition quality", with a profoundly pictorialist style, and that rapidly acquired its own set of rules, standards and fixed values to which an image had to conform in order to have a chance at winning a prize."
Miserachs, Xavier. "El trofeo Luis Navarro", in *Imagen y Sonido*, no. 13, Barcelona, January 1965.

126. «"Artistic" photography arrives at the ridiculous by way of the pretentious. The term "art", having been applied so gratuitously, has lost all meaning in the context of photography."
Maspons, Oriol. "Salonismo" in *Arte Fotográfico*, no. 61, January 1957.

127. From 1970 onwards, the Negtor Prize – the most prestigious commercial competition – began admitting submissions from the more progressive sectors. In 1974, the prize went to a photomontage by J.M. Oriola, and the work of other photographers working in a styles closer to the more avant-garde aesthetics of the time, such as Elias Dolcet, Saturnino Espín, José A. Marín Chacón, Salvador Obiols and Gonzalo Vinagre, were also awarded prizes. For its part, the Egara Trophy for 1973 went to Morgan, a young photographer tending to conceptualism and abstraction.

On the Eve of Reality

128. Cirici Pellicer, Alejandro. From a lecture given in April 1958 and published in the *Afal* newsletter, no. 25, July-August 1960.
Brassaï had already observed in 1932 "Those who safeguarded the purity of photography in their work were the photographers with no artistic pretensions. They were the ones who first questioned the all-powerful nature of art, who usurped the exclusive right to all of the dominions of reality."
Brassaï. "Images Latentes", in *L'intransigeant*, Paris, 15 November 1932.

129. Muñoz Molina, Antonio. Printed in Ricardo Marín's book *Sostener la mirada*, Junta de Andalucía, Granada, 1993.

130. In fact, Smith was aware of the importance of his report from the moment that Life magazine gave him the assignment. He wrote to Carmen Smith Wood on 10 March 1950 "I am now working on one of the most important assignments of my life. I am going to live in a Spanish village and work in the midst of the poverty and fear of Franco's Spain. I expect it to be the strongest and most moving photo-essay of my life." Letter transcribed in Jim Hughes's book W. *Eugene Smith, Shadow and Substance (The Life and Work of an American Photographer)*, 1989.

The Last Portraitists

131. Although the penury of the trade was comparable only to the penury of the times themselves, the reality of those years of punishment could not be fully understood without those itinerant photographers, without their anonymous, modest and unsung work. Julio Llamazares wrote "The photographer would appear at the school one morning with his case on his shoulder and carrying his camera and tripod in his hand. He would set up the tripod in the middle of the classroom, and one by one we would sit behind the teacher's desk, on which we had placed a notebook, a pen, and the globe that was kept in cupboard. For a backdrop, there as a folded sheet and the map that I had helped the photographer hang from the top of the blackboard."
Llamazares, Julio. *Escenas de cine mudo*, Seix-Barral, Barcelona, 1944.

132. Not everyone accepted this photographer's "resurrection". From the pages of El Alcázar: "One cannot forget. A photographer, who had portrayed royalty and great figures of our society, thought it fitting to collaborate with the red press. (...) We find it somewhat grating that this photographer should advertise his name on one of the city's central streets. Let him work, but in silence, because one should not provoke those who have a memory." "Cuidado con la memoria", anonymous article published in El Alcázar, Madrid, 30 July 1942.

133. Julio Aumente wrote in 1962 "The practice of photography in Spain is influenced not only by illicit competition from a large number of unqualified practitioners, but also by competition between professionals themselves, who are mired in an industrial smallholding as is the case with any underdeveloped profession."

Aumente, Julio. In *Boletín Nacional de Artes gráficas*, no. 6, Madrid, November-December 1962.

134. Christian Caujolle writes "This absolute power on the part of the photographer who uses close-ups in excess to emphasise invisible details or stagings with symbolical connotations can also have an irritating effect. (...) It is clear that the most effective images are those that captivate us before we are able to decipher their fabrication and that success is so frequent that certain, more bombastic images can end up being disagreeable."

Caujolle, Christian. "De la realidad del retrato", in the catalogue of the exhibition *Alberto Schommer. Retratos, 1969-1989*, Lunwerg, Barcelona-Madrid, 1989.

The Law of Silence

135. Juan José Pradera wrote in 1941 "With the Press Act, the press, with the necessary purges, was converted into an organ of overall interests, into a press that served, as a soldier, the movement that saved Spain with its military intervention."

Quoted by Gonzalo Dueñas in *La Ley de Prensa de Manuel Fraga*, Ruedo Ibérico, Paris, 1969.

136. The photographer José Núñez Larraz wrote "I had just returned from exile and Juan Aparicio, who was Director-General of the Press at the time, called me. I arrived at his office and he did not even let me sit down. He asked for my (press) card, looked at it, tore it up, threw it in the waste-paper basket

and told me that there was no place for me in Franco's Spain."

Núñez Larraz, José. *Seis décadas de fotografía*, Junta de Castilla y León, Salamanca, 1993.

137. Fabre, Jaume. *Història del fotoperiodisme a Catalunya*, Col.legi de Periodistes de Catalunya, 1990, and Cruañas i Tor, Josep, from various articles published in the magazine *Capçalera*, 1989-1991.

138. Xavier Miserachs writes "Our arrival on the market coincided with the incipient development advocated by Franco's technocrat ministers. We had enough work to make a living and we could be intellectually and materially independent, but we had to be jacks of all trades."

Miserachs Ribalta, Xavier. Op. cit.

139. López Rodríguez, Manuel. "Fotógrafos, ergo periodistas", in *Nueva Lente*, no. 107-108, July-August 1981.

"In respect of photography, the efforts of *El País* have been a total failure", writes Juan Luis Cebrián in *La prensa y la calle*, Nuestra Cultura, Madrid, 1980.

140. A large number of agencies were formed during that period but very few survived for any appreciable length of time. Worth mentioning were Blasón, Delta Press, Pull and Seite Press. Cosmo Press, founded by César Lucas and Setimio Garritano in 1965, was of a somewhat different nature. Cover was distinguished by the creation of a strong commercial structure, a fact that has allowed it to look forward to the future with a certain degree of optimism.

The Thaw

141. According to Salustiano del Campo, at least 3,360,000 Spanish workers were living outside Spain in 1970.

Del Campo, Salustiano. *Análisis de la población española*, Guadiana, Madrid, 1972.

142. Goytisolo, Juan. *El furgón de cola*, Seix-Barral, Barcelona, 1976.

143. Artero, José María. "Nuestra postura", in the *Afal* newsletter, no. 4, Almería, July 1958.
Brassaï wrote in 1932 "The rivals are not painting and photography, but rather photographic painting and pictorial photography. Let them devour each other, let them kill each other off and disappear for once and for all!" From "Images latentes", *L'Intransigeant*, Paris, 15 November 1932.

144. Xavier Miserachs writes "This exhibition had an enormous impact on me. What I had suspected to exist was right there before my eyes. That was what photography was for. The catalogue is still one of my bibles." Miserachs, Xavier. Op. cit.

145. Conde Vélez, Luis. "Lo nuevo en fotografía", in *Arte Fotográfico*, Madrid, February 1953.

146. Juanes, Gonzalo. "Cómo hago mis fotografías", in *Arte Fotográfico*, no. 66, Madrid, June 1957.

Documentary Renewal in the 1960s

147. Miserachs has recently stated "The 'art' in photography was its [the Agrupación Fotográfica de Cataluña's] exclusive preserve and our initial suspicion and later confirmation that there were other, more universal, not to mention more useful, ways of integrating photography into the world of cultural created extreme unease. In fact, the use of the term Modern Photography was a euphemistic attempt at accommodating the same 'artistic photography', but with a bit more formal daring, within the status quo. Of course, this was not the case at all and so in the end we abandoned the photographic associations."
Miserachs, Xavier. Correspondence with the author, 1995.

148. Thevenez wrote in 1956 "A minority group has taken its first step and broken with its sclerotic past, although there is still no real concern for man, showing the more profound aspects of Spain. A certain degree of optimism now follows upon the years when Spanish photography caused us consternation."
Thevenez, André, in *Photo-Revue*, Paris, November 1956.

149. Compare the presence of photographers from the Barcelona group with the total absence of any from the Madrid Group. In fact, in the retrospective exhibition of the *Afal* group, only Cualladó and Paco Gómez were included in the selection of photographers, along with Miserachs, Masats, Maspons, Ontañón, Terré and Pérez Siquier.

150. Carlos Cánovas writes "These societies had taken a greater or lesser dose of realism and adjusted it to the laws of salons-competitions, utilised a few informalist precepts whose origin they were absolutely ignorant of, and zealously protected the same technical suppositions as always."
Cánovas, Carlos. "Entre dos rupturas", in the catalogue for the exhibition *Tiempo de silencio*, Barcelona, 1992.

The Dawning of the Future

151. Bozal, Valeriano. *Arte del siglo XX en España* (vol. II), Espasa-Calpe, Madrid, 1995.

152. Mira, Enric. "La ubicuidad de *Nueva Lente* en la diversidad estética de la década de los setenta", in the records of the seminar on *Nueva Lente*, Madrid, October 1993.

153. Mira, Enric. Op. cit.
Pere Formiguera, one of the most representative members of the *Nueva Lente* generation – known, with a total lack of historical rigour, as the *Fifth Generation* – honestly admitted

this suspicious amnesia. "We looked back in anger without bothering to separate the wheat from the chaff. (...) I still wonder what one avant-garde was doing rejecting the other. What we were rejecting, they (the members of *Afal* or the Madrid school) had already rejected, what we defended, they had already defended, and what we criticised, they had already deplored ad nauseam."
Formiguera, Pere. "De la quinta a la cuarta, con un abrazo a destiempo", in the catalogue for the exhibition *Fotógrafos de la escuela de Madrid*, Madrid, 1998.

154. During that period a dozen photographic galleries were founded that eventually became academies and exhibition rooms. Of these, Forum, in Tarragona, Spectrum, in Zaragoza and Visor, in Valencia have survived, and have now been joined by the bookshops Railowsky, in Valencia, Kowasa, in Barcelona, and Babel in Madrid, all of which have regular exhibition programmes.

Latest Trends: Between Reality and Fiction

155. Eduardo Subirats writes "A new generation was on the threshold of political power. They were young. They were leftist. They believed in their firm resolve to reform. They distrusted Spanish history. Deep down, they distrusted everything Spanish. If a town planning issue had to be dealt with, they would call in an American specialist. If there was some new concept in the field of the media or intellectual pursuits, they would turn to the most banal but latest French model. If they had to take a decision on culture or art, they would opt for an international concept or simply borrow something from the avant-garde."
Subirats, Eduardo. *Después de la lluvia (sobre la ambigua modernidad española)*, Temas de Hoy, Madrid, 1994.

156. Subirats, Eduardo. op. cit.

157. Eco, Umberto. "Lo posmoderno, la ironía, lo ameno", in *Apostillas a El nombre de la rosa*, Lumen, Barcelona, 1994.

158. Formiguera, Pere. In the *Everfoto-5* yearbook, Everest, León, 1980.

159. Pérez Mínguez wrote, in 1974, "These photographers invent an endless array of tricks to ensure their understandable, and, in their view, thoroughly deserved, promotion in the world of culture. For this purpose, on occasion, they paint, cut, transfer and manipulate their images to make them more appealing. It would appear that more processed 'things' guarantee, in themselves, originality and exclusivity (i.e. inaccessibility), just like the old pictorialists. (...) It is a shame that so much effort should come to so little in the end."
Pérez Mínguez, Pablo. "La fotografía... ¿antiarte?", in *Nueva Lente*, no. 25, March 1974.

160. Although many of these events are no longer held, worth mentioning is the creation of a number of new photography centres, such as the PhotoMuseum in Zarautz, the Centro Andaluz de Fotografía, in Almería, the Centro de Fotografía Isla de Tenerife, and the Photography departments at the universities of Cantabria and Salamanca. Most of them also carry out important publishing work. Worthy of note in this area are the efforts by the Centro de Estudios Fotográficos in Vigo (1984), which has publicised the work of several classical Galician photographers, such as Vieitez, Pacheco, Caamaño, and José Suárez.

161. The growing institutional interest in old photography is manifest in the publication of dozens of compilations with a local, provincial and regional scope and in the implementation of different projects for conservation and diffusion carried out by regional organisations, such as the Filmoteca de Castilla y

León, or by municipal archives, such as those of Gerona, Vitoria and Seville. The Culture Department of the Catalan Autonomous Government completed an ambitious project for cataloguing photographic archive, resulting in the drafting of the white paper entitled *Llibre blanc del Patrimoni Fotogràfic a Catalunya*, in 1996. A highly informative source on this subject is found in Bernardo Riego's essay *La historiografía española y los debates sobre la fotografía como fuente histórica*, in the magazine *Ayer*, no. 24, 1996.

162. Worth mentioning in this connection is the admirable initiative of recovering the work of such photographers as Xavier Miserachs, Oriol Maspons, Paco Gómez, Ricard Terré and Carlos Pérez Siquier, begun in 1995 by Lunwerg Editores and the Fundación "la Caixa", being continued at present by Lunwerg on its own, with the publication of two excellent retrospectives in 1999 on Alberto Schommer and Ramón Masats. The monograph dedicated to the forgotten Galician popular photographer Virgilio Vieitez was particularly welcome; it was produced by Keta Vieitez and exhibited at the 1999 Fotobienal de Vigo, which has always paid special attention to early Galician photographers.

Albumen (negative). To solve the problem of poor resolution in calotypes, in 1847 Niepce de Saint-Victor began producing glass negative coated with albumen, to which he added potassium chloride. The plate was then sensitised in a bath of silver nitrate and acetic acid and kept for ten days. The albumen negative was costly and difficult to produce and was not highly sensitive.

Albumen paper. Introduced by Niepce de Saint-Victor and Blanquart Évrard between 1847 and 1850. This paper was coated with egg-white containing potassium bromide and acetic acid. After drying, it was treated in a bath of silver nitrate solution and dried again. The copy was made by contact printing from a negative, with no developing agents. Once fixed and dry, the copy presented a very detailed image in brownish or violet tones.

Ambrotype. Also known as melainotype, the ambrotype was introduced in 1851 by J.R. Le Moyne. It was produced by placing an under-exposed glass negative against a black background. It was quite successful for many years since it provided the appearance of a daguerreotype and was much less expensive.

Autochrome. A colour image obtained through the Lumière brothers' additive colour process from 1903 onwards. A glass plate was coated with a layer of tiny grains of potato starch dyed green, blue and red and then covered with an emulsion sensitive to all colours. The photograph was taken using a yellow filter and processing involved the inversion of the original negative. The system had low sensitivity.

Bromide. A process introduced by R.P. Maddox in 1871 and perfected by Charles Bennet in 1878. A solution of cadmium bromide, water and gelatine sensitised with silver bromide was spread on a glass plate, producing highly sensitive negatives that were easy to handle and long lasting. This was the long sought-after dry plate, with a sensitivity forty times that of collodion plates. This development laid the groundwork for the snapshot and modern photography as a whole. Production of gelatine-bromide papers, using silver bromide, began in 1880. This is the type of paper still in use today.

Bromoil. This process, introduced in 1907 by E.J. Wall and C. Welborne-Piper, consisted of bleaching a silver bromide enlargement in a bath of potassium bichromate and copper sulphate. With one wash, the bleaching bath removed the silver image, but the remaining emulsion absorbed water in inverse proportion to the amount of silver that remained. After removing the excess water, greasy ink was applied with a brush. The wet areas repelled the colour, while the drier areas absorbed it. This created an image in the greasy ink of whatever colour was desired, with the original shading of the original silver bromide print. In addition, the inked proof could be transferred to engraving paper using a press. This variation was known as a *bromoil transfer* or simply a *transfer*.

Calotype. (From the Greek *kalos*, beautiful) A process invented by W.H. Fox Talbot in 1839, also known as the talbotype. Since it involved a negative created directly on paper, it made the sought-after goal of photographic reproducibility a reality. Paper was treated with silver nitrate and potassium iodide and sensitised immediately before exposure with silver nitrate and gallic acid. After developing with silver nitrate and fixing with sodium thiosulphate, the paper was immersed in a bath of melted wax to make it transparent. The texture of the paper negative gave the calotype a grainy effect that was very different from the daguerreotype.

Carbon. A pigmentary process based on experiments carried out by A. Poitevin between 1855 and 1866 using an emulsion of gelatin, dichromate and carbon powder, which was transferred to another paper after development by printing down. The name of this process was also applied to other variations, such as *fresson*, which did not require transfer.

Citrate paper. Manufactured industrially from 1882 onwards, this paper was easy to store and handle. Treatment in a combined developing-fixing bath was very fast and practical. It continued in common use by portraitists until the 1930s.

Collage. A technique consisting of assembling different materials (paper, cut-outs, cardboard, objects, etc.) on a surface.

Collodion. In order to overcome the difficulties presented by albumen negatives, F.S. Archer proposed the use of collodion in 1851. This was a sort of varnish formed from guncotton dissolved in ether with the addition of potassium iodide. This preparation was mixed with a silver bath and had to be applied to the glass plate immediately before exposure. The plate was placed in the camera while still wet, thus the name wet collodion. The photographer then had to rush to his darkroom to develop the plate with iron sulphate and pyrogallic acid before the collodion dried. These operations made outdoor shots extremely difficult, since the photographer had to carry bulky and heavy equipment with him. Taupenot introduced dry collodion in 1855, but, although it simplified the process greatly, it did not come into generalised use, owing to the rapid success of bromide-gelatin negatives.

Collotype. A photomechanical procedure discovered by A.L. Poitevin in 1855. It consisted of exposing bichromate gelatin through a negative. The gelatin became insoluble to the extent that it was exposed to light through the transparent areas of the negative. Since it did not absorb moisture it would hold lithographic ink and a copy could be produced by taking advantage of the difference in ink retention between the parts exposed to greater or lesser amounts of light.

Colour film. Celluloid colour film was introduced in 1932 by the Lumière factories, which then ceased producing glass plates. The new cellulose nitrate support was lighter and unbreakable and had the same characteristics as the autochrome plate, with the advantage that it did not require the use of filters.

Cyanotype. A process introduced in 1842 by John Herschel, consisting of sensitising paper with potassium ferroprussiate. With a yellowish hue when dry, it turned bluish upon moistening with water. For many years it was used almost exclusively for industrial printing.

Daguerreotype. The photographic procedure publicised officially in 1839. It was named after its official inventor, L.J.M. Daguerre, who produced his first images on silver-covered copper plates that were highly polished and sensitised with iodine vapours. The shot had to be taken within one hour after the plate was sensitised. It was then developed with mercury vapour and fixed with common salt. Exposure times could be over one hour at first, although refinements by Fizeau and the introduction of accelerators by Claudet and Bingham helped to reduce that time considerably and made the daguerreotype suitable for portraits.

Dry waxed paper. Processes for obtaining negatives on paper were gradually improved after the concept was introduced by Fox Talbot. One of the greatest improvements was the waxed paper negative produced by Gustave Le Gray in 1851. Pure wax was used to close the pores of the paper and thus increase its transparency and clarity. This paper negative was very useful for views of landscapes or buildings that required exposures of up to five minutes in sunny weather.

Ferrotype. A procedure introduced in 1852 by Adolphe Martin, consisting of coating with collodion a tin sheet covered in black enamel. It produced a unique, very inexpensive image and became one of the most widespread photographic processes towards the end of the 19th century.

Flexichrome. A colour printing system, precursor of the dry transfer system, in which a black and white image was bleached and coloured manually with chemical colourings. These colourings produced shadings that were directly proportional to the original intensity in black and white. The final print was lacquered.

Fresson. A variation on the carbon process, promoted by the French company of the same name beginning 1903. *Fresson* printing was carried out on the basis of developing using damp sawdust to achieve a rough, velvety effect. When this type of paper ceased to be manufactured, Ortiz Echagüe acquired the patent and used the process for most of his work.

Gum Bichromate. A pigmentary process introduced in 1858 that became very popular with pictorialist photographers. Prints were obtained using a photosensitive emulsion of gum arabic, ammonium bichromate and potassium bichromate, and a water-soluble pigment. The parts of the emulsion exposed to light hardened and became insoluble. After contact printing with the negative, the print was developed in tepid water to wash away only the parts not exposed to light.

Heliography. The name used by Nicéphore Niepce for the first positive images that he produced around 1820 using silvered copper plates covered in bitumen of Judea. The copper plates were treated with acid, making them into printing plates similar to those etched with nitric acid. Using this process, Niepce was able to reproduce old engravings, before he succeeded in photographing the view from his window in 1827.

Kodachrome. Introduced in 1935 after research by Leopold Mannes and L. Godowsky. Formed by three layers of emulsion with the colours appearing successively in each one upon developing. The process offered a number of advantages and quickly superseded previous systems.

Noble prints. A generic term applied to the gum bichromates, bromoils, carbons and other pigmentary processes used by the pictorialist photographers. All of them were based on Poitevin's experiments centred on gelatin's tendency to become more or less insoluble depending on the intensity of exposure to light when containing metallic salts.

Photocollage. A technique consisting of the combination of various photographic images by means of direct assembly, breaking up conventional representation of space and perspective.

Photogram. A photographic image formed directly on an emulsion by exposure to light though different types of materials and without the use of any conventional negative. Man Ray called the procedure the *rayograph* and Christian Shad called it the *shadowgraph*.

Platinotype. A process introduced by William Willis in 1873, based on the reaction of platinum salts to exposure to light, similar to the behaviour of silver salts. Prepared using potassium chloroplatinate and exposed in a normal manner, the platinum paper was developed in a very hot bath of oxalic acid. It is still used occasionally and provides a long tone scale and allows selection of the paper's tonality and grain. It has never been a common method, owing to the difficulty of the process and its high cost.

Polacolor. A very commonly used direct photography process. Introduced in 1963, the process is quite complex. A paper tab extending outside the camera is pulled, drawing out the negative and the positive paper, which come into contact with chemicals that spread through the different layers in a matter of seconds, forming the positive image on the final backing.

Salt paper. Used by W.H. Fox Talbot from 1843 onwards, it was extremely simple to produce. The process consisted of brushing drawing paper with a solution of common salt and then sensitising it by submersion in a bath of silver nitrate solution. After drying, the paper was placed under the negative and exposed to sunlight. When the image was sufficiently clear, it was then fixed.

Tinting. The system of hand colouring of black and white photographic prints using anilines, watercolours or gouaches.

Toning. Replacement of the silver making up the photographic image by a different metal or chemical in order to intensify or modify the tonality of the original. There are dozens of different toning processes, each producing different tones.

BIBLIOGRAPHY

ALEIXANDRE, CÁNCER, HUGUET, VERGARA, *Fotografía en la Comunidad Valenciana, 1839-1939*, Barcelona, Lunwerg, 1992.

BARTHES, Roland, *La cámara lúcida*, Barcelona, Gustavo Gili, 1982.

BENJAMÍN, Walter, «Pequeña historia de la fotografía», in *Discursos interrumpidos*, Madrid, Taurus, 1973.

CAMPAÑA I BANDRANAS, Antoni, Texto de Marta Gili, Barcelona, Fundación Caixa de Barcelona, 1990.

CÁNOVAS, Carlos, *Apuntes para una historia de la fotografía en Navarra*, Gobierno de Navarra, 1989.

— *Deriva de la Ría: paisaje sin retorno*, Bilbao-Bizkaia Kutxa, 1994.

— *Paisajes fugaces*, Ivam, Valencia, 1997.

CAPA, Robert, *Cuadernos de guerra en España*, text by Carlos Serrano, Valencia, Institut Alfons el Magnànim, 1987.

CASTRO PRIETO, Juan Manuel, Obra Social de Caja Madrid. Madrid, 1998.

CATALÁ-ROCA, Francesc, *Personajes de los años 50*. Madrid, Ministerio de Cultura, 1984.

— *Foto-grafías A-cromáticas*, Barcelona, Tibidabo, 1995.

— *Impresions d'un fotògraf*. Barcelona, Ed. 62, 1995.

CATANY, Toni, *La meva Mediterrania*, Barcelona, Lunwerg, 1990.

— *Natures mortes*, Barcelona, Lunwerg, 1987.

— *Obscura memòria*, Barcelona, Lunwerg, 1994.

— *Fotografíes*, Lunwerg, Barcelona, 1997.

CENTELLES, Agustí, *Fotoperiodista (1909-1985)*, texts by Fontcuberta, J. Green and A. Balcells, Barcelona, Fundació Caixa de Catalunya, 1988.

CLIFFORD, Charles, *Fotógrafo de la España de Isabel II*, texts by L. Fontanella and G. Kurtz, Madrid, El Viso, 1996.

— *Vistas de las obras del Canal de Isabel II*, texts by J. Benet and P. López Mondéjar, Madrid, Canal de Isabel II, 1988.

COLOM, Joan, *Izas, rabizas y colipoterras*, text by C.J. Cela, Barcelona, Lumen, 1964.

COLOMA MARTÍN, Isidoro, *La forma fotográfica. A propósito de fotografía española desde 1839 a 1939*, Universidad de Málaga, 1986.

CUALLADÓ, Gabriel, *Fotografías*, Madrid, Círculo de Bellas Artes, 1985.

— Gabriel, *Fotografías*, Valencia, IVAM, 1989.

— *Imágenes cotidianas*, Barcelona, Àmbit, 1996.

Cuatro Direcciones. Fotografía contemporánea española, 1970-1990 (2 volumes) texts by M. Santos, Suárez Canal, F. Caja, J.V. Monzó, Barth, Ministerio de Cultura, Lunwerg, 1991.

CHAMORRO, Koldo. PhotoBolsillo. Ed. TF-La Fábrica, 1999.

DÁVILA, Rick. Ed. PhotoBolsillo. Ed. TF-La Fábrica, Madrid, 1998.

DOLCET, Juan, *Retratos de artistas*, C.A. Reina Sofía-Lunwerg, 1992.

ESPLUGAS, Antoni, *El nu femení*, Departament de Cultura de la Generalitat de Catalunya. Barcelona, 1998.

FERNÁNDEZ RIVERO, J. Antonio, *Historia de la fotografía en Málaga durante el siglo XIX*, Málaga, Miramar, 1994.

FERROL, Manuel, *Emigración*, Vigo. C.E. Fotográficos, 1986.

FONTANELLA, Lee, *La historia de la fotografía en España desde sus orígenes hasta 1900*, Madrid, El Viso, 1981.

FONTCUBERTA, Joan, *Estética fotográfica* (Various texts), Barcelona, Blume, 1984.

— *Herbarium*, Barcelona, Gustavo Gili, 1984.

— *Historia artificial*, texts by G. Picazo and J.V. Monzó, Valencia, IVAM, 1993.

— *El beso de Judas (Fotografía y verdad)*, Gustavo-Gili, Barcelona, 1997.

FORMIGUERA, Pere, *Retratos*, Barcelona, Generalitat de Catalunya, 1993.

— *Tal com som*, Museu de Granollers, 1995.

Fotografía pictorialista valenciana, text by José Ramón Cáncer, Valencia, Generalitat Valenciana, 1992.

Fotógrafos de la Escuela de Madrid, texts by J.M. Casademont, P. Formiguera and G. Vielba, Madrid, Ministerio de Cultura, 1988.

Fotógrafos valencianos años 60, texts by P. Benlloc, E. Mira and A.T. Ortega, Valencia, Generalitat Valenciana, 1992.

FREIXA, Ferrán, *Fotografías, 1977-1994*, Salamanca, Universidad de Salamanca, 1994.

FREUND, Gisèle, *La fotografía como documento social*, Barcelona, Gustavo Gili, 1986.

GARCÍA-ALIX, Alberto, *Los malheridos, los bien amados, los traidores*, Salamanca, Universidad de Salamanca, 1994.

— *Fotografías, 1977-1998*. Ed. TF-La Fábrica, Madrid, 1988.

GARCÍA RODERO, Cristina, *España oculta*, Barcelona, Lunwerg, 1989.

— *España, fiestas y ritos*, Barcelona, Lunwerg, 1992.

GERSNHEIM, Helmut y Alison, *Historia gráfica de la fotografía*, Barcelona, Omega, 1967.

GODES, Emili, *Fotògraf de la Nova Objectivitat*, Barcelona, Generalitat de Catalunya, 1996.

GÓMEZ, Francisco, *La emoción construida*, texts by C. Cánovas and R. Levenfeld, Fundación «La Caixa» Lunwerg, Barcelona, 1995.

GONZÁLEZ, Ricardo, *Luces de un siglo. Fotografía en Valladolid en el siglo XIX*, Valladolid, Gonzalo Blanco, 1990.

— *Segovia en la fotografía del siglo XIX*, Segovia, El Doblón, 1997.

HARA, Cristóbal, *4 cosas de España*, Madrid, Visor, 1990.

— *Lances de aldea*, PhotoVision, 1992.

Historia de la fotografía española, (Actas del Congreso de), various, Sevilla, 1986.

Història del fotoperiodisme a Catalunya, 1895-1976, text by Jaume Fabre, Barcelona, Ayuntamiento de Barcelona, 1990.

HERRÁEZ, Fernando, *Vestigis*, Barcelona, Fundación Caixa de Barcelona, 1990.

Idas y Caos. Aspectos de las vanguardias fotográficas en España, texts by J. Fontcuberta, M.L. Sougez. C. Cánovas. M. Gili, C. Zélich, Madrid, Ministerio de Cultura, 1984.

La fotografía en España hasta 1900, texts by Fontanella, Fontcuberta, López Mondéjar, Sougez, Yáñez Polo and Calvo Serraller, Madrid, Ministerio de Cultura, 1992.

La fotografía en las colecciones reales. Texts by Margarita González, Leticia Ruiz and Marie-Loup Sougez. Patrimonio Nacional-Fundación «La Caixa». Madrid, 1999.

La fotografía pictorialista en España, 1900-1936. Texts by Anne Hammond, Elisabeth Insenser and Cristina Zelich. Fundación «La Caixa», Barcelona, 1998.

Laurent-I, texts by A. Gutiérrez and C. Teixidor, Madrid, Ministerio de Cultura, 1983.

LEDO, Margarita, *Documentalismo fotográfico contemporáneo*, Ed. Xerais, Vigo, 1996.

LEMAGNY, Jean C. y ROUILLE, A. (ed.) *Historia de la fotografía*, Barcelona, Martínez Roca, 1988.

Les avantguardes fotogràfiques en España, 1925-1945. Texts by Joan Naranjo. Fundación «La Caixa», Barcelona, 1997.

LÓPEZ MONDÉJAR, Publio, *Retratos de la vida*, Madrid, Mayoría, 1980 (Reed. Lunwerg, 1991).

— *Crónica de la Luz*, Madrid, El VISO, 1984.

— *Memoria de Madrid. Fotografías de Alfonso*, Ministerio de Cultura, Madrid, 1984.

— *Las fuentes de la Memoria-I. Fotografía y sociedad en la España del siglo XIX*, Lunwerg, 1989.

— *Las fuentes de la memoria-II. Fotografía y sociedad en España, 1900-1939*. Lunwerg, 1982.

— *Las fuentes de la memoria-III. Fotografía y sociedad en la España de Franco*, Lunwerg, 1996.

LUCAS, César. PhotoBolsillo. Ed. TF-La Fábrica, Madrid, 1999.

MADOZ, Chema, *Fotografías, 1985-1994*, Madrid, Art-Plus, 1995.

— *Objetos, 1990-1999*. Aldeasa, Madrid, 1999.

MARTÍN, Ricardo (photos) and MUÑOZ MOLINA, Antonio (texts), *Sostener la mirada. Imágenes de la Alpujarra*, Centro Andaluz de Fotografía, 1993.

MASATS, Ramón, *Los Sanfermines*, Madrid, Espasa-Calpe, 1963.

— *Viejas historias de Castilla la Vieja*, Barcelona, Lumen, 1963.

— *Neutral Corner*, text by Ignacio Aldecoa, Barcelona, Lumen, 1964. (Reedición, 1996)

— *Fotografía*, Lunwerg, Madrid-Barcelona, 1999.

MASPONS, Oriol, *El instante perdido*, texts by D. Balcells and LL. Permanyer, Fundación «La Caixa» Lunwerg, Barcelona, 1995.

— *Animales de compañía*, Barcelona, Àmbit, 1995.

— and UBIÑA, Julio, *Toreo de salón*, Barcelona, Lumen, 1963.

MIRA, Enric, *La vanguardia fotográfica de los años setenta en España*. Dip. Provincial de Alicante, 1991.

MISERACHS, Xavier, *Barcelona en blanc i Negre*, Barcelona, 1964

— *Costa Brava Show*, Barcelona, 1966

— *Los cachorros*, Barcelona, Lumen, 1969.

— *1 segundo y 25 centésimas*, Barcelona, Fundación «La Caixa», 1992.

— *Profesiones con futuro, Fotógrafo,* Barcelona, Grijalbo, 1995.

— *Criterio fotográfico,* Ed. Omega, Barcelona, 1998.

MOYA, Adelina, *Nicolás de Lekuona, obra fotográfica,* Bilbao, Museo de Bellas Artes, 1982.

MUÑOZ, Isabel, *Flamenco,* París, Ed. Plume, 1993.

— *Tauromachies,* París, Ed. Plume, 1995.

NAVARRO, Rafael, *Dípticos,* PhotoVision, 1986.

NEWHALL, Beaumont, *Historia de la fotografía* (with appendix by Joan Fontcuberta on Spanish photography), Barcelona, Gustavo Gili, 1982.

NUEVA LENTE (Jornadas sobre), moderated by Rafael Doctor, Comunidad de Madrid, 1993.

ORTIZ-ECHAGÜE, José, *Sus fotografías,* text by G. Vielba, Madrid, Incafo, 1979.

PÉREZ MÍNGUEZ, Luis, *Fotografías,* Madrid, Ministerio de Cultura, 1984.

PLA JANINI, Joaquín, monograph with texts by P. Formiguera and J.C. Lemagny, Fundación «La Caixa» Lunwerg, 1996.

QUINTAS, Ángel, *Fotografías, 1950-1970,* text by C. Zélich, Junta de Castilla and León, 1993.

RAMÓN Y CAJAL, *Recuerdos de mi vida,* Madrid, Espasa-Calpe, 1981.

REPRESA, Jorge, *Retratos,* Barcelona, Ediciones B, 1996.

Retratos, fotografía española, 1948-1995, text by M. Canals, I.L. Permanyer, Joan Naranjo and Vicenç Altaió, Fundació Caixa de Catalunya, 1996.

RIEGO, Bernardo, *Cien años de fotografía en Cantabria,* Barcelona, Lunwerg, 1987.

ROCANDIO, Jesús, *Cien años de fotografía en La Rioja,* Cultural Rioja, 1992.

ROMÁN, Benito, *Duendes, entes y mojigangas,* Madrid, Foco, 1985.

ROMERO, Alfredo, *La fotografía en Aragón,* Ibercaja, Zaragoza, 2000.

RUEDA, Jorge, *Mal de ojo,* Mestizo, Murcia, 1997.

— *Mal de ojo,* Mestizo, Murcia, 1997.

SÁNCHEZ, Gervasio, *Vidas minadas,* Madrid, 1997.

SCHOMMER, Alberto, *Retratos, 1969-1989,* texts by Ch. Caujolle, E. Hosoe and V. Verdú, Barcelona, Lunwerg, 1989.

— *El viaje,* Madrid, Turner, 1994.

— *Antológica,* Lunwerg, Madrid-Barcelona, 1998.

SENDÓN, Manuel, *Imaxes na penumbra (A fotografía afeccionada en Galicia (1950-1965),* Xerais, 1998.

SENDÓN, Manuel y SUÁREZ, X. Luis, *En Galiza nos 50. As agrupacións fotográficas,* Ayuntamiento de Vigo, 1990.

— *Imaxes na penumbra (A fotografía afeccionada en Galicia [1950-1965]),* Xerais, 1998.

SENTÍS, Marta, *Habitaciones y migraciones,* Fundación «La Caixa», Barrcelona, 1993.

SONTAG, Susan, *Sobre la fotografía,* Barcelona, Edhasa, 1981.

SOUGEZ, Marie-Loup, *Historia de la fotografía,* Madrid, Cátedra, 1981.

SUÁREZ, José, *1902-1974,* texts by M. Sendón and X.L. Suárez Canal, Ayuntamiento de Vigo, 1988.

TAUSK, Petr, *Historia de la fotografía* (with appendix by J.M. Casademont on photography in Spain), Barcelona, Gustavo Gili, 1978.

TERRÉ, Ricard, monograph with texts by P. Formiguera and M. Ledo, Fundación «La Caixa» Lunwerg, Barcelona, 1995.

Tiempo de silencio. Panorama de la fotografía española de los años 50 y 60. Texts by C. Cánovas and P. Formiguera, Fundación Caixa de Catalunya, 1992.

Toledo en la fotografía de Casiano Alguacil, texts by Carrero, I. Sánchez, J. Sánchez, R. del Cerro and F. Martínez, Ayuntamiento de Toledo, 1983.

TRILLO, Miguel, PhotoBolsillo. Ed. TF-La Fábrica, 1999.

VALLHONRAT, Javier, PhotoBolsillo, Madrid, 1999.

VEGA, Carmelo, *La isla mirada. Tenerife y la fotografía,* Centro de Fotografía Isla de Tenerife, 1995.

VIEITEZ, Virxilio, *Álbum,* texts by Manuel Sendón and Xosé Luis Suárez Canal, Centro de Estudios Fotográficos, Vigo, 1998.

YÁÑEZ POLO, Miguel Ángel, *Retratistas y fotógrafos,* Sevilla, 1981.

ZABALZA, Ramón, *Imágenes gitanas,* PhotoVision, 1996.

ACKNOWLEDGEMENTS

I should like to express my sincerest thanks to the people who, over more than ten years of research and investigation, have assisted me with their invaluable and generous co-operation: José Aguayo, Eduardo Alonso, José Mario Armero, Pilar Aróstegui, Javier Bersaluce, Santiago Bernal, Joan Boadas, Alfonso Braojos, José Ramón Cáncer, Carlos Cánovas, Martín Carrasco, Manuel Carrero, Juan Manuel Castro Prieto, Sergio Centelles, Elena Cortés, Josep Cruañas, Lorenzo Díaz, Luis Escobar, Lee Fontanella, Miquel Galmes, José Gálvez, Mateo Gamón, Carmen García, Juan Guirao, María Teresa Gutiérrez Barranco, José Huguet, Miriám de Liniers, Manuel López Rodríguez, Bernard Marbot, Basilio Martín Patino, Victor Méndez Pascual, Carlos Morenés, Ana Muller, Manuel Muñoz Clares, José Luis Mur, Matilde Muro, Carlos Ortega, Isabel Ortega, Mario Parralejo, Fernando Pereda, Juan Antonio Pérez Millán, Joaquín Plá y Guarro, Llorenç Raich, Adolfo Ribas Prous, Eduardo Roldán, Rosa Ros, M.ª Leticia Ruiz, Santiago Saavedra, Eduardo Segovia, Manuel Sendón, Alejandro Sosa, Marie-Loup Sougez, Xosé Luis Suárez Canal, Carmelo Tartón, Antonio Teruel, Sonsoles Vallina and Luzzi Wolgensinger. Special thanks to the photographers Juan María Ardizone, Ángel Blanco, Joaquín Brangulí, Luis Rodríguez, Alfonso Sánchez Portela, sadly no longer with us, and Catalá Roca, Joan Colom, Gabriel Cualladó, Jean Dieuzaide, Manuel Ferrol, Eugenio Forcano, Ramón Masats, Oriol Maspons, Xavier Miserachs, Nicolás Muller, Francisco Ontañón, Carlos Pérez Siquier, Leopoldo Pomés, Marc Riboud, Alberto Schommer, and Ricard Terré, from whom I have learned so much and whose work has given me so much pleasure. Lastly, it would be unfair not to mention Juan Carlos Luna and Andrés Gamboa, who conceived this the project for this work with me in the now distant year 1986.

P.L.M.

LUNWERG EDITORES

Editor in Chief
JUAN CARLOS LUNA

Art Director
ANDRÉS GAMBOA

Technical Director
MERCEDES CARREGAL

Layout
MIGUEL A. PALLEIRO

Editorial Co-ordinator
MARÍA JOSÉ MOYANO

English Translation
GERARDO DENIS